Work Without Boundaries

Work Without Boundaries

Psychological Perspectives on the New Working Life

Michael Allvin
Department of Sociology, Uppsala University

Gunnar Aronsson
Department of Psychology, Stockholm University

Tom Hagström
Department of Education, Stockholm University

Gunn Johansson
Department of Psychology, Stockholm University

Ulf Lundberg
Department of Psychology, Stockholm University

WILEY-BLACKWELL

A John Wiley & Sons, Ltd., Publication

This edition first published 2011
© 2011 John Wiley & Sons, Ltd.

This book is a revised and extended version of: Allvin, Michael; Aronsson, Gunnar; Hagström, Tom; Johansson, Gunn; and Lundberg, Ulf (2006) *Gränslöst arbete – socialpsykologiska perspektiv på det nya arbetslivet*. Malmö: Liber.

Wiley-Blackwell is an imprint of John Wiley & Sons, formed by the merger of Wiley's global Scientific, Technical and Medical business with Blackwell Publishing.

Registered Office
John Wiley & Sons Ltd, The Atrium, Southern Gate, Chichester, West Sussex, PO19 8SQ, United Kingdom

Editorial Offices
350 Main Street, Malden, MA 02148-5020, USA
9600 Garsington Road, Oxford, OX4 2DQ, UK
The Atrium, Southern Gate, Chichester, West Sussex, PO19 8SQ, UK

For details of our global editorial offices, for customer services, and for information about how to apply for permission to reuse the copyright material in this book please see our website at www.wiley.com/wiley-blackwell.

The right of Michael Allvin, Gunnar Aronsson, Tom Hagström, Gunn Johansson and Ulf Lundberg to be identified as the authors of this work has been asserted in accordance with the UK Copyright, Designs and Patents Act 1988.

All rights reserved. No part of this publication may be reproduced, stored in a retrieval system, or transmitted, in any form or by any means, electronic, mechanical, photocopying, recording or otherwise, except as permitted by the UK Copyright, Designs and Patents Act 1988, without the prior permission of the publisher.

Wiley also publishes its books in a variety of electronic formats. Some content that appears in print may not be available in electronic books.

Designations used by companies to distinguish their products are often claimed as trademarks. All brand names and product names used in this book are trade names, service marks, trademarks or registered trademarks of their respective owners. The publisher is not associated with any product or vendor mentioned in this book. This publication is designed to provide accurate and authoritative information in regard to the subject matter covered. It is sold on the understanding that the publisher is not engaged in rendering professional services. If professional advice or other expert assistance is required, the services of a competent professional should be sought.

Library of Congress Cataloging-in-Publication Data

Gränslöst arbete. English
  Work without boundaries : psychological perspectives on the new working life / Michael Allvin . . . [et al.].
    p. cm.
  Rev. and extended version of: Gränslöst arbete : socialpsykologiska perspektiv på det nya arbetslivet / Michael Allvin . . . [et al.]. Mälmo : Liber, c2006.
  Includes bibliographical references and index.
  ISBN 978-0-470-66613-5 (cloth) – ISBN 978-0-470-66614-2 (pbk.)
  1. Work–Psychological aspects–Sweden. 2. Job stress–Sweden. I. Allvin, Michael. II. Title.
  HD8574.G7313 2011
  158.7–dc22
                                                                    2010042193

A catalogue record for this book is available from the British Library

This book is published in the following electronic formats: ePDFs 9781119991229; Wiley Online Library 9781119991236

Set in 10.5/13pt Minion by Thomson Digital, Noida, India
Printed in Singapore by Ho Printing Singapore Pte Ltd

1   2011

Contents

About the Authors	vii
Foreword by Cary L. Cooper	ix
Preface	xi
Acknowledgments	xiii

1	The New Work	1
	The new inequality	4
	New markets and new structures	7
	The new work life	13
	What is so new about "The New Work"?	16
	The new and the old work	18
	The purpose and structure of this book	22
2	The New Rules of Work: On Flexible Work and How to Manage It	25
	Flexible work	29
	Flexibility through empowerment	35
	Flexibility through substitution	48
	Separate paths?	60
3	The New Work Life and the Dimensions of Knowledge	69
	The cognitive knowledge demands	71
	The social knowledge demands	81
	The societal knowledge demands	97
	The existential knowledge demands	107
	Some concluding considerations	120
4	The Place of Work in Life	123
	Separate spheres	126
	Competing spheres	129
	Coping with boundaries	130

  Mutually favored spheres   *133*
  New conditions outside work life: the consumption society   *134*
  The moral supermarket   *138*
  The market aesthetic   *141*
  The new family   *144*
  Organizing living   *149*
  Conflict and balance in life   *158*
  An individual matter   *162*

5 Work Life, Stress, and the New Ill Health   163
  Stress as a social problem and research area   *167*
  Stress models for the work life   *172*
  The new work life as a source of stress   *189*
  The new ill health   *205*
  The new ill health, work environment, and the possibility space of work   *212*

6 Some Concluding Comments and Reflections   217
  The deregulation of working life   *218*
  The individualization of working life   *219*
  The heterogenization of working life   *220*
  The new inequality   *221*
  New strains and symptoms   *222*
  Flexibility and power in times of economic recession   *223*
  Future – trust or new forms and fields for external regulation?   *225*

References   229

Index   253

About the Authors

Michael Allvin is a licensed Psychologist and Associate Professor of Sociology at the Department of Sociology, Uppsala University. He was previously at the Swedish National Institute for Working Life. His research centers mainly on new forms of work and organization. He is currently doing research on working conditions within knowledge-intensive organizations.

Gunnar Aronsson is Professor of Work and Organizational Psychology, Department of Psychology, Stockholm University. He was Professor in Psychology at the Swedish National Institute for Working Life from 1990 to 2007. He has carried out studies on many occupational groups, blue-collar and white-collar work, and published several articles and books on work, stress, and health. He is currently participating in research on transfer of learning in work life, illegitimate tasks as stressors, sickness presenteeism, and individual strategies in boundaryless work.

Tom Hagström is Professor Emeritus at the Department of Education, Stockholm University and licensed Psychologist and was formerly senior researcher at the Swedish National Institute for Working Life. His research has focused on people's action and developmental possibilities in contexts of instability and change such as vocational rehabilitation, unemployment, and transitions from school to working life. He is currently engaged in research on sustainable competence and organizational decentralization as well as networking related to mobile ICT in work and non-work contexts.

Gunn Johansson is Professor Emerita of Work Psychology at Stockholm University. Her early research was on psychosocial work environments, stress, and health in white- and blue-collar occupations within a biopsychosocial framework. She later used a similar approach in research on work-related values, retirement, women's career patterns, and the flexibilization of work. She is currently involved in a research and development program on long-term strategic human resources management as a competitive factor in business development.

Ulf Lundberg is Professor of Biological Psychology at the Department of Psychology, Stockholm University, and at the Center for Health Equity Studies (CHESS), affiliated with Stockholm University and the Karolinska Institute. He was Editor-in-Chief for the International Journal of Behavioral Medicine from 1999 to 2006. The general aim of his research program is to identify psychosocial, behavioral, and biological factors linking psychosocial and socioeconomic conditions to well-being and health risks in men and women. He has published extensively on work, stress, and health (more than 200 articles and four books).

Foreword

Studs Terkel as long ago as 1979, in his acclaimed book *Working*, wrote that "work is about a search for daily meaning as well as daily bread, for recognition as well as cash, for astonishment rather than torpor, in short, for a sort of life rather than a Monday through Friday sort of dying." Over thirty years later, we are revisiting what work should be about today, and in the future. *Work Without Boundaries* is an excellent example of this, highlighting where we are, and what our priorities should be for the new world of work. This is extremely important, at a time when we are struggling to cope with the aftermath of the recession and the consequences this had, and will continue to have, on working people not only in the developed world but also in the developing world as well.

The post-recession world will mean that there will be fewer people doing more work, with the demands of new technology and global competition adversely affecting their work and private lives. This book attempts to identify the fundamental drivers of change, the issues that workers at all levels will have to face, and how we should restructure our organizations and working lives to confront these challenges. In the developed world, we will increasingly become a knowledge-based and service-based economy, where technology will play an increasing role in changing the face and composition of our workplaces. This will mean greater demands on the individual worker, the family, and the relationship between the individual and their employing organization. The demands, and in many cases the lack of control over these events, will mean that the stress levels are likely to rise in the foreseeable future, at a time when every person will count toward achieving organizational goals but there will be fewer of them (in an effort to keep the labor costs down to compete with cheaper labor from the Far East and developing world).

These trends have massive implications for the work organization of the future (Cooper *et al.*, 2009). This will inevitably mean that workplaces will have to be more flexible in their approach to their workforce, in terms of where and when people work; they will have to provide a different style of training for their managers, particularly in social and interpersonal skills, and to be more adaptable and less rigid in their management style; they will have to work smarter rather than forcing their employees to work longer and more intensively; they will have to define jobs and objectives better in an effort to provide role clarity; they will have to understand that if individuals are to survive the demands in the future they will need to be managed by praise and reward and not fault-finding or by fear of job loss; and finally, they will have to attempt to provide the two-earner family of the future with great work-life balance and support if they are to retain and attract quality staff, and minimize the impact of the intrinsic stresses and strains of future work environments.

As the great social reformer of the nineteenth century, John Ruskin, wrote in 1871, and it applies even more today: "in order that people may be happy in their work, these three things are needed; they must be fit for it, they must not do too much of it and they must have a sense of success in it." This is our generation's challenge for the future, and this book goes a long way to identify how we might do this – and I congratulate the authors for their important contribution not only to the literature but also to the health and well-being of the workers of the world.

Cary L. Cooper, CBE

References

Cooper, C. L., Field, J., Goswami, U., Jenkins, R., and Sahakian, B., 2009. *Mental Capital and Wellbeing*. Oxford: Wiley-Blackwell.
Terkel, S., 1979. *Working*. New York: Avon Books.

Cary L. Cooper, CBE, is a Distinguished Professor of Organizational Psychology and Health at Lancaster University Management School, Chair of the Academy of Social Sciences, and lead scientist on the UK government's Foresight Project on Mental Capital and Wellbeing.

Preface

This book has emerged out of a long-term research program concerned with the transformation of working life which has taken place during recent decades. The program was performed in collaboration with the Swedish National Institute for Working Life and the Department of Psychology, Stockholm University.

Work Without Boundaries is a metaphor for work that is not restricted by traditional organizational rules like regular office hours, a single workplace, fixed procedures, and limited responsibility. The concept was developed more than ten years ago as the title of the abovementioned research program. Because of its strong intuitive meaning and relevance in the changing landscape of work, it found its way into the public and political spheres as well as the academic discourse. It has become a common way of describing a work situation that escapes any attempts to restrain or even control it. It describes, in other words, a work situation that runs the risk of getting out of hand, of becoming overpowering.

The overall aim of our work has been to explore, describe, and analyze contemporary work by presenting and integrating research from different fields, such as sociology, social psychology, cognition and psychobiology, as well as organization and learning theory. Although there has been a great deal of research within all these fields separately, a comprehensive theoretical framework with the ability to synthesize this research is still lacking. Our ambition has been to find a more integrated outlook and to embrace several perspectives in our analyses.

The book takes as its point of departure the increased dependency on market forces of almost all organizations and their subsequent impulse to increase their flexibility. There are several ways to promote flexibility. It can be promoted through deregulation, decentralization, and delegation, thus empowering the individual, team, or work unit. It can also be promoted through increased regulation, centralization, and standardization, thus making individuals, teams, or work units replaceable. Both of these ways involve a transfer of responsibility from the organization as such, and the terms of employment within it, to the individual, thereby making him/her increasingly accountable for his/her own work and employability.

In order to explore and account for this development, as well as its social and psychological ramifications, the book is organized into four themes: the work organization implied by this development; the skills and qualifications required for it; the work-life balance act involved in it; and the stress and health implications related to it. A central conclusion is that de- and reregulation of work imply an individualization, which is a base for a more heterogeneous labor force and working life.

Since we are all active researchers in Sweden, the book is naturally written from a Scandinavian perspective. However, when it comes to work organization and its effects on working life, the last twenty years of increasing global economic collaboration has effectively evened out many of the distinctive characteristics of that perspective. As a consequence, we are convinced that the content and examples of the book are relevant for a large part of the international labor market.

Michael Allvin, Gunnar Aronsson, Tom Hagström,
Gunn Johansson, Ulf Lundberg.
Stockholm, October 2010

Acknowledgments

We are grateful to our colleagues, Kenneth Abrahamsson and Jan Christer Karlsson, who provided valuable comments, as well as to our Wiley editors, Darren Reed and Karen Shield. Our gratitude also goes to the funding agencies that supported our research program: The Swedish Board of Communication Research and the Swedish Research Council for Working Life and Social Science (grant 2001-0278 and grant 2001-0049). Three students completed their doctoral theses within the framework of the research program: Marika Hansson, Camilla Kylin, and Petra Lindfors. Thanks to them. Finally our gratitude goes to Erika Viklund who provided a draft translation of an earlier Swedish text, on the basis of which this book has been elaborated.

1
The New Work

It's all about "time to market." You're in a hurry and things change all the time. If you can't get your products out in time, they will already be old when they get out. The timeframe between your product idea and one or two competitors getting an equal product onto the market is very narrow. So, when you're piloting a project, you're hurrying, hurrying, hurrying. Always running, not to miss the train.

In a sparsely furnished office in a suburb south of Stockholm, Peter is trying to explain what his work is all about. Leaning forward and gesticulating, he constantly checks his watch. From time to time he is interrupted by his mobile phone ringing or by colleagues poking their heads through the door to ask about something. With a tired look he apologizes each time.

I guess we're at least trying to stay ahead of the crowd but we can't keep up with the trend leaders, so we're probably lagging behind a bit. This means it's always stressful and products are always outdated. The competition is unbelievable.

Peter is one of the founders of one of the many IT companies that started up at the end of the 1990s. He started the company together with two course mates from university. Since then they have grown into a company of around ten employees, but Peter and his cofounders are still there, doing most of the work. This was also the original idea. They have no plans to expand, but rather see the company goal as cooperating and working together. Or, in Peter's words: "we like to race and wrestle one another. We enjoy it."

Peter is a modern entrepreneur. Being one of the founders, the life of the company is his life. He also expects the same commitment from his co-workers. The company runs a profit-sharing system by which everyone

---

Work Without Boundaries: Psychological Perspectives on the New Working Life, First Edition. Michael Allvin, Gunnar Aronsson, Tom Hagström, Gunn Johansson, and Ulf Lundberg.
© 2011 John Wiley & Sons, Ltd. Published 2011 by John Wiley & Sons, Ltd.

receives a certain percentage of the profit. Peter sees this as an incentive for everyone to help out and "do their bit," but he also feels that it comes natural – after all, to them the company is a communal project. The company per se does not interest him. The point is not to create or set up a business. It is rather the particular way of working he likes. He wants to do what he enjoys doing, and to be able to take that initiative by himself. As he says, to get the information you need when you need it, and arrange meetings with the people you need when you need them. For Peter, working with people with whom he gets on well on a common project, and at the same time being his own boss, is what makes his work so appealing. Just the same, it forces him to work a lot. And life outside work, if it exists at all, suffers the consequences.

> On my wife's twenty-fifth birthday, I didn't get home until after midnight. [laughter] I couldn't go home. I just couldn't. We had to deliver next day, and the stuff wouldn't work.

Stella, a colleague of Peter's, also senses the impact of their hard work and has seen her health affected. She suffers from insomnia and high blood pressure. It feels strange to be struck by problems like these when you are so young, and she does not quite know what to do about it. Changing the particular way of working would be difficult. She has only just discovered its appeal, and cannot imagine an ordinary "nine-to-five job." At the same time she is slowly realizing that the problems will not just go away. Still, she and her colleagues have been aware of the risks, and possibly even been challenged by them.

> After all, we have created this situation ourselves, because we're eager for this to work. Then, you'll have to assume a larger role. At the same time we've tried to say that maybe you can't work like this for more than three years.

Running a business in such a competitive industry is, for both Peter and Stella, a way of testing themselves and stretching the limits of their capacity. The company itself is, in Peter's words, just a "tool" to develop yourself and your role in life.

In an apartment not far away, Monica is waiting for the phone to ring. She is employed by the hour by a sizable labor recruitment firm, performing less complicated office tasks.

> If you're lucky you get to know about it the evening before. Around three–four in the afternoon they call and ask if you can work the next day.

> The worst is when they call at half past seven in the morning and tell you you need to be at work at half past seven.

Monica is 45 years old and a single mother. She used to work as a secretary at a larger company but was forced to quit when it was reorganized. Since then she has been back at her old workplace several times in temporary hired positions. Most of the people there are new, but the tasks she is assigned are more or less the same as those she performed earlier. She also does not understand why she was laid off in the first place. Even though she is not particularly fond of the tasks, she has no problem carrying them out. Instead, it is the way in which she has to work that she dislikes: that she can never know when or if she will be working. It is far too uncertain.

Monica has no specific education and does not believe she will be able to get a more "developing" job. In her youth she spent all her time doing sports. Even though she is still active and gets a few jobs coaching junior athletes, there is no future for her in sports. She also finds it difficult to relax and to use her spare time for anything constructive.

> There is no relaxation. You always have at the back of your mind that: I wonder if they'll call? Should I prepare for tomorrow? Should I send away the kid? Even though you're free, you can't unwind. But you're thinking: are they going to call tomorrow? Will it be long until there is a new job this time?

She is registered as part-time unemployed with the national job agency. But she expects no help, at the most "a public labor market measure project, or something like that." In a way it is good, as it keeps her from "falling out of the system," but it does not do anything for her. "If I get stuck with something like that I'll just have to do it. But it's not something I look forward to, if you know what I mean."

Her replies are laconic and overall she gives a rather apathetic impression, adding that she feels exploited, excluded, and discarded.

> Sure, when they want you they want you. But if there's no work, you're no one, and then you can stay home. And *that*, that's exploiting people, isn't it?

Even though Peter, Stella, and Monica perhaps are not representative from a purely statistical point of view, their stories are not entirely uncommon. They certainly represent two extremes, but much of what they describe is in many ways typical of what we would like to call "the new working life."

There is a widespread perception of a fast tempo. There is the very tangible experience of abrupt turns, fluctuations, and constant changes. But there is also the paralyzing fatigue and feeling of uselessness. There is the sensation of having freedom and control, in work as well as in life. But there are also experiences of being imperiled and abandoned. There are expectations of development and future possibilities but also depressing sensations of uncertainty, insecurity, and frustration. On the one hand, the new working life provides expanded possibilities and a new kind of freedom. On the other hand, it can lead to increased exclusion. The life of work increasingly resembles a giant switchboard which either connects or disconnects people.

The New Inequality

But, you might wonder, what is new about this? The life of work has always divided people into those who are above and those who are below, those who exploit and those who are exploited, those who have power and those who lack it. This is of course true and the new work is no different. The life of work has not become less unequal, quite the opposite. What is new is instead the way in which the inequalities are distributed.

In order to explain this, we need to go back to the stories of Peter, Stella, and Monica. We can distinguish three experiences they all seem to have in common. First, there is the experience that time has become more urgent and demanding. For Peter and Stella this means a higher tempo and changing conditions. There is no upper limit for how much, how well, or how fast they are expected to perform. At the same time they must constantly be aware of the conditions and prerequisites. Working a lot, well, and fast with something that is already dated and nobody wants is not just useless, it is a waste of time. Time is stalking Monica as well. But for her it is all about seizing the opportunities that are offered. She is unable to relax as she can never know when, or if, the phone will ring. Conditions are constantly changing, and she never knows what tomorrow will bring. A consequence they all suffer is increasing fatigue, exhaustion, and possibly even burnout.

The second common experience is to have more control on a smaller scale, but less on a larger. For Peter and Stella this manifests itself in that they have substantial freedom at work. No one tells them what to do. At the same time they are subject to the unconditional demands of the industry, market, and competition. These demands rule their work as inevitably and mercilessly as an assembly line, although not in as much detail. What is more, the work is ruled without any regard for human limitations and social obligations. Saying that Monica is in control on a smaller scale may sound odd or insensitive, but her workday is, in a certain sense, not limited by the rules of work, but instead open and dependent on her personal choices. At the same time, these choices are severely constrained by events quite beyond her scope and control. Another way of expressing this problem is that people's control in their work has increased, whereas their control over the conditions of work has decreased. As a consequence they have parallel experiences of freedom and lack of security.

The third experience is the number of opportunities that are offered through work, and all the expectations they give rise to. In the case of Peter and Stella, these concern successes, personal development, doing what you want to do, and having fun. Just how they imagine this is, of course, individual. Their stories, however, hint that the world is at their feet and that everything is possible. A female colleague of theirs at another company describes her plans for the future as follows.

> On the whole, I think I know fairly well what I want to do further on. I know I want to develop this company, and we have discussed having children in maybe three years or so, in order to first get the company going ... Then I would like to get a PhD in the USA, and afterwards I would like to work helping women in the third world ... or some form of international engagement, although not in any traditional organization.

But as the opportunities and expectations skyrocket, our abilities to respond to and benefit from them are still as limited as ever. We cannot do all that we want when we want it. Nor can we do it all at once. There are limits to how much we can work and at the same time lead a meaningful personal and social life outside work. Friends, family, personal economy, time, and finally our body fail us. There is also a limit to how much we can learn and how much we can adapt. Organizations may have become more flexible, but human life still requires a certain measure of stability. Although capital is now transient and global, the workforce is still stationary and local.

Monica had had the same experience too. She had also seen opportunities and had expectations. But in her case the possibility of realization lay not in work, but in sport. She expected her job to provide her with the social and economic stability her self-realization necessitated. But when the workplace was being reorganized, her education, experience, and abilities were not enough. When demands increased, conditions changed, frustrating her expectations. Hence, the third common experience is that the individual, with her physical, cognitive, social, and economic limitations, finds it increasingly difficult to match all the opportunities work has to offer, the expectations it harbors, and the demands that it makes. The result of this growing discrepancy is not just heightened pressure and stress, but also, as in Monica's case, frustration or even depression.

In a certain sense, these three types of experiences are all general, though the perception and awareness of them will of course vary. On the other hand, the consequences differ. Although everyone senses the speed and pace of change, not everyone is exhausted or burnt out as a result of it. Even though the displacement of control at work versus control of working conditions is felt by all, some experience it as enhanced freedom, whereas others experience it as lessened security. Although everybody sees the opportunities and harbors expectations for their work, not everyone is able to take advantage of and realize them. Here yet another inequality materializes. It is, however, not an inequality between those at the top versus those at the bottom as that would require a static order. The fact that some people have not been overcome by fatigue or burnt out by the fast pace and changing nature of the new work does not mean that they never will. Nor is this an inequality between the exploiters and the exploited, the prerequisite of which would be a zero-sum game in which everyone takes part and is needed. The ability of some to take advantage of and realize their possibilities and expectations does not dictate the inability of others. Finally, it is not the inequality of those who have power and those who lack it, which would require two or more hostile parties controlling each other or having a social relation to one another. The relative success of Peter and Stella is, after all, not based on them exercising power over people like Monica.

The emerging inequality is therefore not a social inequality, in that it is not distributed through social relations. Instead, relations between the concerned parties are similar to those between participants in a marathon. In a marathon it is pointless to speak of the differences between the runners in terms of social relations such as power, exploitation, or subordination. Either you are in the race or you are not. As long as you are in the race you can either be in the lead, in the pack, or behind. Each individual participates according to her own capabilities, and needs only the other participants to calculate her relative position. In other words, there is no evident relation between the runners other than their relative positions. The leader of the race is in the lead irrespective of how many runners are tailing him or have interrupted the race. The very last runner is last, regardless of how many are ahead or of how far ahead they are. The race as a whole is completely independent of the individual effort. A slow runner will not lower the tempo of the other runners, but will simply be left behind. Or, to rephrase it, the only one to care, or even notice, if a runner is left behind is that runner.

The new work is characterized by this particular kind of inequality. Stella and Peter are, in Peter's words, lagging a bit behind the leaders, whereas Monica has fallen far behind. Using another sport metaphor, we could even say she is on the bench. The inequalities between them do not primarily have to do with their jobs but with their individual capacities and opportunities. Peter can feel that it is getting more difficult, but there is still hope for a placement. Stella is beginning to notice her body reacting to the pace and worries about having to slow down and get stuck somewhere in the pack. Monica, on the other hand, is having doubts whether she will be able to hang on and finish the race at all. Peter and Stella are both young and well educated. Their mental and physical conditions, however, seem to differ. Monica has the physical requirements, but she is getting old. She does not have any kind of higher education, and on top of that she is a single mother and sole provider. Their opportunities for finishing the race all differ.

Perhaps we should better add that we, in underlining individual differences, by no means deny the existence of widespread power discrepancies and other social inequalities. On the contrary, these injustices to a large extent contribute to the differences in individual opportunities. But differing individual opportunities cannot be reduced to social differences. Differences in personality, attitudes, age, language, and cognitive, economic, biological, intellectual, physiological, and many other differences also play a significant role. Taken together with the "traditional" social differences, they generate the aforementioned individual opportunities. Of interest here, and what makes this more than the trivial statement that we are all different, is that the new work exploits and even presupposes such individual differences.

New Markets and New Structures

If the traditional inequality of work traces its origin to the hierarchical order of the workplace, the new inequality originates rather in the competitive nature of the contemporary labor market. The opportunities of the individual are decided not by her objective position within the organization, but by her relative position on the market. A person who is attractive to the labor market does not have to feel insecure. He or she has the possibilities to negotiate good working conditions, whereas those who are not attractive will be left at the mercy of a callous market.

It is not uncommon to explain this new inequality in terms of work and labor markets being influenced by a more liberalist, even neo-liberalist, policy. This statement is habitually used to claim that deliberate strategic political decisions have invested the market forces with more space for action. The fact that work and labor markets have been partially deregulated as a consequence of political decisions is true, as is that many of the decisions initiating these deregulations were taken within the framework of a neo-liberal agenda. This is valid internationally and especially if focusing on Anglophone countries. But though neo-liberal elements may be identified in the politics of numerous countries, it is still not possible to accuse all countries, including Sweden, of having conducted neo-liberal policies. Certainly, it is also up for discussion just how deliberate and strategic the decisions have actually been. Perhaps it has rather been a series of adjustments to growing pressure from international trade and competition. But it is difficult to deny that market forces have had their influence enhanced in work and on the labor market. Without downplaying the impact of political decisions, we would like to suggest an alternative representation of recent developments – a development where the internationalization of business has been an important driving force.

In Sweden, and in many other European countries, work and labor markets are relatively well regulated. Not only employment and wages but also working conditions and the job environment are regulated by laws and central agreements. These laws and agreements essentially mirror the balance of strength between the different parties on the labor market. They, so to speak, constitute the existing frontier between the parties, and they are changed by the unions advancing their positions on the employer, or by the employer doing the same thing vis-à-vis the unions. In other words, the regulation of work mirrors not only the diverging interests of the parties, but also their interdependence.

At least this can be said to have been the case up until the 1970s, when a substantial portion of the Western world stumbled into economic crisis. When their profits fell, companies were forced to finance their investments through raised prices and increased credit. This in turn led the unions to compensate their members by demanding wage increases, which shrunk profits and pushed prices even higher. The welfare state and bank system, through transfers and credits, acted as buffers by keeping up consumption and production in an inflation-triggering upward spiral. The result was simultaneous stagnation and inflation (aka stagflation).

In order to raise profits and speed up growth, companies increasingly turned to new markets abroad. This was mainly achieved through investment in other industries and in foreign companies. In the 1980s, Swedish investment abroad had already grown to twice the size of domestic investment. Swedish companies merged with, bought, bought stakes in, and entered into alliances and cooperation agreements with companies all over the world. Companies in other Western countries made similar investments. Through this strategy, companies expanded their markets beyond their national borders, first in neighboring countries and the Western sphere, later a few countries in Asia and Latin America, and during the 1990s the former Eastern bloc, followed by China and India. Simultaneously, companies were cutting their previously strong ties to unions and the welfare state in their country of origin. Instead of relying on these institutions, companies have become increasingly dependent on one another, as owners, partners, customers, or competitors in supranational commercial networks. Thus, companies do not necessarily relocate abroad, though this of course also happens, but rather they sign agreements, cooperate, and carry out transactions amongst themselves quite independently of national borders. And this is not only true for large corporations. Small- and medium-sized companies also take part in such transactions, or depend on them as subcontractors, at times several layers deep.

Not only has this worldwide "structural change" reduced companies' dependence on national and cultural roots, it has also increased the impact of the market forces. And the expansion is not just geographical. Parts of the developing countries and the former Eastern bloc have opened up to trade on free market conditions, but the expanding influence of market forces can also be felt in the national economy, between different sectors. In a majority of Western countries, most significantly perhaps in the Anglophone world, the publicly financed sector is increasingly operating on market principles. But the change has increased the impact of market forces in an even wider meaning. This has been done through the growth of the financial economy, through the development of new economic control systems, and through the development of new information technology. We will touch briefly on each of these three areas.

The growth of the financial economy originates, in slightly simplified terms, in companies' need for money to expand on the international market. Between 1984 and 1991, Swedish companies invested more than €22 billion abroad. Investments on this scale, within such a short period of time, require a sizable injection of capital. The lion's share of this capital was obtained through loans and other forms of credit. Traditionally, this has been arranged through a few institutional intermediaries, primarily banks. If a company needs a lot of capital relatively quickly, however, this may constitute a serious obstacle. Hence, during the 1970s, and still more during the 1980s, companies in growing numbers started to bypass these intermediaries and turned directly to investors on the financial market. Consequently, the world stock market's turnover increased dramatically throughout the 1980s. At the start of the 1970s, the turnover of financial transactions was twice that of the trade in goods and services, but in the first years of the 1980s it grew to a ratio of 10:1. By the mid-1990s the ratio was 70:1 (Dicken, 2003).

As companies mortgage their future profits through the sale of shares, the shares themselves achieve a certain value. In order to procure the necessary amount of investment or risk capital from the financial market, a seemingly unavoidable side effect will be the independent trade in shares and other securities. The larger the yield of the shares, the larger the trade will be. By the mid-1990s, an enormous 90 percent of all financial transactions were made up of speculative trade. Only 10 percent were immediately related to trade and the production of goods and services (Dicken, 2003). Speculative trade in shares does not concern itself with company profits per se – it only speculates in the expectations of such profits. This means that companies, in order to procure the capital they need, have to raise or at least maintain expectations of their profits. They, quite simply, must satisfy investors' constant demands for higher and shorter-term yield. Companies, in other words, are drawn into the game of speculative financial trade. This fuels the speculative trading further, as well as making company boards increasingly shortsighted in their actions.

The intrusion of market forces in companies is, however, not just a question of strategy but also of management. As companies expand, develop, take over, cooperate, or in other ways interact with other companies, they also come to span more and more areas and activities, rendering an overview of the activities more difficult. Different and differing products, techniques, competences, languages, and cultures – geographical as well as professional and industry-specific – meet and are coordinated within the framework of the company. It is impossible for the company management to know about every part of and premises for their activities. Instead, the common language becomes money. The company is divided into several self-supporting profit centers, subject to internal demands for returns, and controlled by sophisticated accounting systems. A profit center which does not live up to standards is sold, back-scaled, or closed down, and new activities bought in its place. The directorate sees the company simply as a collection of accountancy entries, which may be combined or manipulated into generating more or less short-term profits. The background for this view of company management is found in big American corporations' countermove to the anti-trust laws of the 1940s and 1950s. To ensure continued growth, companies were forced to expand into different industries and, as a consequence, diversify their activities. In order to control the company, advanced systems for financial control were developed. This attitude and these accounting systems later spread and became increasingly universal as companies in the 1970s and 1980s were expanding abroad (Fligstein, 1990).

However, the sizable financial market and advanced accounting systems of today would not have been possible without the new technology developed in the 1970s. The economic prerequisites of the new work have uninterruptedly developed throughout the post-war years, but they received a decisive push through what Manuel Castells (1996) calls "the information technology revolution," that is, the development of microelectronics, computers, and telecommunication. With the assistance of microelectronics, information processing could be built into all kinds of machines. Personal computers made information processing immediately accessible to individuals, and telecommunication tied them together in global communication networks. The development within each respective area was so fast that it truly deserves the epithet revolution. Microchips shrunk rapidly, while their capacity increased. Computers also became smaller, gained additional applicability, and became more user-friendly. Telecommunication sped up, was expanded, and increased its applicability as well. And to top it off, it all happened in little more than a decade. The development started in 1971 when Ted Hoff, an engineer at Intel, invented the microprocessor and ran until 1983 when researchers at Berkeley adjusted UNIX, an operating system enabling computers to communicate with each other, to the TCP/IP protocols that enabled communicating computers to be linked together in networks. Adding to this the development of other means of communication (satellite transfer, mobile telephony, fiber optics, etc.), we have the basis for the global communication network and a prerequisite for the international economy (Castells, 1996).

What we see here is that the enhanced influence of market forces by and large can be grasped against a backdrop of the international expansion of business. This expansion, in turn, has been an important driving force in the exploding development in financial markets. It has also played a decisive role in the growth and spread of the new economic systems for management and control that now, to a great extent, dominate work. Even if the emergence of the new information and communication technology is not directly derived from the international expansion of business, the continuing development and spread of the former is unthinkable without the contribution of the latter. Without taking any further stand on which is the chicken and which is the egg in this cocktail of factors, we would like to point to a development that, though in clear interaction with political institutions, to a large extent is quite beyond the reach of any effective political influence.

It is also against this backdrop that the labor market, despite existing and still substantial regulation, has grown more individualized and market-like. Although the dominant form of employment is still permanent employment, the number of temporary workers increased from about 10 to 15 percent during the 1990s, and this through a string of contract forms: by the hour and project employment, stand-in and probationary employment, as well as short-term contract employment to meet the temporary needs of the employer. During the 2000s there has been a stagnation and they constitute about 15 percent of the Swedish workforce. A reason for this stagnation is deregulation of public employment services in Sweden, which has resulted in a strong growth of hire agencies, Swedish and internationally based. Workers employed by hire agencies substitute temporary workers. The number of self-employed, that is, those with a private business and no employees, is similarly increasing. The same goes for part-time workers, who now make up more than 20 percent of employees.

Furthermore, we may state that competence demands have grown and changed. Since the beginning of the 1990s there are large losses of employment opportunities in the traditional sector of the manufacturing industry. In the same period, the service sector and the service content of the remaining industry jobs have grown. Qualification demands at work have also increased, mainly through the disappearance of low qualified jobs while other more highly qualified jobs have appeared. It is generally the case that knowledge-intensive jobs increase, while capital-intensive activities decline. One consequence of this development is that many of those who lose their jobs have problems finding new ones. They are simply not qualified enough or they lack the right "competence profile."

At the same time, as traditional jobs in the manufacturing industry become fewer and far between and the highly qualified white-collar jobs are on the rise, the number of low qualified service industry jobs is increasing. The growing service sector, however, has limited opportunities to compensate for the shrinking sector of manufacturing industry. While middle-aged male industry workers who have been made redundant certainly find it difficult to go back to school in order to get the right kind of knowledge and the right attitudes for getting a new job, it is just as difficult for them to fit into the service sector, dominated by young people, women, and immigrants. Today's unemployment is in this sense structural rather than dependent on current fluctuations of labor.

The international expansion of business and the surge in market influence, however, have not changed the labor market solely through the growing demands on and competition for the jobs. The surge in question has also meant that the general demands collectively made on employed industry workers have been exchanged for the individual, or even personal, demands on highly qualified employment or less qualified service jobs. In effect, competition increasingly hinges on individual rather than collective traits. The market forces consequently have not only become increasingly important on the labor market, they have moved closer and become more invasive to the individual.

The New Work Life

In this altered state of affairs, companies have become more aware of competition. As a result, they have also adjusted their organization. They have cut down on personnel to become more cost-efficient and they have sold off, shut down, or outsourced unprofitable segments of their operation. At the same time, the organization of work has adjusted to the various demands particular to the business. In cases where the demands are not obvious, goals not clearly defined, or where their definition instead is an integral part of the job, the traditional organization has become more relaxed, or sometimes even deregulated. Instead new rules and norms have been developed – rules expecting individuals to adjust their work continuously to changeable demands. By contrast, jobs where demands are relatively simple, specified, and repetitive have seen the organization grow tighter and more detailed. The employment relation has been subject to similar adjustments, and at times, as in the case of labor firms, it has been sidestepped altogether. The philosophy behind this is, of course, that employees should be fed in to work as easily as they are shipped out. Thereby the workforce can be adjusted to the fluctuating demands of work.

The continuous adjustments of companies to the market, as well as the subsequent work organization strategies, however, place a great strain on the individual. When the set of rules regulating the individual job relaxes or disappears altogether, the need for the individual worker to plan, organize, and take responsibility for the completion of work becomes increasingly important. The same thing happens, although inverted, when the set of rules is tightened and the employment relation is restricted. The individual is forced to adjust within an ever-shrinking scope of action.

The demands put on the individual are also not clear and straightforward. They are, rather, multidimensional. There is the cognitive knowledge, meaning the demands for "technical" knowledge made on the individual in relation to his or her specific tasks. For certain jobs these demands will be so complex and comprehensive that they overwhelm the individual through the sheer quantity of information, sometimes even exceeding her ability to absorb it. As a consequence the demands are displaced and focus is shifted to the practical capacity of identifying, handling, organizing, and applying the knowledge needed for the moment.

While the requirements for technical and explicit knowledge in that sense become more practical and implicit, the demands for social knowledge, on the other hand, become more technical and explicit. The requirements for social competence, social networks, and social capital become ever more important for an individual to do the job, advance within the organization, and if necessary find a new job. Hence, both the technical and social knowledge needed in the work of today are more personal, portable, and refer to the capacity for adjusting to different situations. As a result, a large part of the universal premises of work disappear. Instead of collective usefulness and community, work becomes more of an individual project for personal development or survival.

The same is true for the relationship between work and private life. The more flexible the organization of work, the more blurred the distinction between work and private life. Where to draw the line becomes a question of negotiation between the parties concerned. It is then up to the individual to establish and maintain personal limits. How the individual shapes her life and relates to her job is hence more and more dependent on individual opportunities and preferences. This also means that conflicts, problems, and the experience of balance in the relationship between work and private life will seem to affect each individual differently.

Stress and other health consequences brought about by working life must also be considered, to an increasing extent, against a backdrop of the plethora of differing working conditions and individual requirements found in work. Health problems generated by companies' demands for flexibility are only to a limited extent attributed to organizational restrictions, low mental requirements, and lack of influence at work. Instead they follow from the fact that individuals strain themselves beyond their capacity in an attempt to meet the demands of a job with no clear boundaries. Further, they concern individuals' feelings of insecurity and uncertainty when facing unreasonable or unformulated demands. These also concern individuals being forced to accept working conditions they normally would not accept for fear of being excluded, marginalized, or sidestepped. Finally, these health problems will not be countered with more information, negotiations, laws, job design, or preventive work environment measures. Instead it is the individuals themselves who have to ration their efforts, make counter-demands, and increase their employability.

We can conclude that the new work is based on individual differences and opportunities. The dynamic of working life is created through the accentuation and exploitation of these very differences. It forces the individuals to compete with one another and in the process accept higher demands. It encourages them to develop and take additional responsibility for their work. It also compels them to exploit their potential and strain themselves to, and sometimes beyond, their capacity. It is perhaps best to point out that this does not necessarily mean that working conditions have deteriorated. Quite on the contrary, measured by traditional standards they have in many cases improved substantially. These working conditions, however, are linked to other conditions. Much more extensively than previously, they are tied to individual performance and responsibility. This is perhaps also the most important difference between the work we have been used to during most of the twentieth century and the new work that is emerging. Working conditions are to a lesser extent clear, unconditional, and universal. Instead they are tied to specific conditions and dependent on individual opportunities, situations, and performances. Previously fixed boundaries are blurred, and it is up to the individual to find new points of reference from which to navigate.

What is so New about "The New Work"?

We have tried to give an introductory picture of what we mean by the new work. Before we go on, however, we should perhaps mention a few things about the expression itself. When speaking about "the new work," two objections are immediately voiced. One objection is that the phenomena in question in most cases have been present previously in one form or another, and that they hence are not very new at all. The other objection is that the difference between the old and new work is exaggerated. Alternatively, that there is no difference whatsoever and that no change has actually occurred. In order to prevent these objections from recurring and annoying the reader, we think that it would be appropriate to bring them up at the start and, insofar as it is possible, explain how we relate to them. Therefore, we will deal with them here, in due order.

Speaking about "the new work" is fraught with difficulties as it implies working life is not what it used to be. Depending on what is meant by "used to be," it is always possible to find traits that are, or at least seem, just like they used to be. A few reservations might thus be in place. The question is: what do we really mean when we speak about the "new" work? Without disclosing the actual content of this book, that is, enumerating phenomena, terminology, and theories we believe are new, we will here just briefly try to explain what we mean by calling them new.

Quite a few phenomena exist, of course, which are categorically new, for instance, information transmission and communication via fiber optics and satellite. Another example is the spread of personal computers and the extensive use of the Internet. Speaking about new information and communication techniques in general, however, can be more problematic as the history of calculators, telegraphs, telephones, and computers is rather long. So again the question is: when can we start calling these phenomena new?

A general answer is when the phenomena in question have grown in scope, become cheaper, smaller, or faster. Computers existed and were used already in the late 1940s, but they revolutionized working life only when they became small, fast, and cheap enough to be used to a significant extent by a critical mass and, not least, when the Internet was fully developed. The same thing goes for temporary employment. This form of employment has always existed, but only lately has it become more common. We could in the same breath mention international trade, relocation of jobs, and the use of flexible techniques of production. It may therefore be claimed that a previously occurring phenomenon is new if it has gone through a significant change in sheer scope and quantity.

But there are also phenomena that we consider new, even though they existed previously to a greater extent. Working from home, for instance, was relatively common before the 1960s. In spite of this, we call telecommuting, in reality a form of work from home, a new phenomenon. It is also not very common, despite the considerable attention given to telecommuting during the 1990s, which could lead to a belief that this is the case. The reason for this misunderstanding is that the old and new versions of work from home have very little in common. Before the 1960s, working from home was mainly a female undertaking, involving women who performed low-qualified part-time office tasks or dressmaking, while at the same time watching children and tending to domestic chores. To this day, private daycare workers and teachers preparing classes and correcting tests represent the most commonly occurring forms for working from home in Sweden. What makes telecommuting a new phenomenon is not just the name, although this is not unimportant. Telecommuting is certainly work performed from home, but it concerns different groups and quite different tasks than traditional "homework." Telecommuters are mainly highly educated, male (at least when the expression was coined in 1970s America) white-collar workers, who have a regular workplace, but who choose to perform certain tasks outside of this workplace. This phenomenon probably existed earlier. Telecommuting was decisively introduced into the new work when it was carried out with the help of new information and communication technology. Using a mobile phone, personal computer, and an Internet connection, a wealth of office tasks can in principle be performed just as well from home as from the workplace. We can therefore argue that a previously encountered phenomenon is new if it has taken on a new meaning, involves new groups and tasks, or if the premises for it are new. We can also claim that it is new if it has gone through substantial qualitative changes.

Yet, a reason for calling an old phenomenon new is if it interacts with other phenomena, which need not be new either, to give rise to a new, more comprehensive phenomenon. Although the individual phenomena are not new, their interaction potentially is. For instance, a company selling part of its business to other companies is not a new phenomenon. Neither is cutting down on personnel or making working conditions worse. Not even closing down factories and moving the jobs abroad constitute a new phenomenon. But when Ericsson sells its manufacturing units for mobile phones to Flextronics, a Singapore-based subcontractor specializing in manufacturing electronic components for businesses worldwide, and Flextronics speeds up the work pace, lowers social benefits for the employees, and finally shuts down several factories all over the world, relocating production to low-wage countries such as Malaysia, Poland, and China, we have a new phenomenon. By outsourcing cost- and personnel-intensive production to a subcontractor, Ericsson avoids both responsibility and fixed expenses. But not only that, Ericsson can also make demands on the subcontractor and squeeze the prices of their products. Instead of increasing the work pace, squeezing the cost of wages, and lowering social benefits in their own factories, Ericsson, through this sale, passes it all on to Flextronics. Similar agreements exist between many other companies.

Several new phenomena can be identified in this deal alone. Delegating production – a sizable, central part of activities most companies, old or new, would consider their very core – to a subcontractor is a new phenomenon. The existence of companies specialized in handling production for other firms around the world, companies that, like Flextronics, can be several times the size of their customers, is also a new phenomenon. Squeezing fixed costs for factories and personnel by systematically moving production to low-wage countries is yet another new phenomenon. A common characteristic for all these new occurrences is that they are a function of the global cooperation of companies. We can hence summarize that previously existing phenomena can be considered new if they are now part of a larger pattern that is new. We could probably go on enumerating reasons for calling old phenomena new, but we hope the ones we have mentioned will suffice. Instead, we move on to the second objection that the differences between the old and new work are exaggerated.

The New and the Old Work

When speaking about the new work one is also, explicitly or implicitly, commenting on the old. Contrasting and comparing to something old is a common technique for pointing out what is new. There is often a pedagogical point to this. Understanding a concept is easier if it is clear how it has evolved. But there are two problems with this way of arguing. The use of contrasts tends to exaggerate differences and creates a schematic and unfair dichotomy. Not only do the old and the new, through this, seem more homogenous, they are also made into each other's respective opposites. The second problem is that an order of succession is implied. The new order, it is assumed, in all significant respects has replaced the old order. Both problems concern social changes and what is meant by it.

One recurring point of confusion when speaking of social changes has to do with the various levels that serve as a point of departure or reference. To put it simply, we can say that social changes unfold on three different levels.

The first is the *empirical* level. By this is meant demonstrable behavioral changes or other material changes. In order to speak about a change in working life on this level, one should preferably be able to show that a majority of companies, workplaces, or employees have assumed significantly new characteristics or behavior. But there may be certain difficulties involved in this, as social changes do not happen overnight. A new phenomenon is also, by definition, a minor phenomenon. When it finally reaches major proportions it is no longer new. That is why one rather speaks of statistical changes. By this is meant a series of more or less distinct deviations in the pattern, for example, for income levels, GDP, or various response frequencies to surveys.

The second level is the *institutional*. This designates changes in or of the rules and norms by which we live. These rules and norms can either be formal or informal. In both cases, however, changes may be difficult to prove, as nothing needs to have changed on the surface of things. For instance, formal sets of rules may be unchanged, and people, when asked, still quote established norms and values. Rules and norms, as is the case, are not always changed by a majority vote. Rather, they can be likened to the rules of a game. The basis of game rules is that everybody follows them and the main reason why people follow the rules of a game is that everybody else does. It is therefore sufficient if one person, or at least a critical minority, no longer follows the rules for the whole game to fall apart. Until this happens, however, players will quote, by force of habit, the old game rules. It can therefore be difficult to find out whether institutional changes are underway by simply asking people about it.

The third level is the *discursive* level. This signifies the concepts and models we use in order to explain how everything ties together. Changes at this level are usually easy to point out, but significantly more difficult to verify on any of the other two levels. A further problem concerns the fact that concepts and models, in a very obvious way, are social constructions. They are formulated in a social context with all that this implies in terms of presumptions, perspectives, and intentions. As a result, concepts and models must always be interpreted and evaluated with this in mind.

Disagreement on concepts and models is hence only natural. When there is no longer disagreement the models in question are probably no longer new.

These three levels or perspectives are of course interconnected, but hardly in any clear, unambiguous way. It may nevertheless be assumed that the discursive level is the least permanent of the levels. New concepts and models are constantly being promoted. The institutional level is rather more sluggish. Rules and norms do not change very easily. In certain respects, the empirical level is perhaps the slowest moving of them all. In order for a new behavioral pattern to be charted, the old pattern must not only be dissolved, but a new one must be established. At the same time, it is at the empirical level that changes originate. They are, however, difficult to detect with comprehensive statistics. In order to detect changes at a relatively early stage, strategically targeted measures, or case studies, will have to be employed. However, these will always be open to criticism for being incorrectly chosen, over-interpreted, or biased.

We have studied changes on all three levels, but our focus is on the institutional level. When we speak about a new work we mean that the rules of work have changed or are changing. "Rules" do not necessarily imply formal sets of rules, laws, and agreements. Instead we focus on informal rules and norms that are consciously or subconsciously used in working life. The individual will experience them in the shape of various demands or expectations that the situation puts on her – and that she puts on herself. Such demands and expectations may be more or less explicit, as is the case with most of the traditional control systems used at work. But they may just as well be implicit and built into our knowledge in and about work.

When we claim that rules have changed or are changing, this should not be taken to mean that old rules are necessarily replaced by new ones. What is happening is more often that new rules and norms are added to the already existing framework. The reason for this development is the changing premises following the development of new markets, industries, and activities. In a long-term perspective this may of course involve the disappearance of old rules and norms. But a surprising amount of "old" rules and norms still remain in working life, although often in a modified form.

A substantial part of the rules concerning work were developed in and through the first factories. There were a vast number of rules for the behavior of workers, consolidated into coherent sets of rules concerning, above all, time and space. As explained by Shoshana Zuboff (1988), the purpose of this was to get the workers to stay in one place and perform consistently within a given period of time. As factories, production, and machines grew and became more complicated, rules were also developed for the procedure of work and its administration. Perhaps the best-known representatives for this development were Frederick Taylor (1911; [1912]1977) and Henri Fayol (1916) respectively. They formulated and theorized rules that together formed what we today call the sequentially and hierarchically ordered "organization," an order dominating working life throughout the twentieth century.

Since the 1970s, however, companies' operating conditions have undergone substantial changes. Attempts have been made to adjust to these new conditions through the creation of more "flexible" forms of organization. The method, which will be discussed in greater detail in Chapter 2, is the introduction of more flexible forms of work in which the individual to a greater extent defines, plans, structures, and takes responsibility for his work. But flexibility is also achieved through more flexible forms of employment, in which the individual to a greater extent becomes replaceable.

But the development of these new rules does not automatically imply the disappearance of the old rules. Many workplaces, possibly even a majority, are still using a traditionally sequential and hierarchical work organization. Even newly established industries and workplaces such as the expanding fast-food industry use it. Other workplaces have deregulated or eased up their rules to a certain extent. Examples of this phenomenon are the spread of flexitime and telecommuting. Yet other industries and workplaces have, as previously mentioned, developed very flexible forms of work. One need only look at the creative jobs characterizing small IT, media, and consulting firms in the 1990s. Working life, in other words, does not develop through the replacement of old rules by new ones. Instead, development comes in the form of additional rules. Rules do not change, they proliferate.

Consequently, we cannot point to an obvious difference between an old and a new working life. Rather, as rules of work are developed the heterogeneity of work becomes more apparent. An important assumption regarding the new work is that we live in a world of several different working orders. Today's work is not a unified whole, but consists of a plethora of simultaneous working orders. In other words, the work of today is distinguished by an augmented differentiation at the same time as we, through the new inequality, can distinguish an increased polarization. This is, in conclusion, how we perceive the relationship between the old and new work. New industries, markets, companies, techniques, and forms of cooperation have developed. These new phenomena, in turn, have changed the premises for other industries, markets, and companies, forcing them to adjust to the new situation. These adjustments, however, occur in different degrees and in various ways. Hence, certain industries, markets, and companies remain relatively unaltered, whereas others have been changed to the core.

The Purpose and Structure of this Book

The field of interest of this book is vast. We will discuss organization and social theory, cognition and psychobiology. Nevertheless, the topics are united, at least in our opinion, by a common perspective. Our constant focus will be the individual, while trying to place her, as well as the theories concerning her, into a social context. The field of interest of this book is wide, also in the sense that we will bring up a multitude of, at times, seemingly disparate theories, concepts, and phenomena. Our reason for the absence of any coherent theoretical frame of reference is, quite simply, that no such frame exists. When our interest in the new work was first awakened sometime in the mid-1990s, many people were talking about it. From a scientific point of view, however, it was, in the popular phrase, all talk and no show. Since then things have definitely changed. A vast amount of studies, concepts, and perspectives, almost impossible to survey, have been introduced and discussed, both within and outside the world of scientific research. But a comprehensive framework on this research is still missing. There is no general agreement about what the new work is all about, what should be included in this concept, or even if there is such a concept at all. This book has been written as an attempt to remedy this situation and to create a comprehensive framework of these perspectives, theoretical approaches, and real working life changes during the last twenty years. We, however, do not make any claims to success in this project. Nevertheless, we hope, through this book, to contribute to the emergence of a greater understanding of this area as a whole.

We are not just researchers, we are also teachers. We educate students, are practicing social scientists, as well as researchers. Hence, the scope of the book mirrors the various parts and kinds of knowledge we believe are a prerequisite for understanding and approaching the new world of work. This also implies that the book should not be seen as a mere study of the various theories, concepts, or phenomena it deals with. *The first purpose* of the book is instead epistemographic, that is, to structure the area of knowledge, and to synthesize rather than analyze its respective parts.

On the other hand this should not be taken to mean that the book is purely descriptive, or that we entirely lack ambitions to theorize. We believe that there are some, more or less distinct, patterns that characterize the work of today. *The second purpose* of the book is therefore to try and demonstrate these patterns and how they recur in several separate areas of the new work.

As a result, the book is structured cross-dimensionally. First of all, it has been divided into six chapters, of which the middle four each treat a separate theme.

- *The first theme* concerns the new organization of work and is discussed in Chapter 2. In this chapter we account for various forms of flexibility and their corresponding organization of work.
- *The second theme* concerns the knowledge needed in the new work and is discussed in Chapter 3. Here four distinct dimensions of knowledge are discussed. First, the cognitive dimension, relating to the knowledge required to carry out the particular tasks. Second, the social dimension, meaning the knowledge needed to relate to other individuals in the work. Third, the societal dimension, by which is meant the knowledge of work as part of society. Fourth, the existential dimension, meaning the knowledge, or the self-image, we entertain of ourselves as employees and workers.
- *The third theme* treats the relationship of the new work to our private lives. This theme is discussed in Chapter 4 where we will briefly treat the various relationships between work and private life as described in previous research. We will then discuss the social demands put on us outside of work. Finally, we show how the relationship between work and private life appears in our research on boundaryless works.
- *The fourth theme* concerns the health consequences of the new work (Lundberg and Cooper, 2010). This is discussed in Chapter 5 where we cover stress research and its relation to a number of social problems. After this we discuss the new work as a cause of ill-health, as well as the new ill-health in society.

Theories and concepts relevant to the understanding of the themes are dealt with in their respective chapters. The chapters are in this way meant to serve as an introduction to their specific areas. In order to provide illustrations to the theories and concepts we treat, we occasionally use results from our own research as examples. The different themes and chapters are, when put together, meant to give a more comprehensive picture of the new work.

But the book also has another structural dimension. Three separate theses on the new work run, more or less distinctly, through all chapters of this book.

- *The first thesis* is that work is subject to a series of alterations in the way that it is regulated. By this we mean alterations aiming to make companies and organizations more flexible.
- *The second thesis*, which in part follows on the first thesis, is that the labor force is being individualized, or even autonomized. The new regulations expect the individual to identify, choose, plan, structure, and take personal responsibility for her work. This, in turn, presupposes certain abilities and talents, or at least the possibility to develop them. These demands collide with and, in certain cases, even break up the collectives and the social identity formed around work ever since the onset of industrialism. Instead, the individual is left to find his own way in an increasingly competitive labor market.
- *The third thesis*, which can also be said to follow from the previous two, is that work has become increasingly heterogeneous. When the conditions of work vary from one industry, workplace, and individual to the other, it becomes increasingly difficult to speak about work in general. Jobs are adjusted to their individual premises and are allowed to vary, depending on the context. This does not necessarily mean that work is flexible in relation to the worker. It might just as well mean that the worker needs to stay flexible in relation to work. The consequence, in any case, is that the variations of work increase.

This book is based on experiences and knowledge gained within the framework of a Swedish research program called "Boundaryless work." The program ran from 1998 to 2006. The book, however, is not an account of the program, or of the studies carried out within it. For such an account, we refer to the reports, articles, and theses that were written within the framework of the program. Instead, the book wants to give a more comprehensive view of the area concerned by the program studies, what we have here called the new work. For this reason, we will, in this book, deal primarily with theories, concepts, data, and research published by other scholars, Swedish and international. They will be presented in the text and referenced in the customary manner. From time to time, however, we punctuate the text with experience taken from our own research. When referring to our own experiences in this manner we imply research conducted and reported within the framework of the program. The function of these punctuations, then, is primarily to exemplify and illustrate, rather than verify, the present line of argument.

2
The New Rules of Work: On Flexible Work and How to Manage It

The Nuer have no expression equivalent to "time" in our language, and they cannot, therefore, as we can, speak of time as though it were something actual, which passes, can be wasted, can be saved, and so forth. I do not think that they ever experience the same feeling of fighting against time or of having to coordinate activities with an abstract passage of time because their points of reference are mainly the activities themselves, which are generally of a leisurely character. Events follow a logical order, but they are not controlled by an abstract system, there being no autonomous points of reference to which activities have to conform with precision. Nuer are fortunate.

(excerpt from E. Evans-Pritchard, *The Nuer*, quoted in Thompson, 1967)

In his classic article about time and work discipline in the youth of industrialism, Edward P. Thompson describes how important time measuring was for the establishment of modern work. Through the introduction of common working hours for all employees in a factory, the coordination of several individual activities into one became possible. Separate but interdependent activities could hence, within the framework of common working hours, be performed in parallel, and with an intensity, precision, and volume which previously had been impossible. And this held true not only in the factories. With the help of pocket watches, timetables, and schedules, activities everywhere in society could be coordinated in a previously unparalleled way. Traveling, transports, preparations, deliveries, and consignments to and from different places and carried out by independently operating actors were coordinated with time and place as primary references.

Work Without Boundaries: Psychological Perspectives on the New Working Life, First Edition. Michael Allvin, Gunnar Aronsson, Tom Hagström, Gunn Johansson, and Ulf Lundberg.
© 2011 John Wiley & Sons, Ltd. Published 2011 by John Wiley & Sons, Ltd.

In pre-industrial society there was no definite concept of time to relate and adjust to. Therefore there also was no set time devoted to certain activities. They were simply allowed to take the time necessary. All activities were embedded, so to speak, in an immediate "here and now," and it was also in this context they acquired meaning for those present. The establishment of a common clock-time as a coordinating principle for different activities, however, means that the independent activities become important to one another only in relation to an abstract system of reference. It is then not enough that a particular activity is carried out; it also has to be carried out at a particular time. Activities performed outside of this time frame are in this context meaningless, they are non-activities. Engaging in such an activity is as pointless as buying a ticket for a train that has already departed.

This was also valid for the place. The establishment of a designated workplace enabled the coordination and cooperation of activities. The workplace was isolated from society at large in order to concentrate its activities and relate them to one another. The workplace itself was subdivided to accommodate for different activities and hierarchies. Preparatory work had its designated place, tooling and product finishing had theirs. The office was in a separate location with its own entrance. Within each section, each worker had their place, and each place had its worker. These workplaces were so organized that those who worked would be in contact only with those who relayed them work to be done, or those they passed it on to. Parallel work processes were kept separated. All workplaces were also arranged so as to enable constant supervision by supervisors. The purpose of this workplace organization was to maximize the functional interaction between separate activities, while minimizing the dysfunctional, or social, interaction.

In pre-industrial society there was no independent, separate place to relate to. Activities were allowed to fill the space necessary for their performance. They were tied to places rather than to one another. Hence there was also no need to coordinate them to any particular extent. Necessary coordination took place in that those involved were physically present. The establishment of a particular workplace, however, meant that separate activities were coordinated using an abstract room principle and they took place quite independently of each other. A worker performing a particular activity in a tooling process never needed to have any contact with those performing another activity in the same process. It was even desirable that they should remain entirely out of touch with one another, so as not to disrupt the process and disturb concentration. Independent activities were related and became mutually meaningful only in the context of their common physical location.

Activities that are subjected to an abstract structure of time and place, while taking place independently from the immediate needs of life, first become a wider phenomenon within the context of industrialism. Here another form of work also makes its first appearance: wage labor. Wage labor is hence something taking place in relation to an abstract structure of time and place. Also, the term wage labor did not imply any specific activities or results of activities, but rather all activities taking place within a particular time frame at a particular workplace. This is also what the workers were paid for. The employee was nothing more than labor. The first job of management was to control the availability of said labor, or in other words their personnel's attendance.

The establishment of attendance as an absolute work rule in the factories meant the birth of industrial work organization. Physical presence had been necessary also in agriculture and artisans' trades, but in the factories it took on a whole new meaning. Attendance was here defined with an exactitude previously known only within the armed forces. Factory work was synonymous with remaining in one place and performing consistently for a sufficiently long time. Whoever left their designated place during working hours, if only to speak to whoever worked the neighboring machine, or to go to the washroom, was subject to steep fines in the form of wage deductions. This strict regulation of time and place has accompanied work throughout the ages. Today, the majority of work is still measured, defined, and coordinated through some form of regulated working hours (opening hours, telephone hours, overtime, emergency duty hours, meeting hours, and holiday working hours) and a similarly regulated workplace.

During the latter half of the 1800s the premises of work changed. Markets were growing, and with them production and factories. New inventions, such as electricity and the internal combustion engine, meant that factories became independent of daylight and of natural power sources, such as streams and steam. Production could hence be placed almost anywhere, and organized to preferences. Demands, not only for coordination but also for the rationalization of work, increased. Up to this point, more complicated tasks had been performed by skilled professionals. The character of their work was rather similar to that of artisanship, and they knew their machines like the palm of their hand. But they were an obstacle to the increased productivity of the factories. Toward the end of the 1800s, planning engineers started rationalizing work by breaking down skill-demanding tasks into smaller pieces, and then putting these pieces together in new, more efficient ways. In this way a simplified, universal means of work regulation was developed, that is, the *work task*, predefined and independent of the individual performing it.

Leading and administrating the workforce responsible for performing these new work tasks became a profession in its own right with its own relevant area of knowledge: labor management and work organization respectively. A pioneer within this area of knowledge was Henri Fayol, a French mining engineer. Fayol (1916) formulated a number of administrative principles for the management of larger organizations, 14 of them to be exact, which in various ways emphasized the importance of the submission of the individual to the larger whole, and to an absolute direction. Social interaction within an organization must be vertical and not horizontal in nature. Fayol's principles were, consequently, a set of rules for *hierarchy*.

This set of rules, together with the work task regulations, supplemented the original regulations of time and place. Taken together, this set of rules formed what we today know as the hierarchical and sequential "organization." Ever since, this form of organization has been so evident that, for the larger part of the twentieth century, it has for all intents and purposes become synonymous with wage labor. "Work" is quite simply what we do within the framework of an organization of this kind. It is what we do during our working hours and at our workplace. It is what we do when we perform our predefined work tasks and when we make decisions within the framework of our limited area of responsibility. Wage labor is, in other words, what we do when following the rules of work, not more not less.

During the past 20–30 years, however, this form of organization has come to be questioned as the obvious choice for regulating labor. The reason for this development is the changing conditions companies now face, demanding quicker and more flexible action. For this purpose, new rules and management forms are being developed to replace or add to the old ones. These new rules and management methods form the topic of this chapter.

We believe that these newly developed and developing rules do not differ from previous rules in that they regulate different things. To a great extent the new rules still regulate time, place, work tasks, and social interaction. Rather, what is new is that the character of the rules has changed. They are looser and more goal oriented. They are also not predefined or external in origin. The regulation of work is, to an increasing extent, handed over to the individual, who then, to a varying degree, personally defines, plans, structures, and takes responsibility for their work.

Parallel to this development is another, seemingly opposite trend. It involves the tightening and spread of work regulation to professions that previously were not so strictly regulated, or that were regulated through different, professional sets of rules. The sharpening of these sets of rules is often linked to the breaking up of traditional forms of employment. In other words, work becomes more constricted and conventional while workers become more loosely tied to their work. These separate developments are both commonly justified with the argument that companies constantly have to adjust to the terms of the market.

In this chapter we will describe the background for what is popularly called flexible work. By flexible work we mean, by and large, the impact on work by companies' adjustments to market demands. We will then go through the two tendencies of development and describe them as two separate ways for achieving flexibility. One of these ways we have called flexibility through empowerment, the other, flexibility through substitution. Both of these ways, however, entail a breach of the traditional set of rules governing work. We will therefore also describe some of the new tools for managing and controlling work. By way of conclusion, we will discuss the respective differences of these two ways.

Flexible Work

When the American researchers Michael Piore and Charles Sabel (1984) introduced the term "flexible production," they were concerned with the pre-industrial craftsman's mode of production. This form of production is not characterized by the functional division of work and the pronounced standardization of industrial mass production. When, during the latter part of the 1800s, mass production was being developed and productivity was increasing, traditional artisans' production became largely neglected. The Piore and Sabel thesis is, however, that although artisanship was marginalized with the breakthrough of industrialism, it did not cease to exist. Instead it was modified and developed in those areas where mass production proved impossible. An artisan's mode of production was hence used, for instance, in the production of luxury goods, experimental products, machines, specialized tools, for repairs and maintenance, or for those products where markets were too insecure for the enormous investments necessary for mass production. Artisanship was, consequently, not just a "rest" category. It survived as a complement, a lubricant, and an innovative accessory within the framework of industrialism (Piore and Sabel, 1984, p. 206–207).

The element of artisanship in industrial production, however, varied between industries and countries. When markets wavered, and the economic infrastructure that mass production relied on started to come apart in the 1970s, it was the technically intensive workshop industry in Japan and Germany, countries with a relatively large element of artisanship in their industrial production, which acquired a leading position on the international market (Coates, 2002).

The point of mass production is that the cost per unit drops as the amount of units produced increases. The more is produced, the more profitable the products become. As the production series are the least profitable right at the start, long series and few adjustments are the essential factors to making production really profitable. The problem with this mode of production is that it is sensitive to disruption and it cannot handle sudden changes in demand. In Japan, however, a series of techniques had been developed in order to, for example, cut the time needed to readjust workshop machinery (change-over time), reduce faults and cassations in the process of production, and to reduce inventory costs (Gronning, 1997; Kenney and Florida, 1988; Hutchins, 1988; Ouchi, 1981). The Japanese techniques enabled the cost-efficient production of short product series within the framework of industrial mass production. In this way, the seemingly impossible was attainable: flexible mass production.

These techniques quickly became much discussed, in demand, and were spread throughout the world under snappy by-names such as *Kaizen*, *Just-In-Time*, *Kanban*, *No Buffer*, *Quality Circles*, and *Poka Yoke*. However, Japanese business executives and rationalization experts tried to play down the importance of individual techniques for the benefit of the comprehensive production philosophy of which they were part. The important thing was not to introduce a specific rationalizing measure, but rather to understand the purpose of the measure in question (Shingo and Dillon, 1989). In order to implement and combine the techniques, each worker in production had to know and constantly be aware of what the other workers in the production process were doing. The industrial division of work and the clear distributive lines between individual tasks that it entails was, accordingly, an obstacle to a more flexible mode of production and made inefficient use of the available resources.

The same conclusions had been drawn in the German industry, but from a different perspective. In Germany it was, above all, increasing automation that forced a more artisan attitude to production. As automation accelerated, so did the need for qualified machine tenders. In time these workers became increasingly central to the production process as a whole, leading to production being organized around them rather than the other way around. As industries were being automated they were also becoming more knowledge intensive and employees more qualified (Kern and Schumann, 1987).

Owing to the Japanese and German examples, industrial development henceforth implied an increasing integration of work tasks, instead of the previous differentiation. Concurrently with its success on the international market, this conviction spread to other countries and industries. In Sweden, a country which always has been very dependent on exports, the new way of thinking was adopted early on. In a policy publication from 1979, the Swedish Employers' Confederation described it as the production method of the future. This reception of the new reasoning was certainly not only a reaction to increasing international competition, but also to union demands for industry work with more possibilities for development. Nonetheless, the industrial production in Sweden was developing toward a more process-oriented organization and semi-autonomous work groups (Sandberg, 1982). During the 1980s serious efforts were made to integrate work tasks and to, through organizational measures, eliminate time-wasting impediments to the production process. Renowned examples are the Volvo car assembly plant in Kalmar and Uddevalla (Sandberg, 1995; Berggren, 1992).

But the crises of the 1970s also opened the door for realizations reaching beyond the rationalization of the process of production. When mass markets yielded it became obvious that putting out products as fast as possible was not enough; they also had to be sold. The revenue from a product comes not from its production, but from its sale. This realization led to an increased awareness of the role of the customer in the value-creating process. Hence it became increasingly important to, at an early stage, involve the customer in the process of production. This was achieved through highly developed marketing, which also was integrated in production. Among the methods used were sophisticated customer group analyses, wider product ranges with special "niched" goods, letting customers specify their own articles, and packaging the products as lifestyle accessories.

But the most far-reaching advances were made within the growing service industry. The production of services differs from manufacturing on many points. To start with, service is intangible, which means it cannot be generated, handled, distributed, or sold anonymously. Instead, it presupposes direct contact between vendor and purchaser. Service also consists of a series of actions, or rather interactions. This means that service is produced simultaneously and in the same place as the consumer consumes it. It all takes place in the meeting with the consumer. Customer contacts can hence be considered the service production equivalent of the product manufacturing "work processes."

From this follows a series of consequences for the organization of service production. The first is that service cannot, unlike manufacturing, be centrally produced and then distributed to the consumers. Instead it has to be produced locally – on the spot. A service organization is therefore also a distributed organization. The new technology, however, has for the last twenty years partially changed this reality. Phenomena such as Internet selling, call centers, and telemarketing can be said to have made services independent of location. Another consequence is that the consumer is drawn into production as one of its factors. This may happen in several different ways. One of them is that the customer takes part in the specification of the service he or she buys. This is true for instance of the health service industry where the patient participates in making the diagnosis. But it is also valid for other service areas where the service is customized for the individual consumer. The customer can also be made to participate in the actual production, which happened for example when railways make the transition from having personnel sell tickets on the train to letting their customers buy and stamp their own tickets in vending machines. Another example of this phenomenon is the Internet banks which have made cash counter service superfluous. Yet another way is to involve the customer in the quality control of the service. Richard Normann (2001) writes:

> When cleaning companies substitute cleaning outside office hours for daytime cleaning it is not only because they save labor costs. When cleaning is done while the client looks on, there is an element of quality control built into the service delivery system. (p. 118)

A third consequence for the organization of service activities is that they become customer managed. This, in effect, turns the organizational hierarchy upside down, and reduces, at least in rhetoric, the administrative apparatus to a purely supportive function with the service personnel on the "frontline" and "the customer in the center" (Normann, 2001).

An early example is that of the Scandinavian airline, SAS, in the 1980s. After having run at a loss for quite some time, Jan Carlzon was recruited from the then largest domestic carrier in Scandinavia. He became synonymous with the transformation of the company from a travel to a service provider. Carlzon (1987) describes, among other things, how central offices were closed and how all activities were moved to the airport, where the various categories of personnel got to teach each other their respective jobs so that ticket vending, check-in, telephone, and customer service could be handled by all categories of personnel. According to Carlzon, not only did these measures save money, they also improved service.

> In fact, service is probably better because the organization is more flexible. Now that everyone knows each other's jobs, there is always someone around who can handle the problem of the moment. And for many employees, work has become more fun and challenging. (p. 60)

These and other experiences contributed to a wave of decentralization, where tasks, responsibility, and resources were pushed downward in the organizations: from general management to individual branches, working teams, and sometimes down to individual workers. The rationalization of activities came to mean the same thing as the breaking down of internal barriers between separate functions within the process of production, between production and administration, and to the benefit of the business process (Ashkenas, 1995; Hammer and Champy, 1993; Stalk Jr. and Hout, 1990; Womack, Jones, and Roos, 1990).

The renaissance of artisan production in what Piore and Sabel call flexible production, or flexible specialization, implies, as stated, bridging the division of work within the production process. The idea is that the process will become more flexible when the workers are allowed to adjust, develop, and switch between different functions when and if they believe it to be in the best interest of production. In this way, the workers become increasingly versatile and assume a larger responsibility, and gain more of a say in company matters. Flexibility also came to be regarded as a prerequisite for the future of both industrial organization and service – a prerequisite described and advocated in more or less optimistic language by various authors, not least by Piore and Sabel themselves.

At approximately the same time, that is, the latter half of the 1980s, reports criticizing the development toward increased flexibility started surfacing. There were those who were critical toward the concept as such (Pollert, 1991), and those who took a critical stance to whether a development of this character really was underway (Wood, 1989). But there were also reports dealing with the negative sides to the development toward greater flexibility. The majority of these reports came out of Great Britain, which had experienced major cut-downs and market adjustments in the wake of the 1979 accession to power of the conservative government under Margaret Thatcher. The center of, and quite often the subject of, these critical reports was the English researcher John Atkinson.

The reason for this can be found in the reports about the "flexible firm" that Atkinson and others wrote in the mid-1980s (Atkinson, 1984; Atkinson and Meager, 1986). When Atkinson speaks of flexibility he means, in contrast to the previously mentioned discussion on flexibility, not primarily how production can be organized, but how the labor force can be utilized. Here Atkinson differentiates between three types of flexibility in the labor force.

- *Functional flexibility*: This refers to the versatility of the labor force in their ability to assume many and differing work tasks when prompted by circumstances. The workers must therefore have generalist abilities and wide-ranging competence, allowing them to appraise the situation more or less independently, and to assume the tasks which need to be carried out at the moment. This is pretty much the ability Piore and Sabel associate with flexible production.
- *Numerical flexibility*: The possibility to vary the size of the labor force depending on variations in demand. There is, in other words, a need for a labor force with only loose ties to the organization that can be taken into and out of use at short notice.
- *Economic flexibility*: The possibility to vary the remuneration of the labor force according to performance and demand. The labor force must, consequently, have individual and market adjusted wages.

Atkinson's division has been very influential in that it has spawned widespread debate. The debate, however, has been concerned to a large extent on how to interpret his ideas. The question has been whether Atkinson's division is to be understood as fundamental, normative, or descriptive. As a consequence of this the division has later been criticized on theoretical, ideological, or empirical grounds. We will not here enter this debate, which is not entirely new, but only state that Atkinson has identified an essential and recurring distinction when discussing flexible work. What is interesting about Atkinson's division – which, by the way, is also found in American studies, and then without reference to Atkinson (see for instance, Harrison, 1994; Storper and Scott, 1990) – is that it gives us another method for understanding and achieving flexibility in business. This method is as plausible and well documented but considerably more controversial than the method advocated by Piore and Sabel. If we disregard the economic flexibility – the purpose of which, according to Atkinson, mainly is to facilitate the functional and numerical flexibilities – Atkinson distinguishes between the flexibility achieved when the labor force has several functions and independently adjust their work according to the requirements of production and the flexibility that is achieved when the labor force as such can fluctuate with the demands of production. In the first case we may speak of flexibility through empowerment, and in the latter of flexibility through substitution. Without in any way complying with or further developing Atkinson's model we would like to use this distinction for structuring our subsequent exposition on flexible forms of work.

Flexibility Through Empowerment

By flexibility through empowerment we mean the kind of flexibility resulting from workers being allowed to manage their own work. The concept of empowerment established itself through management rhetoric in the early 1980s. The concept offers increased self-determination for workers in exchange for organizational commitment and job involvement. When removed from its rhetorical context, however, it becomes clear that the self-determination referred to is restricted to the individual or, at most, the work group level and does not involve any influence beyond that (Wilkinson, 1997). It is also in this way that we will continue to use the concept.

The advantages of self-determination are not in themselves a discovery of the 1980s. At the start of the 1950s, for example, the American management consultant Peter Drucker formulated the principles for a more "humanist" division of labor. The idea was that the personnel, primarily professionals and subordinate managers, should take responsibility for their own work. The role of management was to determine, in understanding with the personnel concerned, the appropriate objectives for their work. The managerial principles were consequently labeled Management by Objectives (MBO) (Drucker, 1954). At about the same time, but on the other side of the Atlantic, Eric Trist and Ken Bamford (1951) in a study on Welsh coal miners showed that, under certain circumstances, it could be more efficient to transfer the planning of work to a work team, rather than to direct each individual in detail. The study gave rise to what later became known as the "socio-technical school" where a series of projects with so-called semi-autonomous work groups were carried out.

The increased self-determination advocated by the socio-technical approach was very influential in the attempts to democratize working life in Scandinavia during the 1970s and 1980s. But however important these attempts were – for research, work environment, and co-determination legislation – their practical impact was limited to the time periods and workplaces of particular projects. A substantially larger and more lasting impact was probably attained through changes granting workers limited influence, which were implemented on the initiative of individual employers. Workers, for instance, gained greater influence over their working hours through the introduction of different forms of flexitime. And from the USA the idea of telecommuting arrived as a means of settling the problem of traffic jams and environmental damage in big cities. Also, the possibilities for working at home greatly increased with the breakthrough of personal computers in the 1980s. The decade also saw an increase in awareness and demands for general participation in various developmental projects in the workplaces. Through "quality circles" and local projects, relatively large groups of workers acquired first-hand experiences of a limited but practical self- and co-determination. But even though a substantial number of workers saw their traditional rules of work loosened a bit, the aim of these changes was never to achieve a more flexible production. Instead, the aims varied between everything from cost reduction to personnel encouragement.

However, the dividing line between the limitations of traditional mass production and the promises of flexible production emphasized the importance of distinguishing between two types of efficiency: internal and external. Internal efficiency meant producing goods as cheaply as possible. This was the kind of efficiency traditional mass production always strove to achieve, and for which flexibility always was of subordinate value. But in the 1970s, when the stable markets of the post-war era started swaying, and the manufacturing industry kept churning out products no one wanted or could afford to buy, the limitations of focusing on the internal efficiency became evident. Instead, external efficiency, producing goods that are possible to sell and that will yield a profit, gained in importance. For this kind of efficiency, however, a flexible mode of production was a prerequisite. The idea of external efficiency became topical in the 1980s when companies were forced to compete in specialized and unstable markets, and even more focal during the 1990s in what came to be known as *the new economy*; so focal, as it turned out, that the idea dwarfed itself. Prospects became more important than profits.

When Kevin Kelly (1997), as the editor of *Wired* magazine, gave the new economy its name, the phenomenon already was not new. It could be argued that the phenomenon came to general notice at the start of the 1990s when operators started to sell mobile phones considerably below cost, providing that the customer simultaneously signed up for a long-term subscription with the network operator. Selling such a technically advanced product as a mobile phone at a loss, a product that could be linked via satellite that orbited Earth, in exchange for an "ordinary" telephone subscription through which calls could be made for a bit of pocket change, seemed to defy all reason. But telecommunication, like the sale of computer programs, information systems, and Internet services, follows a different logic from that of traditional mass production. The customer does not pay for a commodity but for access to a communication network. The phone itself, the hardware, is just the doorway. The actual product is the medium of communication, that is, the software. The value of the software increases with the number of users. The very first fax machine, although highly innovative and expensive to produce, was in itself worthless. It first acquired a value when it was hooked up to another fax machine thereby establishing a communication link. The value of the individual machines then grew with each new machine being added to the network. In other words, the more people who use the network, the larger and more valuable it becomes, and the more people will want to use it, which again will increase the size and value of the network. The new economy, or the network economy, maintains that it is in this kind of self-accelerating spiral that value increase takes place. The network with the highest rate of growth will attract the largest number of subscribers, and in this way decimate or crowd out any competing networks (Shapiro and Varian, 1998).

This effect is reinforced by the fact that the software, as a product, is very costly to create, but costs next to nothing to replicate. Production is, in other words, all about innovation. During the 1990s, the development in work organization as a result came to be concerned with various possibilities for encouraging innovation and creativity. The delimitations of work in the guise of, for example, a given workplace, working hours, work regulations, or area of responsibility subsequently became synonymous with obstructions.

The 1990s also saw an increase in qualification and self-determination in work. This was not primarily a result of job design, but of the creation of new and more qualified jobs, and the simultaneous disappearance of old and less qualified jobs (Hansen, 2001; Ekstedt, 1999). Jobs appeared in new and growing industries, such as the computer, telecoms and media industries, Internet development and service, biotechnology, and games and entertainment. They also appeared in more traditional industries where larger companies established their own sections for services, research, education, data, and organizational development (Castells, 2003). A common feature among these new jobs was that they deviated from traditional patterns – they explicitly aimed for flexibility. Some of the jobs created in this period made a point of being extremely flexible. In our studies of these jobs we found the traditional sets of rules for delimiting and defining work to be entirely absent (Allvin, 2008).

Boundaryless, or indefinable jobs

When we asked various consultants, leaders, organizations, and system developers about their work they described a situation entirely different from the traditional (Allvin, 2008). Work or work-related activities were performed at any given time and any given place. There was no particular work order in the form of manuals, specific work tasks, defined results, or fixed goals. In other words, there was no direct guidance as to what needed to be done and how. Neither was there any direction as to what was or was not part of the job. The job, however, usually existed on market terms, within the framework of a company or some comprehensive operation, and was hence guided by more or less general demands of the industry, customers, or the market. On the other hand, these demands were formulated in such general terms that they implied a continuous and focused process of interpretation. A system developer described the work group as "purpose oriented."

> We're probably more purpose oriented than goal oriented. We're sort of trying to achieve something, but what we then do with it is up to us. We report to a management board about once a month. We account for what we've done so far. They function both as a sounding board and as mentors. They give us constructive criticism on what we're doing. So, in this way our work is guided. (System developer)

The formal division of responsibility within the organization did not seem to matter too much to the work they were doing. They had no fixed job titles or positions, and several of them even had difficulties identifying their formal boss. Their work did not seem to be guided by any formalized system of direction and feedback. They had, of course, work mates, but no colleagues they routinely cooperated or interacted with. Neither did they, in their practical work, seem to be bound by any other functions within the organization.

Moreover, their work did not seem to entail any significant amount of "system reproducing" activities, such as regular participation in recorded meetings and committees, and writing and reading of periodical communications, memorandums, notes, and accounts. Nor did they take part in coffee breaks, lunches, and informal meetings on any regular basis, that is, all the activities, big or small, that lend a structural continuity to the organization and a regularity and predictability to the job. The same was valid for the continuous social interactions and exchanges in the form of coffee room chats, corridor talk, gossip, and "bullshitting" that above all serve to reproduce an informal spirit of community. Several interviewees, who previously had worked under more traditional conditions, even pointed out the absence of such system- and community reproducing activities as one of the major advantages of their way of work.

> I'm spared all the internal muddle and prestige rubbish of so many workplaces. I'm completely free from that. No meetings! No committees. Imagine all the papers I don't have to read. I can concentrate on reading what is productive. I don't read any reports. Just imagine all the reports and memos you've read and written in your time. (Former head of personnel, currently leadership consultant)

Evidently these people had virtually no traditional limitations or regulations in their work. This, however, does not mean that their work lacked structure – quite the opposite. Our interviewees consistently emphasized the importance of planning, structuring, and instilling discipline in their work to prevent it from "drifting." Several of those who worked outside of their official workplace choose to work at the office a given number of weekdays in order to have the opportunity for meeting with colleagues and management. Their work at home also seemed to adhere to certain fixed times. They turned off mobile phones at a certain time, did not read e-mails before or after a certain hour, etc. Furthermore, they adjusted their working hours to customer and market demands, global time differences, family needs, and personal preferences. The same thing was valid for place. Virtually everyone had a designated workplace at home. The workplace was well equipped for both writing and communication. They all had mobile phones, laptops, and wireless connections and consequently carried their work with them at all times.

The combination of high performance requirements and vague working conditions made substantial claims for efficiency and focus. It means that work was generally characterized by determination and concentration. This determination can be described from two different angles. On the one hand it entailed a constant demand for initiative on the part of the employee, who constantly had to formulate new objectives, "stay tuned," and remain "on edge"; "market" themselves; push the evolution rather than be pushed by it. On the other hand, the determination implied pronounced demands for responsibility. Not only did the employee have to initiate her own work, but also plan it, structure it, and maintain discipline. She not only had to actively look for new information, but also structure, order, and digest this information in order to make it useful. Moreover, it was not enough to initiate and start projects; she also had to take responsibility for its advancement and successful completion. Nor was it enough to approach professional contacts; the employee also had to maintain and develop them. All of the above demanded a constant need for order in the form of agendas, address lists, meetings, invoicing, and deadlines (Allvin, 2008).

Managing indefinable jobs

The examples of flexible working conditions above are extreme, and perhaps conditioned by the period. But that does not necessarily mean that they are any less interesting. As in a laboratory experiment they rather expose the complexity of the problems and uncover their mechanisms. What we see here is that the absence of the traditional work organization's set of rules meets with another, more individual and case-dependent regulation of work. Instead of fixed working hours and a given workplace the employees must individually decide and motivate when, where, how often, and how much to work. Instead of defined work tasks and a given working order laying down the process of work, the employees must individually define, initiate, plan, and take responsibility for the performance and completion of work. Instead of leaning on a given set of colleagues and a formal hierarchy the employee has to seek, establish, and maintain the social contacts necessary for the work himself. In the absence of an external set of rules the individual has to rely on a corresponding internal and self-imposed set of regulations.

Administrative resources. Assuming full responsibility for one's own work, however, is no easy task. This becomes especially noticeable for those who decide to be self-employed. In a study on freelance journalists they, among other things, described how much time, effort, and money is used on things that are freely accessible at a regular workplace (Allvin and Aronsson, 2000). There is no archive, no technical support, and no one to do the cleaning. The workplace has to be personally funded and furnished. Computer equipment has to be personally chosen, bought, maintained, and updated. The freelancers also have to provide their own administrative service, go to the bank, the post office, as well as order and pay deliveries. Papers and money have to be kept in order and they have to be punctual and make deliveries on time.

In addition to all this, they have to plan their own work and maintain their contacts. Methods for achieving this vary. Some professed to set their own deadlines, others made weekly schedules. For this purpose there are also the usual tools of office administration, such as personal organizers, card indexes, and address books. But the most useful tool is the computer with peripherals (programs, printer, and Internet connection). With the help of the computer, routines for bookkeeping, planning, word processing, and layout can be simplified. Contacts are forged and maintained, articles delivered, and research carried out via Internet and e-mail.

Another instrument, a step in the direction of cooperation, is to share a workplace with others who are self-employed. In this way, responsibility for telephony, IT, coffee making, and cleaning can be shared even if the individuals in other respects have little in common. An instrument taking yet another step toward increased cooperation is to share a workplace with people in the same situation and industry. In the case of the freelance journalists this meant forming or joining a freelance group. Groups like this share not only a workplace, but also working conditions and work itself. The freelancers can share and benefit from each other's experiences, give each other advice and work. They can do joint research and work together on projects. One freelancer also described the importance of having support and social contacts in the group.

> Getting support when you have writer's cramp, or when you are drowning in too much research and can't find your way out, is something invaluable.

Seeing that periodically it strikes everyone is also comforting. (Freelance journalist)

Individual control and regulations. So far we have spoken only of various administrative resources for work performance. Another type of instrument is one that more directly aims to govern the performance of work. One example of such instruments is the governing established as a response to work that is distributed, that is, not carried out within the confines of a single workplace, as in the case of telework. The introduction of telework does not mean the deregulation of activities in order to let people work as they please. Instead, the very establishment of telework means that a range of new instruments directing work are gradually adopted. It was noted in a study of professionals with the opportunity to work from home or a nearby office that various instruments were employed to govern the work (Allvin, 2001), for instance, administrative resources in the form of common travel and remuneration conditions, issued office and computer equipment conformed to company standards, work environment conditions, and insurance policies in compliance with the rest of the industry. But except for these resources other methods were also being used.

- Central management took the initiative for a comprehensive *mapping* of everyone's tasks and duties so as to have a better overview and to limit the moving of work tasks out of the office, in other words increased transparency.
- They arranged for *common training programs* in order to impress common routines, a common outlook, and a common organization culture.
- Furthermore, they insisted on everyone being, if not present then at least *available*, and charged local management with implementing and following up on these demands.
- The demands for availability were also followed up and evaluated centrally in the first of several subsequent *regular follow-ups*.
- They also tightened up *departmental meetings* and imposed a strict discipline of assembly.
- A far-reaching *re-organization* was carried out with the aim of improving the coordination and integration of all projects.
- Central management started developing routines and instruments for increasing their *knowledge of employees*. Examples of such routines and instruments were more systematic and deliberate selection and job

interviews, not least with newly recruited managers. Other examples included periodic career talks with subordinates in order to be informed of and integrate their professional life choices with the plans of the organization, instead of being surprised by them (Allvin, 2001, p. 37).

In contrast to previously mentioned administrative resources, these instruments offer not just a method for structuring work, nor are they as generally formulated and undemanding. These instruments are leveled directly at the individual, laying down what is expected from each person. Implied in these instruments is therefore an indirect warning that non-compliance may lead to consequences. These instruments are often developed in response to or concurrent with a specific situation. They can also be interwoven with each other to a greater or lesser extent. With this, we enter yet another method for managing work, that is, the company-spanning context of which all these methods are part, and in relation to which they receive their direction, force, and legitimacy. It is doubtful whether this really is an instrument in the traditional sense. It is more of a conceptual and consolidating cognitive background, a corporate culture.

Corporate practices, symbols, and language. By a corporate culture we mean something close to a corporate-related identity: an identity within which the framework of the individual's work, role, and behavior acquires meaning. The corporate culture consequently ties the individuals to the company and makes them part of the greater whole (Kunda, 1992). The interesting thing here is perhaps not the identity per se, but rather the way in which it is manifested, communicated, and reproduced. This takes place on several different levels. At the most formal, but simultaneously also the most indirect, level it takes place through all the various *institutionalized practices* we ordinarily associate with the "organization" of the company. Examples of such practices are methods of recruitment, wage systems, and principles of promotion (Hendry, 1995). In addition to being formal administrative routines, these practices at the same time tell us something about the expectations from the company of its employees.

On a more informal level, but at the same time more intimately associated with the corporate-related identity, we find all the *symbolical practices* permeating individual companies. In a case study of a consulting firm, Mats Alvesson (1995) describes various values, norms, and rituals common for the company. Among the typical values that were praised and conveyed were openness, loyalty, friendship, "informality," and a basic positive tone. But, similarly to the norms – that the boss always should be available to the consultants and that all employees must be ready to work overtime – these values were not always unambiguously expressed. Rather, they were expectations one became aware of only by the fact that everyone behaved accordingly. Values and norms became explicit only if or when they went unobserved. Alvesson also gives examples of certain rituals underscoring the social identity of the company. It was, for example, traditional for new employees to sing a song at one of the company's morning meetings. The singing was complemented by the legend that "it is OK to lose face," implying the purpose of creating a sense of community behind this childish ritual of stripping the new employee of their professional façade. Other rituals were regular morning meetings, quarterly conferences, Friday "five o'clock beer," and the yearly all-staff meeting with a compulsory party afterwards (Alvesson, 1995, ch. 7).

Symbols are, generally speaking, an important part of the corporate identity. When, as a consequence of international competition, companies to an increasing extent are forced to offer their goods and services in other markets than their local market, they also face a need to communicate with the world in new ways. It becomes ever more important for the companies to be seen and associated with a positive message. As the companies are not able to represent themselves by virtue of their material presence, demands increase on the symbolic presence. Above all, the symbol used by companies to this end is their trademark, their brand. Aided by their trademarks, companies establish a distinct identity, project a positive image, and target their customers. A strong, established trademark, such as Rolls Royce or Harley Davidson, may hence be worth more than the material assets of the company. Companies like Coca-Cola, which live by their brand, consequently monitor their brand equity continuously (Aaker, 1991, 1996). But a trademark not only projects its idealized image outwards to the market. It is also inwardly directed, as an example and urging for the employees to emulate. The employees are expected to represent and embody the business, to be its "face to the world." The employees are, at the same time, encouraged to see themselves in the image projected by the company. The image and identity projected by companies through their trademark and other symbolical messages are, in other words, not only expectations projected on their employees; the image and identity are also an attempt to bring the employees together and captivate them in a symbiotic relationship. The distributed organization may be compared to a circus, where the show consists of a collection of artists, whose individual performances are tied together into a larger whole by the circus introducing them all in its name. In the same way, separate operators can be tied together into a common company within the framework of an all-embracing trademark (Uggla, 2000).

In the same vein, companies try to establish a *common language*, communicating their expectations to their employees. Here, too, the idea is to formulate the company image as an intermediary link between the world surrounding the companies, and their employees. Perhaps the most obvious example is that of the omnipresent concept of the customer. According to Paul du Gay and Graeme Salaman (1992) the concept of the customer dissolves the traditional distinctions between production and consumption, between the in- and outside of the company, between work and non-work. With the assistance of the concept of the customer, the market can be introduced directly into the organization where it undermines the bureaucratic principles of organization, circumvents the traditional responsibility of the direction for the work of the company, and makes its demands directly on the individual. By that, companies convey to their employees an image of the surrounding world as capricious, demanding, and changing. But through the redefinition of patients, parents, passengers, and students as customers, it is at the same time a surrounding world where all social differences and moral considerations have been erased. In this way, companies can demand attention, quality, and performance from their employees, while at the same time distancing themselves from these demands with reference to outside conditions. Within the framework of these demands, and with the help of their own experiences from social interactions or as customers, the employees can then perform their work in an independent way (du Gay and Salaman, 1992).

All these symbols and language usages are formulated within one or several stories in or about the organization in question. The stories may be about the founding of the organization or about its founder. They may concern the new or altered conditions that the organization faces at the moment. Or they may tell about changes that have taken place or are going to take place. A common feature of these stories is that they present a context against the backdrop of which a particular action acquires meaning. By painting a past, these stories not only explain and give meaning to the present, they also point out a possible direction for the future. Stories of this kind are found everywhere in an organization. Generally speaking, each employee has a story with the purpose to convey something essential about the organization and their personal role within it. These stories can be said to form the self-awareness of the organization. In this sense, the stories are part of the identity of the company (Czarniawska-Joerges and Gagliardi, 2003; Czarniawska, 1997). Most interesting here are the official stories sanctioned by the direction. Although these stories are not always unchallenged, they are still an important instrument for achieving integration, purposefulness, and commitment. They can also be prescriptive by legitimizing the above instruments for governing work and by representing a canon for everyone to comply with or at least relate to when performing their tasks.

To sum up, we see here that the absence of organizational limitations to work – time, place, performance, and social relations – increases the demands on the individual's competence to make decisions of her own. But this does not mean that the individual is free to do as she pleases. Instead, other instruments of governance come into play. In contrast to the setting of limits in the traditional organization, however, these instruments do not form a functional whole. Rather, they have the characteristics of specific techniques. Nor do they focus the employees as a labor force, a collective, but as individuals. Hence, they do not form a social context capable of stabilizing and coordinating the behavior of all individuals. We have here rather a motley set of tools to be used when the need arises and with the only purpose to be as efficient as possible within their respective areas. Three levels of techniques have been identified.

1. First, they appear as more or less generally applicable administrative resources for structuring work, for example, personal computers and common administrative software.
2. Second, the techniques appear as instruments targeting the individual at work, for example, personal career development talks and departmental meetings with personal debriefings.
3. Third, they appear as strategically motivated and company-spanning systems of symbols to direct and motivate the common work and to legitimize the techniques on the previous levels. Trademarks, corporate cultures, and a common language use are all examples of such systems of symbols.

One important consequence of these new techniques is the effect they have on traditional organizations. Although the new techniques can be said to replace the rules of the traditional organization, it does not mean that they are introduced after and as a consequence of the dismantling of these rules. Rather, new techniques are either developed concurrently with the starting up of new activities, or introduced as a directive mechanism in parallel with an already existing mode of operations. A problem of the last case is that the new techniques may not work together with the rules of the traditional organization. The techniques may undermine the authority of the traditional rules, since the authority of the traditional organization is built on the fact that everyone adheres to the same rules. In other words, people follow the rules because everyone else does. When people look to each other as points of reference it also means that everyone subordinates themselves to the communal whole.

But the new techniques do not recognize a communal whole. They are applied when need arises, within limited confines, and only to the extent that they prove to be effective. They are wedged into the traditional system of references and they make it fall apart. This is partially intentional. The techniques are introduced precisely to make people reorganize their points of reference: from the rules of the organization to its aim, from the procedure to the result, from the colleagues to the customer. But problems arise when the rules of the traditional organization and the new techniques exist simultaneously. If the organization does not manage to define sufficiently the effective area of the techniques, it may lead to competing demands, social tensions, and conflicts between individuals, professional categories, workplaces, or organizational units. It is, for example, not uncommon for a group of teleworking individuals working in an otherwise traditionally organized workplace to become the object of envy, suspicion, and slander (von Schéele and Ohlsson, 1997). Conversely, an individual maintaining traditional working conditions in an otherwise flexibly organized workplace may encounter irritation. The existence of parallel systems of governance may also give rise to conflicts between established and new knowledge within the individual employee (Allvin, 2008).

The new rules of work, then, are a consequence of the introduction of new techniques for governing work, rather than the other way around. This may entail social friction and the fragmentation of the organization. At the same time, this is an expressed purpose of the new techniques: the breaking down of borders, habits, and routines in the interest of making the organization more dependent on the individual and adapted to the circumstances that, it is hoped, will lead to greater flexibility. But this is, as previously stated, just one way of increasing flexibility. Another way is to create routines that curtail dependence on the individual and make individuals replaceable.

Flexibility Through Substitution

When we speak of flexibility through substitution we mean the flexibility that follows when the company frees itself of the relative importance of its individual employees. Here it is the employee, not the work, that needs to be flexible, and the set of rules which is being undermined is that of the employment relationship. It is a strategy with a longer history than that of self-determination. "Independence" from the individual is implied in the functional division of work and hence a prerequisite for industrialization as such. The assembly line, introduced at the beginning of the twentieth century, not only made the production more efficient but also made it independent of the individual effort. The background for this was the steady flow of immigrants, lacking any specific qualifications, passing through the industrialized American east coast on their way west. They were farm workers and had not come all the way to America in order to toil in the factories. Neither did they stay for any longer time period. The labor turnover was often 100 percent in less than a year. The less production had to rely on professional individuals, the faster new workers could be trained to achieve their maximum capacity and the less production was affected by the varying quality of the labor force.

The principles behind this were predominantly developed by Frederick Taylor (1911). Taylor was a product of the American movement for rationalization toward the end of the nineteenth century and his ideas made a major impact on the whole Western world in the beginning of the following century (Kakar, 1970). What later, to the displeasure of Taylor, became known as Taylorism is an extreme division of labor, where the individual job is broken down into its smallest elements, and then reassembled into a single predetermined task. This requires the absolute separation of planning from execution and of the execution of work ("direct" work) from its preparation ("indirect" work), where the preparations insofar as possible should be carried out by assisting and cheaper labor. Consequently, professional skills and schooling are reduced to a minimum. Taylor also advocated a professional control system where the individual task not only was to be engineered, but also developed and directed by a designated planning division. The control system hence contained a sophisticated time management system whereby the workers were required to fill out work- and time cards, and then return the cards to the planning division for the planning and rationalization of the work, as well as a piecework system based on the effort ascribed to the particular task by the same planning division. However, British sociologist Craig Littler (1978, 1982) claimed that perhaps the most important aspect of Taylorism was the minimum interaction that this type of employment relationship brought about. The aim of the minimum interaction employment relationship was exactly to minimize the dependence of production on the labor force, thereby maximizing the possibilities for its rational use.

Taylor's starting point is quite simply that if production and labor can be made independent of one another, they can also be optimized in relation to one another. The more standardized the work tasks, the more replaceable, cheaper, and predictable the labor. Consequently, labor is, as Harry Braverman (1974) succinctly put it, reduced to a commodity on which a downward pressure on prices is applicable. The terms and conditions for labor hence become more market-like. If there is ample supply of labor, the price for it will decrease. Short-term employment may be profitable in such cases as prices can be continuously squeezed. If, on the other hand, there is a labor shortage, the price of labor will increase. Here, in contrast, permanent employment pays off, as there is then no need to compete for workforce. The larger the part of production that can be standardized, the larger the part of the labor force that can be treated in such a manner. In this way, capital increases its scope of action and its flexibility in relation to labor. It can make more demands on the workforce, pay less for work, or move operations to where labor is cheaper and more compliant, without obstructing production.

This, as already stated by Marx, is a fundamental logic for market capitalism. But during the larger part of the 1900s, and especially during the post-war years, capitalism "compromised away" a large part of this logic in negotiations with unions and the welfare state. The logic, however, came into favor again during the recession hitting the Western world in the 1980s. As we already discussed, companies tried to come to terms with the receding markets through new, flexible concepts of production, investing in skills and personnel. But the realization that the personnel are the greatest asset of the business entails the realization that it is also the greatest expenditure. Another way of dealing with the recession was therefore a more structural approach. And, starting in the USA, a wave of strategic mergers and acquisitions began in a wild chase for market shares and opportunities for economy measures. In the wake of these mergers, but also as an independently conceived measure, there was substantial downsizing. The wave also swept Europe, where considerable privatization was added to the action program. Although these measures did not all yield the results company leaders and economists had intended and hoped for, but instead mainly instilled fear and insecurity within the organizations, they heralded the return of a more minimal relationship to labor (Cascio, 1997; Hudson, 2002; Martin and Freeman, 1997).

Managing the lean organization

In order to be more competitive and to meet the market demands for a most cost-efficient way, companies started "trimming" their organizations. With this end in view, companies started developing various systems for the optimization of labor usage. These systems were to guarantee that the personnel were put to use only when needed, where needed, and in the way it was needed.

The working hours. Perhaps the most common way of optimizing labor usage is to vary working hours to suit the needs of the company. This is readily achieved through existing personnel working overtime. Another frequently used method for achieving flexibility is working shifts, weekends, or "emergency" duty. Systematic use of irregular working hours is, however, less commonplace. Instruments for exploiting this opportunity may include the use of working hours by year, or different forms of pooling working hours. The idea, of course, is to work when there is a need for it, and to take leave when there is no or smaller need (Olmsted, 1996; Olmsted and Smith, 1994).

A considerably more controversial method for achieving flexibility, however, is the systematic use of part-time employment. When there is a need for a limited workforce in many different places it may be advantageous to have many part-time employees instead of combining different tasks into full-time occupations. One alternative here is to let two people share one full-time job, so-called job-sharing. This is a more controversial method, however, as those who work part-time usually are part-time unemployed, and hence cost the state money without being available to the labor market as are full-time unemployed. Part-time employees earn less, and there is always the suspicion that the employer over-exploits the workforce. Part-time work, moreover, is more common among women, and in low-paid service occupations.

Theoretically, the greatest flexibility is achieved by not having any permanently employed staff at all, but instead engage labor according to need, for a limited time (e.g. by the hour), or for a limited assignment (project employment). This can be realized by employing temporary workers. However, the problem with this is that the workers are unknown, and that they have to be introduced and instructed. An easier and more risk-free solution is therefore for the business to hire workers from private job contractors, or staffing firms. The job contractor is responsible for the workers they contract out, their administration, competence, and conduct (Barley and Kunda, 2006).

The workplace. Another method for achieving flexibility is to vary the place of work. Depending on which units we are concerned with, we may distinguish between distributed operations and flexible offices. By *distributed* operations is meant the possibility of placing entire operational units to locations outside the organization. An organization may of course lack a real center and hence be entirely distributed. The point is that the place for the respective operations can be changed according to need. Examples include relocated units, satellite offices, subsidiary companies, and branch offices. Another example are telephone units or call centers. Relations to the distributed operation may vary from being a central part of the organization's operations to being engaged for a continuous but separate task. Nevertheless, a common feature is that they, by virtue of being distributed, have achieved a looser (more flexible) connection to the organization as a whole (Avery and Zabel, 2001).

By *flexible offices* is meant an office solution without fixed workplaces. This, of course, need not be limited to offices, as similar designs have been implemented in the manufacturing industry (Berggren, 1992). The solution, however, has been most commonly employed in offices. A distinction should be made between offices that have been organized for a particular purpose and offices for regular work. Offices organized for a specific purpose imply that the personnel do most of their work elsewhere. The office is where one goes for meetings, writing reports, and administrative tasks. The office provides resources for these purposes, without these being tied to any particular individual. Here, the office works rather like a sort of headquarters and may be very small in relation to the number of employees. But offices for regular work may also be flexible. An early form of this are the office landscapes of the 1960s and 1970s, where individuals and workplaces could be regulated according to need. A later form is the office that facilitates cooperation in more or less temporary constellations. People, who at the moment work together in groups, teams, or projects, could, for instance, easily be placed together so that they, when cooperation ends, just as easily may be relocated in new constellations (Worthington, 2006). What all these types of offices have in common is that the individual does not have a fixed place. Both the individual and the workplace are, in a sense, mutually free of ties.

The performance of work. A consistent problem in the design of work since the infancy of industrialism has been the control and minimization of individual deviations in the performance of work. The reason for this is that variations in performance lead to varying results, in quantity as well as in quality. The problem has been handled in two ways: through the mechanization of performance (whether by machines, organization, or training) and through spot-check controls of its results. The idea that results should be checked continuously throughout the production process came originally from America. It was, however, the Japanese who first took the idea seriously and implemented, developed, and learned to master it. The Japanese saw it as a kind of philosophy, but when American companies rediscovered the idea, owing to the successes of the Japanese industry during the 1970s and 1980s, they started to package and market it as a general "method" called Total Quality Management (TQM).

TQM is an organization-spanning method for the continuous mapping, classification, standardization, and supervision of all the processes included in production. There are many versions but the general idea is that everyone should be aware of the quality of the results of their work. The unit, team, or person working downstream from them in the production process is essentially their customer. As such they have the right to demand quality. When applied to the organization as a whole, it means that everybody is customer to everybody else and, hence, has the right to demand quality from each other. In other words, everybody becomes a quality inspector and controls each other's results. The continuous "inspection" and the mutual feedback following from it will lead to, or so it is assumed, the successive adaptation and improvement of performance. The method has been developed within the manufacturing industry. During the late 1980s and 1990s, however, it started to filter through to other industries, notably the social service and professional industries (Morgan and Murgatroyd, 1994; Tuckman, 1994). Within these industries the effects of the method have been especially noticeable.

The transformation of highly qualified professional jobs to market-based service jobs is a process involving several phases. In the first phase the client (patient, student, parent, citizen, etc.) is turned into a customer. In order to achieve this, the client must consistently be addressed as a customer (du Gay and Salaman, 1992; Dean, 2009). This means that the client must become aware of his or her own agency, the fact that it is his or her choices, experiences, and satisfaction that ultimately motivate the interaction with the professional. Clients can, for instance, be subjected to customer satisfaction polls, appeals for making suggestions on how to improve the operation in question, and presented with the treatment in terms of choices. In order to recognize and evaluate their own satisfaction, clients must be "informed" on the subject of the service, the conditions of it, and their options toward it. In health care, the client could be supplied with easily available information on illnesses, ailments, and disorders, as well as instructions, procedures, programs, and alternatives for treatments, all of it articulated in layman terms and presented in brochures or on the Internet. Clients should also be made aware of their options, should they not be completely satisfied with the service. They must be informed, for instance, of their right as a patient to get a second opinion, how to contact patient safety groups, file a formal patient report, or complain to patients' boards. The ultimate option is of course to take the professional to court, if, as the Swedish National Patient Safety Agency suggests on their web site, "you have received poor service or need help; if you think the organization is poor; if you think staff have made a mistake; if you feel you are entitled to compensation."

In the second phase the professional's job is made transparent. Transparency is achieved through different means. On a more principal level it may be summarized in terms of regulations, accountancy, and scrutiny. This involves the setting of standards and guidelines, as well as conducting evaluations, rankings, and giving out rewards (Blomgren and Sahlin-Andersson, 2007). All of this presupposes, however, the existence of corresponding measurements. Measurements like this are obtained by encapsulating the activity in a finite number of key performance indicators. Such indicators are typically measured at an organizational level and involve financial, operational, progressive, as well as customer aspects (e.g. Kaplan and Norton, 1996). However, if the indicators are to be effective they must implicate all the employees. This means that the indicators must be translated into practical measures immediately recognizable by everyone, such as waiting time, throughput time, concluded cases, complaints, credentials, availability, reception, and general conduct of professionals. Examples from the health care business would include: Patient satisfaction comprising, for example, transfers, retention, referral rate; Mortality index; Complications index; and Infection rates (Kocakülâh and Austill, 2007).

The third phase is, in effect, a continuance in the pursuit for transparency, as it introduces agencies and instruments for assembling, assessing, and comparing measurements from these performance indicators. The measurements are gathered in intra- and/or extra-organizational databases allowing for comparisons (benchmarking) between organizations, subunits, teams, and even individuals. The databases are in turn searched, operated, and contributed to by various agents acting in the interests of different clients, the general public, or themselves. Examples of such agencies are accountancy firms, standardization institutes, interest groups, government agencies, councils, boards, and researchers. Through these agencies the different measurements are analyzed and fed back to the industry or market as standards, rankings, norms, and regulations for performance. In the health care business this includes the establishing of best practices for therapeutic treatments, recommendation for prescriptions, classification systems, and diagnostic instruments like, for example, Evidence-Based Medicine (EBM) and Diagnosis-Related Groups (DRG). Together they make up a regulatory infrastructure controlling, directing, and standardizing the performance of professional jobs (Hasselbladh and Bejerot, 2007).

The introduction of TQM is carried out, as we can see, with the help of a number of techniques that preclude one another, and that are applied in steps. Competition and comparison with other organizations presupposes recurrent revisions of the quality of operations, which precludes the continuous measuring of customer satisfaction, which in turn precludes the measurability of performance, which precludes its standardization – all this then means that the individual becomes replaceable. As in Scientific Management, it is all about the mapping, classification, standardization, and monitoring of the work process as such. And, as in Scientific Management, this implies that the organization is disconnected from the individual. But, unlike Scientific Management in its original form, this also includes social and professional relations, which have not previously been standardized. Activities such as health care – where professional standing, and in particular that of physicians, has made it impossible to micromanage – can now be reduced with the help of these systems to a purely technical activity with a clear purpose and an optimal mode of operation. In other words, it can be reduced to a set of activities where the individual, regardless of her professional standing, is substitutable.

Social relations. Social relations as such may also be standardized and separated from the individual. This includes relations to customers, clients, students, and patients, as well as those to colleagues and co-workers. That the relation to customers may be standardized is fairly obvious to anyone who has ever visited a McDonald's hamburger restaurant. The relationship is here largely determined by the standardized options a customer has from which to make their choices. The options are in turn determined by the pre-programmed cash register through which all orders are channeled, and to which all interaction must be adapted. The actual customer contact follows six predefined steps: (1) greet the customer, (2) take the order, (3) assemble the order, (4) present the order to the customer, (5) take payment, and (6) thank the customer and wish him or her a nice day. These routines include a certain number of possible phrases, to use or not use. Furthermore, there are explicit instructions to smile, be pleasant, and submissive (Leidner, 1993; Ritzer, 1996; Schlosser, 2001; Royle and Towers, 2002; Forseth, 2005).

The standardization of social relations is, if possible, even more apparent in service relations over the phone to and from call centers. For surveys and telemarketing there are fixed scripts for the personnel to follow. The same goes for computer support, inquiries, complaints, orders, and counseling. They consist of a series of questions that must be run through in the correct order and with the correct kind of response in order to enable the completion of the interaction. Any attempt by the customer to disrupt the order and convey their business in their own words results, at first attempt, in a number of excuses constructed to generate sympathy for the operator's situation, and the issue is then quickly brought back to the prescribed order. Any subsequent attempts will, without fail, result in the customer being redirected and finally cut off. The actions of the service personnel are here limited by their script, which in turn is written to ensure that customers are handled as efficiently as possible. In addition, there are control and reward systems, continuously measuring personnel productivity (Huws, 2003c). Just as social relations can be optimized for productivity, with the help of modern telecommunication, they can also be personalized. Information regarding the customer contained in the telephone number can digitally connect him or her directly to an operator speaking the same language, and even the same dialect, in order to give the customer a more personalized service. The same techniques can even prepare the operator with a variety of personal and contextual information about the customer, such as local events and weather conditions, before the conversation (Huws, 2003b).

Arlie R. Hochschild (1983) has also described in a classic study how flight attendants are chosen, trained, and managed to be the airline's face to their customers. The recruitment of flight attendants is determined by the specific customer group of an airline. An airline that focuses on families, for instance, will, when choosing, decide against busty applicants. As flight attendants are to convey a reassuring sensation, anyone with a seductive appearance is dropped. At Delta Airlines, where Hochschild conducted her study, flight attendants additionally had to submit to regular weight tests. At another company, their hips and thighs were measured. Furthermore, the flight attendants had to accept certain fundamental rules of conduct, such as to control their personal spending and not get in debt, never drink alcohol or go to a bar while in uniform, not get friendly with or accept gifts from passengers (Hochschild. p. 99). Above all, flight attendants were regularly trained to control their own emotions so as to be prepared at all times to deal with angry, unpleasant, frightened, rowdy, intoxicated, or infatuated passengers with the same mild amiability.

These interactions, it is true, tend to be relatively brief and of limited scope, but longer and more complicated relations have also been subjected to a corresponding rationalization. Teachers are evaluated and ranked with the help of student questionnaires. Nurses' and doctors' treatment of patients is, as previously mentioned, continuously documented, evaluated, and rationalized by means of patient surveys. Even such intimate relations as those between therapist and client have been systematically rationalized through a number of cognitive and behavioral techniques.

As more companies create internal markets, renting the services of other companies and of personnel, market-like relations are established between co-workers and colleagues. Colleagues from different departments become each other's customers. Co-workers in the same department may have entirely different conditions of employment, or be employed at altogether different companies. This makes for more formal social relations at work, manifested for instance in the increasing use of uniforms, company logos, and name tags. In our study of nurses in the staffing business we saw how a single ward could be manned with staff of different functions, different types of employment, and from several different employers. An outsider would notice this only from the name tags worn by the personnel and, if one was very perceptive, from the somewhat formal atmosphere between the personnel categories. Several staffing nurses also described, in interviews, the distance and specific expectations signaled by the name tag with its company logo. The name tag was hence a means of protection, enabling the delimiting of social relations and commitments to include only what were demanded by the contract (Allvin, Jacobson, and Isaksson, 2003).

One consequence of the standardization of social relations at work described here is that in these relations individuals are increasingly substituted by functions. At the same time, this is the inevitable and indirectly intended outcome of, what we may call, the "social management" of labor.

Casual employment. When speaking about flexibility through substitution, even flexibility in general, it is usually the different forms of time-limited employment that are referred to. This was also Atkinson's (1984) idea when contrasting functional and numerical flexibility. It may thus be a good idea to describe these phenomena in a little more detail. Atkinson imagined the center of the company as a permanently employed workforce in possession of key competences and skills necessary for the company. The jobs in this center are supposedly more varied so that the personnel are able to handle a multitude of tasks. Surrounding this center are a number of more or less loosely tied groups of temporary workers. These are employed and made redundant as the need arises. The idea is that companies, by having a core group of long-term employment contracts and peripheral groups of short-term employees, will be able to balance the needs for stability and control as well as flexibility and a capacity for adaptation.

An additional function of the model is that it explains how organizations can increase their ability to absorb risk and uncertainty by distributing it, that is, by forcing it on a periphery consisting of short-term employees and subcontractors (Aronsson, Dallner, and Gustafsson, 2002; Aronsson, 2004). The fact that more women than men have temporary employment, and that they are also younger, just shows who are doing the distributing and who are doing the absorbing in this equation. Temporary employment has been a growing phenomenon in the labor market since the 1980s (OECD, 2006, 2002). Within the EU, however, the growth has slowed down and leveled out during the last years and is currently gravitating around 15 percent of the workforce (Eurostat, 2009). The actual level differs between countries though. Spain is the country with the largest proportion of temporary employees.

Making international comparisons is, however, not entirely unproblematic. First, the concept of employment itself has different meanings in different countries. In Great Britain, Ireland, and Denmark, for instance, employment security is virtually non-existent, which means the concept of time-limited employment contains no real meaning (Bergström and Storrie, 2003; Robinson, 1999). Second, there exists, in statistics and research, a complicated concept hierarchy, the origin and function of which are unknown. "Temporary" employment is here a subgroup of "contingent" employment. The concept of contingent employment in reality concerns and is sometimes also called "precarious" employment, which includes everyone employed without a long-term contract whose working hours fluctuate in a way which is beyond the direct or indirect control of the individual. Contingent employment is in turn a subgroup of what in a labor market statistical context is simply called non-standard types of employment. The whole matter is further complicated by the fact that employees with staffing agencies, who in Sweden, for instance, are permanently employed within the staffing company, sometimes are included among the temporarily employed (Allvin, Jacobson, and Isaksson, 2003).

We have so far described two separate ways for achieving flexibility in an organization (Table 2.1). The first is via empowerment. Here, the flexibility intended is that which is generated when decisions about work to a significant degree are delegated to the workers themselves. The other road is via substitution. The flexibility intended here is that which is achieved when the organization tries to become independent of its individuals. We have described how both these ways have been manifested in the occurrence and spread of working hours and the workplace, and in the performance of work and social relations. Further, we have identified a number of instruments for achieving flexibility in both these senses. Similarly to the hierarchical organizational structure, they are instruments for managing and controlling activities within the organization. Management instruments within the hierarchical organizational structure are, however, primarily functional in character. We do not confront them individually but rather as an integrated whole, a functional "organization." The new management instruments, on the other hand, are instrumental in character. They are constructed with a specific purpose in mind, and they may be used independently of one another. Telecommuting, for instance, does not presuppose project work, and vice versa. Instead, their legitimacy follows exclusively from their relative success. Therefore, they should not be understood in terms of a social structure, as a work organization, but rather as separate techniques for managing work. The techniques are not part of the organization. They are introduced into the organization, so to speak from the side, and applied whenever and wherever there is a need. As such they are also globally distributed and to a growing extent on a commercial basis (Sahlin-Andersson and Engwall, 2002).

Table 2.1 Examples of different techniques to achieve ...

	...flexibility through empowerment (individual-dependent)	...flexibility through substitution (individual-independent)
Working hours	Individual hours	Part-time, overtime, emergency duty hours
Working place	Telecommuting	Flexible offices, office landscapes
Performance of work	Independent projects	Continuous measuring of customer satisfaction, revision and standardization practices
Social relations	Professional networks	"Social management"
Employment conditions	Consultants, freelancers	Staffing personnel and temporary employees

Separate Paths?

We have described the two roads to flexibility as mostly separate. In daily usage as well as in the context of policy they are also treated as two alternative roads to flexibility. These may then be described as "the high road" and "the low road," where the previous corresponds to what we have called flexibility through empowerment and the latter to flexibility through substitution. An example of the latter is often given as the substantial increase in low-qualified service jobs in the US, resulting from the "Reaganomics" of the 1980s, while the former represents a more home-grown (Continental European) ambition to develop a knowledge-intensive workforce. Contrasting the two "roads" in this fashion, however, presumes two things. The first assumption is that the two "roads" correspond to a difference between good and bad jobs. The accentuated self-determination of the first road is also closer to the concept of the good and developing work, whereas substitution is commonly seen as a re-Taylorization of work. The second assumption is that the two roads also imply a choice of direction, and that the choice between them is a question of political will and determination. By way of conclusion, we would like to take a look at these assumptions in the light of our experience from, among other things, our own studies.

Good and bad jobs

The idea that work is inherently good and self-actualizing is essentially built on the critique of industrial work developing since the 1950s. The critique centers on the psychological and social limitations following the industrial division of labor. We are thinking in particular of the so-called horizontal division of labor between planning and execution, the division of responsibility between different hierarchical levels, and the fragmentation of cooperation and social interactions between fellow workers. A number of studies have also shown what consequences these limitations may have on, for example, stress and health (Karasek and Theorell, 1990), intellectual development (Kohn and Schooler, 1983; Kohn, 2006), leisure (Meissner, 1971), and even democracy (Elden, 1981). But concluding that an industrial division of labor has a series of negative consequences is quite different from assuming that the opposite, that is, job-enrichment, empowerment, and social integration, has the corresponding positive consequences. For a long time, the latter has been regarded as self-evident in both scientific and political discourse.

In our own studies of various free jobs we have been able to demonstrate that this is far from self-evident. Even though these jobs are not subject to divisions and fragmentation, but quite on the contrary are as inclusive as one could possibly wish for, it does not mean that they are free from serious psychological and social consequences. These are, however, a different type of consequence, a different type of stress, intellectual strain, and disruption of the personal quality of life. When the organizational framework associated with the industrial division of labor is broken up, leaving the individual accountable, he or she is forced to define, initiate, plan, and assume responsibility for the work. One consequence of this process is that the individual is subjected to tremendous time pressure. She has to find the time to do everything herself. She must also be able to deal with all the uncertainty that was previously absorbed by the organizational framework. Another consequence is that the work and the life outside of work are compressed into one. The individual is hence forced to delineate, plan, and take responsibility for her private life in the same way as for her work life. And in the wake of all this follows a number of potential conflicts: social conflicts at home and at work, as well as inner conflicts between her will, endurance, and ability. In facing this, the individual is left to herself in a way that was not the case when the conditions of work were dictated. We consequently see an emerging source of conflict and stress in the increasing difference between those who can handle this situation and those who cannot (Allvin *et al.*, 1999). We will have the opportunity to return to this in the following chapters.

Although many assert that they never want to return to a traditionally organized job, many have also experienced the uncertainty following from the liquid boundaries of flexible jobs and wished for a more visible organization and direction for work. On the other hand, we have also demonstrated that jobs based on replaceable performances do not necessarily involve the mental and social restrictions associated with the industrial division of work. In our interviews with staffing nurses they, for instance, described how their limited responsibilities and their detachment offered them the opportunity to decide under which conditions and with what amount of dedication they would carry out their tasks. They could, within obvious limits, choose when, where, how much, with what, and with whom they wanted to work. When work is adapted to personal preferences in this way, it will also be shaped by the individual's attitude toward it. The detachment brought about by their interchangeability simultaneously gave them a certain kind of freedom in relation to their work, a freedom which the permanently employed – with their considerably wider job description, larger influence, and deeper social roots – lacked completely (Allvin, Jacobson, and Isaksson, 2003).

As we can see, empowered jobs are not necessarily "better" than substitutable ones. The difference between good and bad jobs is in both cases whether the individual is qualified and attractive on the labor market. The difference between good and bad jobs is, in other words, also a question of employability. Whether a job is good or bad, then, is not entirely independent of the person who has to do it. Characteristic of flexible jobs, regardless of whether we by that mean empowered or substitutable jobs, is perhaps exactly that we cannot appraise them without also taking the individuals who work into account. Whether a job is good or bad is not only about estimating the demands of the job. It is also about estimating the individual's ability and aspiration to meet these demands. If we take this into consideration we must conclude that flexibility through empowerment does not necessarily mean better working conditions than flexibility generated through substitution.

Can we choose one or the other?

Since one form of flexibility is not necessarily better than another, it is not obvious that we ought to choose one over the other. But even if we, on a general level, would like to make such a choice, it may not be possible to do so. Several authors, including Atkinson, describe the two types of flexibility as mutually dependent.

The flexible firm, as conceived by Atkinson and others, relates the two forms of flexibility within the framework of a single organization. The idea is that flexibility is achieved by balancing the two forms in a way that is optimal for the organization in a specific situation. This can be achieved by segmenting the labor force into groups that are more or less central to the business. The nuclear group maintains the continuity of the operation and is empowered to make decisions about their own work to a relatively large extent. This group, in Atkinson's terminology, is flexible in a "functional" sense. Around this group, and connected to it, we find various support groups, which may be more or less replaceable, or flexible in the "numerical" sense. According to Atkinson (1984; Atkinson and Meager, 1986), they do not amount to a homogenous group, but may consist of several different categories. He mentions three such categories. First, there are workers (or clerks) performing relatively simple tasks, who, even though they may be permanently employed, have neither career opportunities nor any substantial employment security within the company. Sales clerks, assistants, switchboard operators, and chauffeurs are all examples of such jobs. Second, there are workers who may be highly qualified but not necessarily essential to operations. Examples from this category are computer technicians, lawyers, economists, and various forms of consultants. Third, there are workers performing various forms of maintenance, who are seldom permanently employed at their place of work, for example, cleaners, security guards, or canteen personnel.

Atkinson's model for the flexible firm has, as previously stated, attracted extensive criticism, which we will not go into any further (for an overview, see e.g. Legge, 2005, ch. 5). We will only call attention to the fact that Atkinson with this model has shown that the two forms of flexibility are, or at least may be, interrelated. He points to the mutual dependence between a core team and a constantly present, but replaceable, support crew. Even though Atkinson himself does not frame it like this, and his critics definitely do not, he draws attention to an important correlation. Free and autonomous jobs, to a certain extent, require an adaptable support service. Free and autonomous workers most often do not have the time, opportunity, or economic means to find, prepare, and administer the basis of their own work. The freelance journalists we interviewed complained that the support and administrative service, freely available to their editorial staff colleagues, was so cumbersome and time-consuming for them that they felt they had to work twice as much and twice as fast in order to achieve the same thing. The same can be said about the staffing nurses we interviewed. They were often called in to give the regular staff an opportunity to take part in the long-term development of the ward, or just to take a well-earned holiday. In order to benefit from the opportunity for work development, co-determination, and other rights, a support crew was needed to maintain the day-to-day operations, exactly because it did not enjoy the same opportunities.

The same type of mutuality can be found on a more societal, even global, level. Outsourcing, hiring, and buying parts of the activities are today well-established modes of operation in the strategic repertoire of business (DiMaggio, 2003; Castells, [1998]2009; Reich, 1992). The best-known example is the car manufacturing industry, where manufacturers maintain a vast network of manifold subcontractors (Smitka, 1991; Clark and Fujimoto, 1991). Although the relationships between manufacturers and subcontractors are not on equal terms, they are prerequisites for and dependent on one another. Working conditions, however, may differ substantially. That, for instance, Volvo several years ago trumpeted the good working conditions in their Uddevalla plant meant little for the working conditions of those manufacturing the car parts delivered to the plant for final assembly. Dramatic differences have also been shown between the heart (product development) of the sport shoe manufacturer Nike in Oregon, USA, and the actual manufacturing of the shoes contracted to, for example, Taiwanese companies and placed in China (Klein, 2000). But it is not only the bad, dangerous, or labor-intensive work tasks that are outsourced. Russian companies, assuming monotonous programming tasks for big companies in Europe and the USA, for instance, often hire large American firms to handle their accounting. The accountancy firm is here both bigger than their contractors and enjoys substantially better working conditions (Huws, 2003a).

The division of labor that traditionally divided work tasks according to technical and administrative principles within the framework of a single organization now instead divides them according to market requirements and between different organizations. This means that even if a company chooses to increase its flexibility through empowerment it will probably require other companies whose flexibility is more substitutable. Around companies with autonomous jobs there also soon emerges a market for various adapted and more labor-intensive services. Autonomous jobs, free of traditional limitations in time and space, may for instance require restaurants, service stores, call centers, support units, and Internet banks that are open around the clock. We can also indirectly link the development of autonomous jobs to the rationalization of the common public sector, and the standardization of its functions with which we illustrated flexibility above. It is the growing, privileged, and well-educated middle class whose individualized work experiences are distancing them from other groups on the labor market. Being relatively well paid, they are shouldering an increasing burden of the common and tax funded welfare that, at the same time, is of decreasing importance to them. It is among these groups that the political demands for rationalizing, streamlining, and cutting down on the public sector spending gain their support (Clarke and Newman, 1997; Lasch, 1996).

Even if we prefer one type of flexibility over the other they are, as we can see, not mutually exclusive. Nor does a development toward increased flexibility of work involve a choice between the different types of flexibility. In the introduction we referred to Piore and Sabel who claimed that industrial work, despite the spread and attention it won during the twentieth century, never completely pushed out artisan manufacturing, but instead was dependent on it as a support mechanism and lubricant. It seems that we can now claim the opposite with regard to the twenty-first century. Although focus today is on jobs that are free and independent, their development tends to bring about an increase in a multitude of labor-intensive support activities with a more standardized labor content. These support activities, however, need not be performed within the framework of the same company. They may just as well, or perhaps better, be performed by independent companies, even in other countries. As a consequence, the development toward flexibility ought to be seen as a general development toward more heterogeneous or even polarized working conditions.

So, how many jobs are we actually talking about?

We have in this chapter discussed the forms and meaning of flexible work. Before bringing the discussion to a close we should perhaps ask ourselves just how frequent flexible jobs really are. This may seem like a relatively simple and adequate question, and a question that the subject literature should be able to give a straightforward answer to. Unfortunately this is not the case. There is, to put it shortly, no consensus on how to explain, define, and assess flexible jobs. Rather than try to compare other, and largely incomparable, studies we will therefore just use our own studies to give a rough idea of the proportion of flexible compared to non-flexible jobs.

We define flexible jobs as not being directly regulated by the organization. Hence, a job is flexible in the sense and to the extent that a worker can regulate the job herself, the assumption being that an increase in self-imposed rules presupposes a corresponding decrease in externally pre-scribed rules and limitations. Furthermore, a job can be flexible in different ways. We therefore divide and assess the job in four basic dimensions: time, space, performance, and cooperation. When a worker is able or required to regulate and delimit her work to a large extent in one of the dimensions, that dimension is regarded as not being regulated. And, vice versa, when a worker claims to be unable to regulate and delimit her work in one of the dimensions, that dimension is considered to be regulated.

Thus, unregulated conditions of work are less likely to involve regular working hours, a fixed place for work, standardized operating procedures, an unambiguously defined area of responsibility, a clear chain of command, and provisions of collaboration, while high-regulated conditions of work are more likely to involve such conditions.

We considered a job high regulated if the working conditions are regulated in all four dimensions. A job is low regulated if the working conditions are not regulated in two or three dimensions. If the working conditions are not regulated in any of the four dimensions we consider the job to be unregulated, boundaryless or indefinable.

Data were collected in 2005 by giving a questionnaire to a randomly selected sample of 4,000 individuals representing the working population in Sweden between ages 23 and 65. Of these, 1,000 were classified as employers, including freelancers being self-employed, in Statistic Sweden's databases. The response rate for the sample of 4,000 individuals was 68 percent. After exclusion of unemployed, people on parental- or sick-leave, students, etc., the analyses were based on about 2,200 individuals: 53 percent were men and 47 percent were women.

As can be seen in Table 2.2, about 10 percent of employed men and 4 percent of employed women have unregulated work conditions. Employees were found to experience higher levels of regulation as compared to employers and the differences between sexes were much smaller in that category. The high proportion of unregulated work among employers is not surprising since it is, after all, part of the employee–employer contract that the latter has the right to tell the former what to do, how to do it, as well as where and when to do it.

As can be expected, and as has been shown in numerous previous studies, regulation is highly related to the prevalence of Taylorist and Fordist modes of production. The auto industry and healthcare sectors have the highest levels of regulation, whereas IT-consultants and researchers have the lowest levels of regulation

Table 2.2 Regulation of work – percentage distribution ($n = 2,216$)

Degree of regulation	Employees Men	Employees Women	Employers Men	Employers Women	Total
Unregulated work	10	4	31	24	8
Regulated in 1 dimension	21	12	39	47	17
Regulated in 2 dimensions	23	21	19	14	22
Regulated in 3 dimensions	31	45	8	14	37
Regulated in 4 dimensions	15	18	3	1	16
Total	100	100	100	100	100

Source: Allvin et al. (2010).

The majority of men in Sweden work in the private sector, whereas the majority of women are in the public sector. Men working in the public sector are more often in government employment, which is characterized by low levels of regulation, whereas women publicly employed more often work on a regional or local level. Generally men are more often found in sectors that have lower levels of work regulation.

The study also showed that employees who are regulated in all four dimensions receive substantially lower salaries than those who are regulated in fewer dimensions, at merely 60 percent of the average annual salary of those having unregulated working conditions.

Other findings from the study showed a strong linear relationship between the degree of regulation and the right to overtime pay. Only 33 percent of the employees in the unregulated group had this right compared with 86 percent among those with work conditions regulated in all four dimensions.

Employees with unregulated working conditions were also much more dependent on having access to electronic mail. In that group 81 percent estimated it as very important compared to 19 percent among those who were regulated in all four dimensions. The same strong tendency was found for e-mail use outside normal working hours. In the unregulated group 64 percent often or sometimes used the e-mails on Saturdays and Sundays, compared to 10 percent among those with high-regulated conditions. This tendency was the same for use of electronic mail on weekday evenings: 77 percent compared with 13 percent.

The image of the low and unregulated jobs that emerges is fairly consistent with the results of existing case studies. These jobs are well-paid, male-dominated white-collar jobs that are mainly located in big cities and within the expanding service sector, in particular within the more knowledge-intensive services employed by business. The results are also consistent with the critique often leveled at many of these case studies, a critique arguing that unregulated, or boundaryless, jobs may have a high profile in the ongoing debate, but that they are atypical in real life. In summary, the results showed that a low proportion of the workforce reported having jobs that are entirely unregulated. However, if flexibility is regarded as a matter of degree and something that may be found everywhere, the labor market becomes covered with non-regulated *working conditions*, even if non-regulated *jobs* are fairly rare.

With a broader definition, 47 percent of the jobs on the Swedish labor market can be characterized as low or unregulated, which means that almost half of the Swedish workforce is subjected to a more indirect form of management that to a substantial degree leaves them accountable for their job. Inversely, the results show that less than a sixth of the jobs on the Swedish labor market are subject to working conditions that may be characterized as traditional and fitting with an industrial model of work.

So, even if the occurrence of flexibility is difficult to chart and predominantly flexible or unregulated jobs are fairly rare, it seems that flexible working conditions have expanded throughout the labor market and are now, in effect, the rule rather than the exception.

3
The New Work Life and the Dimensions of Knowledge

Knowledge and learning are and have always been a central part of work. The industrial revolution, starting in England in the 1700s and arriving in Sweden about a century later, was to a great extent about teaching people how to relate to the new industrial work. Of importance was then not to teach people to perform the tasks that they had been charged with as these tasks were generally self-evident or very simple. Rather, it was teaching them to respect working times and to behave accordingly in the workplace. This was, however, not education in the conventional sense. Demands on the labor force were instead conveyed through simple rules that were generally written down and pinned to the wall so that everybody could see them. Typical rules were in the form of prohibitions and enforced with the threat of fines. There were rules against singing, whistling, swearing, shouting, or opening windows. The workers were not allowed to spit, to be dirty, and to show aggressive or sexual behavior. Neither were they allowed to pass water, to seduce women or be inebriated at the workplace (Zuboff, 1988). What workers primarily had to learn were not the actual work tasks, but attentiveness, concentration, and self-discipline.

As in the army, the labor force of early industrialism had to adapt to an order that was considerably more regulated than what they were used to. And as in the army, they had to adapt to rules that, from their viewpoint, often seemed perfectly incomprehensible. But what was important was not that the workers understand the purpose of individual rules, it was rather that they continuously notice, respect, and follow the established rules. It was, in other words, obedience to rules in itself rather than regulated behavior that was to be established. In his study of the disciplinary institutions of the Enlightenment, Michel Foucault ([1974]1991) summarizes the logic of the regulation of industrialized work.

> One is as far as possible from those forms of subjection that demanded of the body only signs or products, forms of expression or the result of labor. The regulation imposed by power is at the same time the law of construction of the operation. Thus disciplinary power appears to have the function not so much of deduction as of synthesis, not so much of exploitation of the product as of coercive link with the apparatus of production. (p. 153)

But maintaining this kind of discipline also requires continuous self-motivation. The first workers hence needed to adopt a set of appropriate values and new morals. A serious problem for the first industrialists was, namely, that the workers did not return to their workplace once they had received their salary, or they returned only when the money was gone. They also needed several days of rest to sleep off drink (Thompson, 1967). In order to be able to operate the factories the employers had to change the behavior of the workers outside the workplace, too. A sober and conscientious life was here a prerequisite. Even more important was to know to postpone one's immediate desires and to think long term, not to spend the money one earned but to save and reinvest it. According to Marx, this is the most central characteristic of capitalism. Capital should not only be maximized, but accumulated. In his classic text on capitalism and the protestant work ethic ([1934]2003) Max Weber shows how this decree resulted from traditional protestant or, rather, Calvinist values. It is also fundamental to the work ethic, which is the basis of industrial society. Submitting to the demands of wage labor was hence not just the duty of the individual; it was a prerequisite for the normative system of industrial society.

We here see how industrial work, apart from the remuneration it brought, also conveyed a behavioral code, a set of norms, and common morals. Entering working life in other words socialized people into a larger pattern of values and social relations. Knowledge and skills generated in working life therefore not only concerned the actual work task, but developed on several different levels. Many of these skills were not rooted individually, but socially. They were developed, legitimized, and conveyed primarily at the work place, in the community, and through social institutions. The knowledge also signified a development of people's consciousness. But people were not always conscious of it as acquired knowledge.

Rather, it consisted of practical habits, obvious behavior that was taken for granted and never reflected upon.

This is also how we view knowledge in the new work life. In order to understand working life and its consequences it is not enough to emphasize the technical skills the individual needs in order to perform her work tasks. Work also contains, and always has contained, skills for relating to other people, to society, and to oneself. This is how we view learning, too. By learning we mean the process through which human beings adapt to conditions new to them. We will in this chapter account for the knowledge demands that the new work life places on people – in four separate dimensions (see Hagström and Hanson, 2003):

- The cognitive dimension of knowledge, by which is meant the technical knowledge demands placed on the individual in relation to work tasks.
- The social dimension of knowledge, by which is meant the knowledge demands placed on the individual in relation to other people at work.
- The societal dimension of knowledge, meaning the knowledge demands placed on the individual in relation to the social and cultural context of their work.
- The existential dimension of knowledge, implying the knowledge demands placed on the individual in relation to herself as labor.

We consider such a broad understanding of knowledge demands and learning processes as necessary, not only to understand the demands for knowledge per se, but also to understand why and how they are to be regarded as new. Each of these demands is often found in more traditional contexts. Thus, our ambition is to discern characteristics relevant for the new working life in each of the dimensions. However, we also think that the interplay between them is of importance: how they form one whole that appears as new in many ways, generating new problems and possibilities. We would therefore like to widen the meaning of the knowledge demands posed by work and show their relative importance. We will start with what we normally think of when we speak of the knowledge demands of work, that is, the purely technical knowledge demands posed by the work process.

The Cognitive Knowledge Demands

Through the establishment and gradual institutionalization of social relations in working life, they also, as far as knowledge was concerned, soon took a back seat. Instead, professional knowledge and skills took a more prominent position. The fast development in production technique increased the demand for and the demands on knowledge of the actual work process, and how to act in order to advance it. Until the start of the twentieth century, this knowledge, to a large extent, had been nested in the professional skills of workers. The development of production technique and organizational skills, however, separated it as an independent domain of knowledge. Throughout the early twentieth century, the battle for this knowledge was raging between workers and employers. New techniques with ensuing rationalizations led to work and its planning being located in different places. Thereby the planning, regulation, and evaluation of work came to be virtually taken over by engineers. Ever since, knowledge of the work process has been developed on the side or diagonally above the work place in planning, drawing, and development departments, so as to subsequently, if the need arose, be conveyed to the workers in the form of directed instructions or educational programs.

As a consequence of this, work was divided into a number of elements, devoid of shared meaning and goals. Similar divisions have of course always existed in industrial work, but in the infancy of industrialism, factories were small and the production process lucid enough not to assess comprehensively. Hence the individual work effort could still be related to the whole and thus be comprehensible. But as products became more complicated and factories larger, the individual worker lost that comprehensive overview. And the individual work effort was accordingly cut off from the larger whole, isolated and incomprehensible. Already in the 1800s, Marx had borrowed the term *alienation* from Hegel in order to describe how through the industrial division of labor the individual is separated from the products of her own labor, and thereby from herself (Israel, 1971; Mészáros, 1975). In the 1970s, Harry Braverman (1974) described the same phenomenon with reference to the Taylorist division of labor.

Space for action and control

Around the same time as Braverman, German labor psychologists were analyzing how the fragmentation of work brought about by the industrial division of labor between planning and performance also drains work of its intellectual content (Frese and Zapf, 1994; Hacker, Plath, Richter, and Zimmer, 1978; Volpert, 1989). Individual jobs were diagnosed with respect to the scope for action and decision they allowed. They were graded on a scale from purely automatic action, over simpler planning, and to an independent formulation of the work goals. If work is limited to mere performance it demands only sensorimotoric ability from the worker. If the job involves a certain element of planning, it demands, apart from sensorimotoric, also an ability to follow rules. And if work involves more unconditional planning, perhaps even the formulation of goals, it demands, apart from sensorimotoric and rule-following abilities, also an intellectual ability.

In other words, the more advanced and complicated the job, the more space for action and determination it allows. The size of that space can also be formulated as a question of control. The larger the space for action and determination the work allows, the more control it requires from the performing individual. For a long time this was a central question for the study of work. In one way or another it has been attempted to relate almost all problems brought about by working life to this very question. Many studies, for instance, have claimed that curtailments of the individual's control over her actions have a negative effect on motivation stress and health on the individual's free time, personality, and personal development as well as on her wage development, possibilities to influence, and democracy. Analyses of the space for action and determination of work are very detailed and technical. One consequence of looking at work in this way, however, is that the picture of the industrially organized work process where the course of action allows itself to be broken down into clear and sequentially organized elements becomes the norm for all jobs. And this gives a very narrow and peculiar picture of all those jobs that are not organized industrially and do not involve machines and physical things, but instead human beings and symbols. Another consequence is that the cognitive abilities of the individual come to the forefront. All effects work has on the individual will hence follow from the cognitive demands posed by the job. Whether work has positive or negative effects in other words depends on whether it poses high or low cognitive demands, whether the work is intellectually stimulating or just routine. Besides, one has focused almost without exception on the negative consequences of low cognitive demands. By accentuating the cognitive dimension per se one also tends to assume, explicitly or implicitly, the opposite connection, that is, that high cognitive demands automatically will have positive consequences.

An increasing rate of work combined with more complex choices may overload the intellectual regulation of actions and decrease the space for reflections. At the same time complex work tasks also may promote learning and development. Ellström (2001, 2002) argues that developmental learning is promoted by work tasks providing tentative, experimenting and critical reflecting, identifying, formulating, and defining problems, and consequently being able to master complex situations and decisions. Such learning processes may interplay more or less dynamically with rule- or routine-based reproductive learning. Thus developmental learning is assumed to be promoted by tasks and challenges that allow us to break out of predefined categories and procedures, constructing new patterns of thought and actions. This seems to indicate a transformative learning process. However, providing space for action and reflections at work can be regarded as a necessary but not sufficient condition for such processes. Intrinsic motivational and more personal drives related to, for example, attitudes, values, and meaning may become more important; deciding if and how such action and developmental possibilities are perceived is worth utilizing. Value, motivational, and developmental aspects will be further elaborated in relation to the societal and existential demands below. Before that we will focus on other aspects of the cognitive and social demands.

Tacit knowledge

In part as a reaction against this limited view of knowledge in work, a discussion was developed, mainly during the 1980s, on the kind of knowledge that fell outside this boundary and was made invisible by the industrially organized work life. This type of knowledge was therefore appropriately called "tacit knowledge." Tacit knowledge is the type of knowledge that is accumulated in the body through experience. The knowledge is personal and the individual is not conscious of having acquired it. Neither is it possible to articulate, and one can therefore not systematize it, convey it, or formulate exactly of what it consists. It is the knowledge one constantly uses, every day, without thinking about it. It is, in brief, a habit.

All work also requires some kind of habit. However much one learns about the job before starting, some form of familiarization is always needed before it is possible to do it properly. Certain jobs are more dependent on familiarization than others. These are above all tasks based on physical activity, but also those relying on social relations. In jobs based on the employment of symbols, the element of familiarity is, however, smaller, and in jobs where conditions are constantly redefined, familiarity may even be an obstacle. Here we may detect a conflict between the cognitively defined knowledge, pointing to the importance of variation and intellectual stimulus, and the tacit knowledge of familiarity, which instead emphasizes continuity and experience. Asserting the one inevitably seems to infringe on the other.

The discussion on the tacit knowledge has also developed to a large extent in opposition to the increasing demands for conceptual knowledge and academic merits in the work life. Research around tacit knowledge has showed how invaluable this knowledge is in a majority of jobs. Research, in other words, has assumed the paradoxical task to make the invisible visible, to formulate that which cannot be formulated, and to give a language to the tacit. Not uncommonly, this has been done to defend professions and work tasks against rationalizations or automatizations. One problem, however, is that this research has come to appear as a romantic and conservative protest. It does not add to the development of working life; it only defends that which is about to be lost. Another problem is that research, through this defense, actually opened the door for what it claims to wish to avoid: continued rationalization.

The knowledge of tacit knowledge can be invoked, for example, in work division, such as when graphics workers were rationalized away as their professional knowledge could be incorporated into the computer systems that the journalists used to write their articles (Ehn, 1988). Yet another problem is that this knowledge, by defining itself as the antithesis of symbolic knowledge, writes itself into and affirms the cognitive dimension of knowledge. Tacit knowledge hence becomes no more than the response to the sensorimotoric demands of work, while symbolic knowledge corresponds to the intellectual demands. Common for both the cognitively defined knowledge and the tacit knowledge is also their one-dimensional focus on the work process, that is, the actual course of action in work.

What do we really need to know in flexible work?

When we speak of knowledge and learning in relation to the work process we mean the ability of the individual to do his job independently. We can briefly say that this independence may be divided into the individual's ability to do the job by virtue of his experience and to do it by virtue of continuous analysis and planning. At the one end we thus find the knowledge of familiarity and at the other the intellectual knowledge. But in principle both types of knowledge lead to the individual being able to do his job independently. Whether this is also the case in practice depends primarily on whether the conditions of work, and thus the work tasks, are stable or not. If the conditions of work remain the same, the individual, regardless of the complexity of said conditions, will be able to perform tasks independently as familiarity with them increases. Familiarity knowledge is hence enough to assume that the individual will be able to carry out tasks independently, if we simultaneously assume that working conditions are more or less stable. Potential intellectual demands will then decrease as familiarity increases. If, however, working conditions are unstable, the individual will be able to work independently only if he is able to analyze these changing conditions and thereby formulate his own tasks. Here, the changing conditions sabotage all attempts at establishing familiarity with the tasks.

Flexible jobs are also characterized by inconsistency, either through working conditions or the composition of personnel being changeable. As a consequence, familiarity knowledge will not be too useful, with the demands on employees' intellectual abilities all the higher. In our studies of flexible working conditions with, among others, consultants, higher employees, and freelance journalists, the high demands for qualifications are quite tangible. Not only are the work tasks complex and increasingly abstract, but they are also unstructured and unpredictable. Most work on projects or under project-like circumstances. This means that the individuals, to a certain extent, personally have to define, plan, and structure their work. And the conditions of work often vary. This is, above all, the case for freelance journalists, who may receive or be forced to take on assignments at very short notice. They therefore need to be ready to reconsider and reorient their work. This also poses demands to acquire new knowledge and understanding of new fields. With reference to the above-mentioned cycle of action we may state that these jobs need intellectual abilities in the shape of advanced problem solving as well as creativity (Hanson, 2004).

However, that the work demands intellectual ability does not mean that it does not demand familiarity knowledge. The freelance journalists specifically emphasized the importance of experience and genuine professional skills in order to complete their assignments. This is particularly true for brief and relatively simple assignments given at short notice. The unpredictability and short preparation time here require a habit on which to fall back. On longer, more complicated and extensive assignments, however, this need is not as pronounced. Familiarity knowledge is important, but in itself not enough (Hanson, 2004).

As these jobs to such a large extent pose high cognitive demands on the workers, one might expect them to approach the ideal of the good work and that they, at least regarding knowledge development and learning, are relatively free from serious limitations. But this is not always the case.

Just-in-time learning. This is because the work organization and technique that enable developed learning, through the breaking down of traditional limitations, affect learning in other ways. The extensive use of projects and project-like work forms, for instance, creates a very limited knowledge focus. The knowledge needed on the job is generated with the help of the project group, with regard to project-specific problems, and within the timeframe of the project. It is, quite simply, the knowledge the group needs in order to complete their task. All knowledge that falls outside these specifications will not be followed up, or just ignored. As projects in some sense always start from scratch and have a specific goal, for example, the relative advantages of extensive previous knowledge will not be very significant – in a certain sense all project co-workers start from the same point. Neither are there any demands for the knowledge generated within the project to be related to a wider context, or to be integrated with the other knowledge of the individuals. Quite on the contrary, there is almost always a lack of time and resources for, and interest in, establishing this new knowledge firmly and comprehensively.

New information techniques create a similar problem. What information one needs is generally so easily accessible, and at the same time so changeable, that it seldom pays off to try and turn it into "knowledge" by remembering it. Information about companies, their personnel, customers, product selection, and prices is, as advertisement has it, just a click away. Internal and external emailing systems also make it relatively simple to establish and maintain a contact network for the mutual exchange of information. Systems and interface are also becoming increasingly standardized and pedagogical, which means that most people are able to understand and use them.

The Swedish researcher Kurt Lundgren has very aptly named the learning brought about by project organizations and new technique "just-in-time learning." One gathers the knowledge, data, or information needed for that moment, uses it, and forgets it or files it away. Learning is for the moment, not for life – not lifelong learning (Lundgren, 1999). When he contrasts this short-term learning with a more long-term method a number of questions and problem areas arise. How quick can learning be and how much can it be compressed? It is obvious that the techniques for quickly putting together, integrating, and starting a project group have developed immensely, making it possible to speed up the take-off considerably. In the same way, the techniques and forms of direction, follow-up, and result presentation have developed and streamlined the process. The construction of the computer interface with the help of pictures, several dimensions, and intuitive functions has also made it considerably easier to profit from vast amounts of information and complex contexts in a short time.

In our studies of freelancers and telecommuting employees, both these groups reported a lack of what we may call space for reflection. This particularly concerned a lack of feedback, a feeling that no evaluations or comments on their work were forthcoming. Instead, work was dominated by what we correspondingly may call "feed forward," that is, the part of the action cycle where the individual tries to influence her surroundings in concordance with her goals. The reason for this imbalance was quite simply that it was, in the end, they who by themselves decided and set limits to the scope of their work and assessed its quality. For the freelancers, the lack of feedback from outside originated in the absence of forms and stages for this purpose, while this, for the telecommuting employees, above all was a question of time scarcity. The consequence for both groups, however, was that much time and energy was spent planning what to do, but less reflecting over what had been done (Hanson, 2004).

Information anxiety. Forcing knowledge development and learning in this way may have unwanted consequences. In a job where the problem is evident and the task consists of finding the "right" solution, learning may be compressed in a number of ways. In jobs where the problems are not distinct, but the task entails first defining the problem one has to solve, streamlining learning is not as easy. In such jobs there is a need for time: time to gather information, time to experiment and reflect, time to share experience with others. When the pressure of time is too great it may lead to tunnel vision and a return to ingrained routines and traditional patterns. Time pressure may thus have the effect to stop the development of knowledge (Ellström, 2002).

In other contexts this is often called tech-stress, information overload, or information anxiety, that is, the fact that the sheer amount of possibilities and information may have a negative effect on people. This may in turn concern anything from not finding the information one needs, to not understanding or not being able to take in the information one has

(Wurman, 1991). Common for all is the insight that more information does not always entail more knowledge or a more informed conduct. Instead, a wealth of strategies appears for screening the information. The consequence of this is that the major part of the information quite simply passes us by, or, in the worst case, that we behave more irrationally than we would otherwise do (Tidline, 1999).

Meta-learning and organizational learning. Another question is whether instances of short-term learning can be linked together and its knowledge accumulated. Even though short-term learning is becoming more efficient, this does not mean that knowledge acquired in this way can be built on to achieve a more long-term knowledge development. The traditional method for achieving this long-term knowledge development is that the short-term knowledge is integrated into and by the individual. But when time is scarce and an increasing part of the integration takes place in the information technology medium, it reduces the need and ability of the individual to take in and process all the information that is presented. Instead of being integrated to becoming knowledge, information then amounts to nothing more than continuous white noise. Therefore, the knowledge that becomes important in flexible and constantly changing activities is not primarily all the individual knowledge and its constant flow, but rather a course of action to generate, handle, and use this stream of knowledge. What we learn, what is accumulated in us as knowledge, is not the information per se, but rather how we find, organize, and use the pertinent information. What we learn is hence a kind of practical knowledge or "know-how." The practical, or tacit, knowledge is here again in focus, but on a more comprehensive level. We are not learning more and more things; we are learning how to learn. It is this kind of meta-learning that learning in flexible jobs is all about. It is also through such meta-learning that knowledge may be accumulated.

This accumulation of knowledge, or meta-learning, may then happen in different ways. It may take place within the framework of an individual's career or life span. It implies that the individual, so to speak, gets used to always searching and always being open to new knowledge. In other words, the individual should always be prepared for changes and accept the development. Such marathon-learning is sometimes described as "lifelong learning," a concept that mirrors development optimism as well as a fear of falling behind in the new work life (Lundgren, 1999).

Another way in which knowledge may be accumulated is through so-called organizational learning. It may take place directly through an institutional accumulation of knowledge, which means that knowledge is stored in various institutional solutions. Examples include internal company routines, internal mail, intranets, databases, customer registries, brands, and various technical solutions. Licenses, patents, and copyrights are other examples.

Such institutional organizational learning, however, differs from the more informal and indirect learning in social relations, groups, or networks. Here, learning is taking place between individuals sharing a practical community (Wenger, 2000). Learning results from the fact that individuals doing something together also adapt to each other. This simple fact is sometimes also called professional socialization, contextual learning, or "situated learning." Knowledge generated in this process is then not individual, but common. The knowledge is the way in which the community performs, regards, thinks, and talks about and relates to work (Brown and Duguid, 1991; Tsoukas, 2001).

As the knowledge is not individually but socially rooted, it means that the order or structure that knowledge constitutes does not appear in the individual's mind as, for instance, a mental representation or schedule. Rather, it is the conditions of participation that have a particular structure or follow a certain order. Learning is therefore synonymous with learning to participate. Participation is then in itself a kind of knowledge that makes it possible to move between and profit by knowledge from different social contexts and communities (Orlikowski, 2002; Tennant, 1999).

Examples of this were seen in our study of nurses in the staffing industry. The more experienced nurses found it relatively easy to change between different workplaces and work groups, as hospital wards look largely the same wherever one goes. Routines are also the same. And not only that, but also the social constellations, the attitudes to work, the employer, the patients, the colleagues, and other professional groups were the same. Discussions and comments in the coffee or smoking rooms were so similar that it was at times difficult for the staffing nurse to know in which ward he was, and whether he had been there before. But through participating in the discussion in the proper way he gained access to the community and its knowledge.

> It all comes down to your attitude. If you are humble and show pleasant, positive behavior and that you want to help, they will return the favor... As a nurse you can never know everything. You always have to trust and help each other. (Staffing nurse)

Developing, directing, and managing organizational learning for strategic purposes is regarded as increasingly important for businesses and organizations. This is also a growing area within industrial management and business economics, and has been endowed with a name of its own: Knowledge Management (Alvesson and Kärreman, 2001).

In conclusion, there are two things we have wanted to point to concerning the cognitive knowledge demands in flexible jobs. The first is that practical knowledge about the work processes is far from being counted out. On the contrary, it seems to become ever more important. However, it is to be found on a higher level. It does not primarily concern the almost sensuous familiarity that artists and others have with the object of their labor, as it was often described in the mid-1980s. Rather, practical knowledge concerns the ability to search for, handle, and convert information to move purposefully forward in the information jungle and to have information experience. In this is also included the ability to see through rhetoric and "information recycling," that is, when old information is presented in new packaging. It also concerns the ability to adapt relatively quickly to and start working under new conditions, a kind of adjustment familiarity. We have called it meta-learning, which implies increased familiarity with the learning process per se.

The second thing we have wanted to point out is that learning is not necessarily something that takes place in the mind of an individual. Learning is also a social phenomenon in the sense that knowledge is generated and exists within a social context. This context may be a formalized structure of rules deciding what may and may not be done or an informal community at the workplace where the knowledge is identical to the rules of participation. A common feature, however, is that the knowledge does not work or does not make sense outside its social context. This will bring us to another type of knowledge demand posed by the new work life, namely, the demand to be able to relate to other people in a constructive and frictionless way. We hereby leave the cognitive and enter the social dimension of knowledge.

The Social Knowledge Demands

When we speak of the social dimension of knowledge we mean the knowledge and learning in relation to other people that the new work life demands. In traditional work this knowledge and learning in all essentials concerned submission, what Richard Edwards (1979) has called the bureaucratic control in the workplace. The individual, as labor, was but a cog in the machinery and expected to follow the rules, know her place, and resign herself to her lot. The "good worker" had to have a strong sense of duty, be predictable, and loyal. As a reward he or she was offered lifelong security and a continuous improvement of the personal working conditions. In this way the bureaucratic organization manipulated and secured the labor force.

> Bureaucratic control brought an organizational logic to the systematic dispensation of higher pay, promotion, more responsibility, access to better or cleaner or less dangerous working conditions, better health benefits, longer vacations, assignment to work stations with more status or comfort, and other privileges that corporations now bestow on favored employees. Positive incentives greatly heightened the workers' sense of the mobility within the firm that lay in front of them. (Edwards, 1979, pp. 142–143)

If the traditional work expected the worker to subordinate herself to the relations at the workplace, the flexible work expects her to participate in them. And in order to participate it is not enough to partake passively. The employee has to be able to take her place in and influence these relations according to her own wishes. That the demands on knowledge and learning in relation to other people in this way have changed and become an increasingly important part of work is mainly due to two things. One is the development of service jobs and the other the increased importance of spontaneous cooperation.

All work is service work

In the past 30 to 40 years, the service sector has seen a dramatic growth in the entire Western world. At the end of the 1990s more than half the working population of Sweden had jobs in workplaces where activities were centered on producing some form of service. Naturally these jobs vary, from plumbers to waiters and waitresses, to consultants of various denominations. Moreover, all the "helping jobs" that constitute the public service and healthcare sector belong to this category. What this diverse group has in common is that their work is decided not only in relation to an employer, but also to a customer, a client, or a patient. Characteristic of service production is, as we pointed out in the previous chapter, that the result of the work is produced and consumed simultaneously, and that the quality of the result in the last instance is defined by the consumer.

As the work is carried out immediately and in situ, there can hardly be any chances of redoing it or correcting any mistakes. It has to be done properly the first time around or, as one of the slogans of the McDonald's hamburger university has it, you never get a second chance to make a first impression. The actual service is supplied in what is popularly called "the moment of truth." The moment of truth is a term borrowed from bullfighting and signifies the moment when the bullfighter and bull are alone in the arena and become the center of everyone's attention. Time stands still and the matador is left to his own means. The former SAS (Scandinavian Airlines) CEO, Jan Carlzon was also fond of the above expression (1987), but did not push the analogy as far as to equate the customer with the bull that is to be forced to kneel, but spontaneously the thought still arises. The intent is otherwise to point to the specific conditions implied in service production. All preparation, investment, organization, and training lead up to, and are entirely dependent on, the encounter with the consumer. In that encounter, only the service personnel count for something. If anything goes wrong in the encounter with the consumer, everything else has been a waste. A service business must hence be directed toward and organized so that it works as backup for the "front personnel" (yet another term implying that the encounter with the consumer is a matter of life and death).

The conflicting demands of service work. The moment of truth, however, confronts the service personnel with conflicting demands. On the one hand, they are the dividing line of the company vis-à-vis the market. Not only are they to sell the products or services of the company, but they also have to represent the company as a whole. As they are in the public view they have to behave in accordance with the company's self-image. The behavior of the personnel is carefully directed and entirely decided by the company. On the other hand the consumer expects the personnel to be made up of independent individuals, people he or she can relate to in the same way as to other people in life. Service personnel therefore also have to be individual, confidence inspiring, and generally sympathetic. Above all they have to express a certain independence toward the company they represent. Otherwise, they do not function as a communicative counterpart, but are reduced to impersonal puppets. Service work demands that the service worker be both a co-dependent representative of their company and an independent individual to whom the consumer can relate (Leidner, 1993).

These conflicting demands force the personnel to a continuous balance act. In simpler service jobs this balance act is facilitated by the actual interaction with the customer being more or less prescribed. In work at fast food restaurants the interaction, for instance, is limited by the choices the customer is given in the menu. But there, too, and even more so in complicated interactions it is not enough that the service personnel simply perform their duties correctly; they also have to give the impression that they like it. The personnel have to look like they really believe in the company and its products. If the personnel look bored or behave unpleasantly, it immediately reflects on the product they are selling or the company they represent. If, on the other hand, their behavior becomes too mechanical or dependent it affects the credibility of what they say. The service relation becomes credible only if it seems to be honestly intended. These conflicting demands are mirrored in Arlie Hochschild's (1983) description of service work as "emotional labor."

There are three fundamental modes of conduct the personnel may adopt in order to deal with the dilemma they face due to the conflicting demands (see Hochschild, 1983, p. 187). The first is to become emotionally involved in one's work. This does not mean only to let oneself be persuaded by the company or the organization one represents, but also to assimilate the self-image of the company. Of course, this may mean a more or less uncritical submission, but it may also be the conscious choice of the individual to acquire the values of the company or to read one's own values into the corporate ones. It may also be the result of a socialization process. In any case, this may be very stimulating as long as the emotional engagement of the individual is not shaken. Moreover, it may be rewarding as it is recognized both by consumers and employers. But the emotional engagement is, by necessity, unilateral. For the employer, the personnel will always be labor to be used. Sooner or later there will also be something undermining the emotional engagement. And when it cracks, the reaction will also be emotional. The frustration is interpreted as a letdown and an insult, resulting in anger, dejection, and, in time, burnout.

The second possible method for dealing with "the emotional dilemma" in service work is instead to dissociate emotionally from the work. This mode of conduct may be the result of a conscious choice or a reaction to defunct emotional engagement. It may also be a means for limiting a job where setting limits is difficult. In a study on healthcare workers, Wanja Astvik (2002) describes a string of strategies care workers adopt in order to limit their emotional engagement and to define their work in the face of what is seen as the limitless need of the care recipients. The various strategies are captioned by telling quotes and expressions: "Give your little finger and they take the whole hand," "I'm no bloody maid," "We have to put up with everything," "You can't put on airs," "I clean for them and nothing else." But the strategies care workers here employ to dissociate themselves emotionally are often counterproductive in the sense that they give rise to more emotional reactions than they shut out. Moreover, these strategies often have a negative effect on both the care workers and the quality of their work.

The third mode of conduct for dealing with the emotional dilemma is professional. The point here is to keep the conflicting demands separate, to be simultaneously a co-dependent practicer of a profession, an independent person, and communicative counterpart. Simply put, there are different roles. This is sometimes described as social competence.

Social competence. Many have noticed that the concept of social competence has been used and abused so often that it has lost most of its meaning. One reason for this is that many of those who use the concept seem to prefer emphasizing the social per se, in order to open the door for everything that is somehow linked to it. Not only does it give entry to a vast field of knowledge, but it is also a relatively unexplored field within work pedagogics. Nevertheless, it poses certain problems. The concept gets a tendency to swell beyond all limits when it is associated with everything from discourse and communication theory to the most fundamental conditions of moral acting. Another problem is the lack of distance it results in. When the concept becomes sweeping, it is also left wide open to individual projections. Constant associations to good or bad things turn the concept into something unnecessarily normative, controversial, and generally cumbersome.

Attempts have been made to circumvent this by coining new concepts that largely mean the same thing. Daniel Goleman, for instance, has adopted Howard Gardner's notion of "emotional intelligence" (Gardner, 1983). Goleman (1995) tries to develop the concept by formulating it as a psychological theory. According to this theory, social skills require a social consciousness, which, in turn, requires self-regulation that, in its turn, requires a consciousness of the self. In order to influence other people one must be responsive to others and the prerequisite is that one is responsive to oneself. A minor industry has subsequently developed around these profound remarks, as well as diagnostic instruments, training courses, and programs (see e.g. Cherniss and Adler, 2000).

Another method for circumventing the erosion of meaning and simultaneously get a much-needed distance to the concept is to focus on the tension between the social and the more instrumental concept of competence. We may state that this social competence is not necessarily a particularly commendable talent. With reference to Goffman (1959) we may argue that social competence means knowing how to interact with others so that one is able to control the impression one makes on other people. Thus it can be regarded as an instrumental skill, a technique for achieving one's aims in relation to other people. Psychopaths not uncommonly command significant social competence. We may also say that social competence can be conceived as the ability to play a game, a responsive game, certainly, but nevertheless a game. In this game, the self is not exposed in other ways than through one's aims. We here have to make a distinction between the individual as a person and the game he plays.

After his publications about emotional intelligence, Goleman has further elaborated on the concept of social intelligence (Goleman, 2007). He takes a departure in broad tendencies toward "social corrosion" or "social autism," due to, for example, people's absorption in virtual reality (iPods, cellphones, Internet, etc.). Moreover, he frequently bases his reasoning on empirical findings from social neuroscience, an increasing research field emanating from the early 1990s. He suggests that social intelligence can be organized into two broad categories, namely social awareness (what we sense of others) and social facility (what we do with that awareness) (p. 84). He claims social intelligence should not only include sensitivity toward other people, receptive listening, emphatically understanding another person's thoughts, feelings and intentions, etc., it should also include actions and interactions in accordance with such feelings, based on real concern for the other person involved.

This more altruistic conception of social intelligence provides an alternative and more sympathetic interpretation of what it can qualitatively mean. But it does not solve the problems developing and applying such a competence in relation to demands in the new work life. Social competence, in a somewhat more superficial way, is a necessary skill in today's society and we all, to a greater or lesser extent, use this skill in our everyday lives. Each day we encounter cashiers, drivers, colleagues, bosses, salespersons, officials, and neighbors whom we in various ways are dependent on and with whom we are forced to establish limited but often decisive relationships. In order to conduct our lives and get somewhere in society we depend on all these limited relationships working smoothly and developing as appropriately as possible. Hereby we may also achieve insight into what social competence means to service work.

All these people whose work it is to meet and provide services to others, in order to carry out their duties, have to adopt a professional mode of action based on social competence in some form. In order to deal successfully with the emotional dilemma that the conflicting demands of service work impose on the personnel they have to be able to keep these demands separate. In other words, they have to play the game.

However, a number of studies point out that it is not possible to play the game on these conditions indefinitely without certain problematic consequences. Hochschild (1983) describes, for example, how service work may lead to the personality traits used at work causing an individual to feel alien and false. She speaks of an alienated and instrumental relation to personal feelings as a possible consequence. Robin Leidner (1991), in her study of insurance agents and McDonald's personnel, also shows how many service jobs require and encourage stereotypical gender patterns. In another context she describes how the norms for social interaction through service work are relativized. This may, according to her, lead to the blurring of the line between moral and manipulative in relation to others. She further speculates whether social interaction in general, as a consequence of this, would be more affected and manipulative (Leidner, 1993).

> But playing the social game is not just giving service to customers, clients and patients. It is also, perhaps most importantly, cooperating with others. The enhanced need for auto-initiated cooperation is another reason for the dimension of social competence becoming an increasingly important part of working life.

How spontaneous is spontaneous cooperation?

Companies and organizations strive for what we in the previous chapter have called flexibility through empowerment; conditions for cooperation are to a large extent the responsibility of the individual. In traditional and bureaucratically ruled organizations, cooperation between individuals is more or less specified by their organizational positions and/or the physical and technical systems employed in production. Cooperation is, in other words, independent of the individuals taking part. In order for activities to be flexible, however, individuals will have to contact one another and independently initiate cooperation with the people or functions needed to carry out the task in question. This means that the forms of cooperation will vary depending on the individuals taking part and the task they cooperate on. The forms of cooperation hence assume a character akin to a social network.

Social networks. A network is characterized by its temporary character and mostly informal integration. As a form of cooperation in working life it poses specific demands on the workers. A traditional organization, so to speak, is the way it is. Individuals are normally not able to influence it. Its task is channeling cooperation into specified routes. What social relations the organization consists of take a back seat and we are mostly not aware of them either. A social or professional network, on the other hand, is part of the cooperation and hence always present. And since a network is defined by the individuals it consists of, all cooperation must be conducted in relation to them as individuals.

In our studies of free jobs (Allvin *et al.*, 1999) it transpired that this may facilitate work.

> Well, you're a bit married to each other. If you've worked together a long time, you know each other. So in that way there's a certain safety working with people you know from before. Then they don't need to feel this heavy responsibility to keep everything in check. (System developer)

At the prospects of getting work,

> Quite often it's the stage designer who says that "I would like to work with him or her." Often you've worked together earlier and know each other. Well, it's chemistry, that, too. (Stage design assistant)

At the same time it demands a lot from those involved, demands that are not really connected to the work one assumes. One consequence is that work becomes more emotionally charged. Just as professional successes may strengthen the self, setbacks and backlashes in the cooperation may hit it. It is not enough to deal with the backlash. One also has to be able to deal with the emotional and social consequences. Furthermore, one needs constantly to be aware of one's proper social position. There is a need for a personal stance vis-à-vis all the groupings, relations, and intrigues that make up the social infrastructure. In order to navigate these circumstances one needs to be conscious of, and know how to relate to, all the unspoken expectations one constantly encounters of which but a fraction actually concern work. Neither is it enough to have a social position, relations, or networks – they also have to be maintained and, preferably, developed. This means a continuous need to guard one's place, to take various social initiatives, and accept those of others (Allvin et al., 1999).

The social game, furthermore, takes place against a serious backdrop that one does not always perceive. While a network includes those involved in a community, it also effectively excludes others. There are no formal criteria for admission to the network and people who are left outside can never really know why. Even within the framework of the community, qualification, praise, and sanctions are often distributed on unclear and irrational grounds. Self-generating communities also tend to have a conserving effect. They develop their own internal systems of values and norms, their own focus and blind spots. Cooperation is thus stuck in a social pattern and involvement in their social roles. If cooperation takes a negative turn it will be difficult to rectify as everybody involved has invested so much of their self. Rather, the cooperation will be dismantled, leaving those involved with a bitter aftertaste.

Social capital. We will see that spontaneously initiated cooperation requires knowledge that will hardly be mentioned in a work description. More specifically, it requires that the individual know how to behave and relate to a specific social context. If we look upon this knowledge as a resource we may describe it in terms of social capital. The concept has been used mainly in politics and sociology in an attempt to specify or classify how various social networks can be a resource for individuals, organizations, or societies. One of the earliest, and possibly best, definitions of the concept is provided by Pierre Bourdieu. According to Bourdieu (1986), social capital concerns the actual and potential resources in terms of relationships and contacts commanded by an individual – in brief, "liaisons." Characteristic of social capital is that it, similarly to economic capital, consists of resources that may be converted into something of admitted value. Bourdieu treats social capital as an individual resource. Social relations are used by the individual to achieve what she tries to attain. In other words, they have an instrumental value for the individual (Portes, 1998).

The American sociologist Mark Granovetter (1973, 1983) shows, in a classic study, that a large part of the highly qualified labor force obtained their current jobs through social liaisons (weak ties). These liaisons are to be kept separate from the close relations (strong ties) we entertain with relatives and friends. Granovetter's point is that many loose liaisons are often more significant for the individual and society than a smaller number of close relations. His argument is that many looser liaisons form thin but extensive networks binding together groups in the social space. This gives the individual entry and qualifications for many different contexts. She can thereby get new information and a social overview which is not possible through close relations. Close relations will quite often exclude others and isolate groups from one another. Therefore, a society where individuals have many and loose relationships is more open to new ideas than a society where individuals have a limited number of close relationships. Many loose relationships, in other words, expand the perspectives and possibilities of individuals while a small number of close relationships limit them.

This distinction was often pointed out by the staffing nurses we interviewed (Allvin, Jacobson, and Isaksson, 2003). The staffing nurses often compared the possibilities and the broad-mindedness their own loose relationships entailed with the lacking outlook and limited community of the permanent employees.

> It's a lot of fun. You get to mix and to see things you never would otherwise. You get to broaden your range of skills and use your entire registry. (Staffing nurse)
>
> I've got to say it's a relief to escape it [the community of colleagues at the ward]. I mean, women are all good and stuff, but sometimes it's just too much granny talk. (Staffing nurse)

Working as staffing nurses, they covered a relatively large area and built up an extensive network of contacts. And as they were not tied to any specific workplace, they regarded themselves as more open to changes than those with permanent employment. The staffing nurses claimed that permanent staff were often locked in their relationships and perceptions. Therefore, one way to motivate their role as staffing nurse was as a little light in the darkness, either in the shape of new knowledge from outside, or through their therapeutic function as unbiased conversation partners.

Loose relationships could hence be a resource for others than those directly concerned. It may even contribute to organizational learning. One part of the workforce being loosely tied to the work place significantly implies not just a risk, but a possibility for the organization, which opens up to the world around in a way that otherwise would not happen. Personnel turnover is therefore not a disadvantage only. Part of the new knowledge benefiting the organization enters or is generated in the periphery of the organization by unconventional and convention-transcending people

(Garsten, 1999; Tempest and Starkey, 2004). This happens in part by knowledge being introduced "from outside" through the convention transcenders forcing the workplace to take the activities into consideration. People with a large contact network may also be a resource for employers looking to employ new personnel. Employing personnel on recommendation not only simplifies recruiting, it also enables keeping control of who is employed; it simplifies communication with potential employees and increases chances of them fitting into the social environment at the workplace (Fernandez, Castilla, and Moore, 2000).

But in order for a contact network to work as a resource all individuals in this network have to be prepared to help one another regardless of whether this entails immediate personal gain. Even if there is an instrumental purpose to the contact network, participation has to be mutual for it to work. Social capital is in that respect a resource for the network as a whole. This is also how the American political scientist Robert Putnam speaks about social capital. According to Putnam (1993, 2000), mutuality in the relationships of individuals will cooperate and affect the network as a whole and, by extension, society. The larger the number of similar relationships making up society, the less risky it will be to act in said society. People quite simply trust and expect others to help and behave more or less the same as they themselves would. Putnam describes this in terms of a "citizenry spirit" based on mutual cooperation and mutual trust.

Trust. With the concept of "trust" we are getting closer to the psychological basis of flexible work. The concept is frequently discussed and enthusiastically used in connection with the new work life. It is claimed, for instance, that the capacity for trust is one of the earliest and most fundamental human characteristics. However, trust may not necessarily be interpreted in terms of such basic needs. The phenomenon of trust appears in the context of social relations consistently becoming more ambiguous, problematic, and, above all, invisible. In other words, the fact that trust has become a factor in the new work life does not mean that relations in working life have become more trusting, but rather the opposite.

Niklas Luhmann (2000a, 2000b) makes an important distinction between confidence and trust. Both confidence and trust refer to a credence given to the actions of human beings and the consequences of these actions. By confidence is meant a more or less unconsidered attitude that these actions and consequences will remain the way they always were: possible to take for granted. Trust, on the other hand, according to Luhmann, is always related to risk. It presupposes that actions may have unforeseen consequences. Trust, as opposed to confidence, always includes an awareness of the possibilities of unexpected consequences of people's actions. This means that trust, but not confidence, presupposes awareness of independent actions, or, more specifically, that actions entail independent choices. Driving, for instance, presupposes trust in the actions of other drivers. We trust others to stop at red lights, to follow traffic rules, and not to cut into our lane when we approach. In other words, we trust other drivers to have full control of their actions, to be responsible and not malevolent. At the same time we are aware that this may not always be the case. Other drivers in principle always have the option to break traffic rules. Even the car may, due to construction defects or other unforeseen errors of the manufacturers, break down or start behaving incongruously. Still we put our trust in the car for the simple reason that we have no reason to expect the unexpected. We know that the unforeseen may happen, but if we have no direct reason to expect the unexpected we put our trust in what we may expect. Our trust is consequently based on such explicit and rational reflections.

Trust is therefore not just an existential category, but also a method for dealing with the insecurity of social life. Through trust, social relations are established and maintained, and actions may be carried out, which otherwise would be impossible without sizable transaction costs.

We see here that trust in a strict sense is not related to other people at large, but to their actions, or rather to the practical consequences of their free choices, or even more specifically to our rational expectations of their practical consequences. Trust is in other words a rational way to deal with the freedom of others. A small child consequently, according to this way of reasoning, does not feel trust but rather confidence with trust appearing much later. It refers to the credence independent human beings in a social system give each other.

According to Luhmann, trust as well as risk is a consequence of the modern and socially unforeseeable society. In all things essential, trust was substituted for what pre-modern societies thought of in terms of luck or destiny. Modern society has instead made us dependent on the actions of other people. Human beings have always been dependent on the actions of others, but because of these modern notions, we more than ever became dependent on human actions that are invisible to us. According to Anthony Giddens (1990) it is specifically the absence of actions in time and space that makes trust so important to us. We do not need to trust visible actions around us as we are able to control them. We have to relate differently, though, to invisible actions. We have to imagine them in order to position ourselves relative to their consequences and it is only afterwards that we will know whether our expectations were correct. This is a rational and calculating attitude. With the advent of modern society people also became more generally aware of taking risks and not just being hit by natural events or divine intervention. One became aware of having an individual say in the course of events and not just being affected by occurrences beyond personal control.

After this we may also start to understand the importance of trust in flexible work. Trust is a way for the employers to deal with the increased self-determination of employees as well as a way for employees to deal with employers' demands for flexibility. In traditional and bureaucratically managed organizations the need for trust is not as pronounced since work in these organizations mainly consists of following prescribed rules and the trust will be limited to people's disposition for following these rules. Trust, in other words, is reduced in familiarity.

In flexible organizations, on the other hand, the regulation of work is subject to the more or less independent choices of the individual. In spite of this, the employer must be able to trust the individual to behave predictably. But as this situation lacks an absolute system of rules for everyone to relate to, the employer needs to find a new basis for his or her trust. Grey and Garsten (2001) have suggested that the prevalent discourse within the organization or field of knowledge concerned may function as this basis. In order for the employer to trust the individual employee, such an employee needs to accomplish results in their work as well as partake in an identity-shaping process by continuously positioning themselves in relation to the current discourse. For instance, by speaking the language of management, by being familiar with activity trends, techniques, jargon, and symbols, one credits and enters a common discourse that offers a basis for trust and predictability. However shallow and clichéd the discourse, even as acknowledged by those involved, it still functions as a common system of reference against the backdrop of how to relate to others. Trust in the actions of others at work may be established in flexible organizations based on such parallel shaping of identities.

Psychological contracts. As previously stated, trust follows from a rational consideration of what we may expect from others. But such a consideration does not necessarily result in the establishment of personal relations with others. It may just as well result in a calculating transaction with others. Such a transaction also allows the relation to become predictable although more limited in scope. What one expects from others is, in other words, an open question. In an analogy with legally binding employment contracts and other formal agreements one therefore speaks of "psychological contracts" when more informal, but mutual, expectations binding employee to employer and the individual to the organization are intended.

Denise Rousseau (1995) has tightened the meaning of psychological contract to include only concrete duties rather than general expectations. What is included in these duties, of course, varies. However, she claims that these concrete duties to an extent are part and parcel of certain contract forms. There are, according to her, two principal types of psychological contracts: transactional and relational. Transactional contracts are self-interested and focused mainly on the actual exchange between the parties. Demands on the employer consist primarily of concrete rewards, for example, money, career paths, and opportunities for development. Transactional contracts are normally also limited in both time and content. They do not involve any offers of commitment and loyalty other than in clearly delineated forms. In this they differ from relational contracts where commitment and loyalty are the distinguishing components. Here, focus is on the relation per se, and the demands on the employer are not as clearly specified. Nor are relational contracts as delineated, but instead imply a long-term, mutual relationship, where commitment and loyalty are offered in exchange for security and opportunities of promotion.

When the employee perceives that the employer has certain concrete, if informal, obligations toward her, she will hold the employer responsible for fulfilling them. If an employee feels that the employer does not fulfill her part of the agreement we are faced with a breach of contract. Breaches of contract have been reported as a fairly common although internationally varying phenomenon. In cross-national comparisons spanning 13 countries the tolerance levels regarding the fulfillment of contracts terms have been found to vary considerably (Rousseau and Schalk, 2000). Such differences seemed to be related to, for example, different societal-cultural conceptions of promises and promise keeping as well as different traditions in governmental regulations of employment. Central agreements, negotiated collectively and limiting the variation of psychological contracts, were found more often in societies that were more negatively oriented toward societal inequalities and more concerned with regulating unequal power balances between the parts in the labor market.

Even if violations appear as a rather common phenomenon, complying with the unspoken demands of each employee seems to be an impossible task for an employer. Breaches of contract may be so common because employees are normally unaware of the contract and only become aware of its content when the employer acts in disregard of it. In any case, a breach of contract will result in a decrease of the trust that the employee has in the employer. Consequences of this may in turn be that the employee is not as committed, does not feel obliged to fulfill her part of the contract, or simply leaves the relationship. We may also expect employees with a relational contract to react stronger than those with a transactional contract, as a relational contract is built on mutuality and loyalty. Morrison and Robinson (1997) also differentiate between the cognitive realization that a breach of contract has been committed, and the emotional reaction to such an event. The emotional reaction is more serious and similar to reactions to an insult or violation. This was also made clear in our interviews with staffing nurses (Allvin, Jacobson, and Isaksson, 2003). The majority started working as staffing nurses as they were disillusioned by the way the County Council acts as employer. Several of the staffing nurses spoke explicitly about the violations they had experienced, and how ruthlessly they had been treated.

> You just have to do more and more, but you don't really get any service, backup, or help. There are just more demands on you. And then these wages, and the inflexibility, and awful working hours and . . . no, thank you. (Staffing nurse)

This group was contracted in a relational-type character to the County Council as well as to its care work in general. The departure from the County Council and the subsequent employment in the staffing industry were, for them, an expression of a changing relationship to their work, a change that can be described as a change of contract – from relational to transactional.

In our study the shift toward a more limited and transactional psychological contract is evident. But whether this is the case for flexible jobs in general is more difficult to say. Judging from our other studies we may conclude that even those who worked under very free forms, distinguished by what we have called flexibility through empowerment, gave evidence of a markedly transactional contract. Concrete obligations in these contracts, however, did not primarily involve money or working hours, but rather opportunities for development. Others who have examined flexible jobs seem to have observed something similar (Guest, 2004). The question arises whether a possible shift toward more limited transactional psychological contracts is a reaction to the employers' demand for flexibility or an expression of a general shift in values in society. Perhaps it is even so that the demands for flexibility at work and certain value shifts in society are two sides of the same coin.

In the cross-national comparisons referred to above (Rousseau and Schalk, 2000) observations indicated that the transactional types of employment were increasing. The authors associate these indications with increasing performance demands in the global capital market related to more flexible employment relationships including mixed forms of relational and transactional arrangements. However, they do not conclude that strictly transactional contracts necessarily predict a future main trend. The picture is more complex, they claim, since local values provide different meanings to seemingly similar practices. Such differences can be determined in context-sensitive studies. Research in this area has been criticized in terms of both unsatisfying theoretical bases and inappropriate approaches (e.g. frequent use of cross-sectional data and questionnaire surveys) (Conway and Briner, 2005). These authors especially underline the need for conceptualizing psychological contracts, more in terms of a process. This would, they argue, enable the researchers to detect changes of content, exchange, and fulfillment in a psychological contract in changing (planned or not) conditions when looking at human resource practices (p. 185).

With this, we leave the social dimension of knowledge and enter a more comprehensive societal dimension of knowledge. But before we do, we may state, in conclusion, that the social knowledge in flexible work seems to have developed into the opposite direction from the cognitive knowledge we described in the previous passage. The social knowledge involved in traditional work was, in all things essential, implicit and decided by the collective identity generated through work. The development of this knowledge also had the character of long-term processes of socialization. Social knowledge in traditional work in other words consisted of tacit collective knowledge. In flexible work, however, the demands for social knowledge have become more explicit and taken a more central position. At the same time as social knowledge has become more important, the employees have also become more aware of the demands they consequently face, and have developed various methods for dealing with these demands. Social knowledge has therefore become increasingly individualized. By this we mean not only that it has become more individual, but also that it has become, to an increasing extent, the topic of individual reflection. Social knowledge has thereby acquired a character akin to a "social game" and has become a more explicit target of rationalization.

The Societal Knowledge Demands

When we speak of the societal dimension of knowledge we mean the knowledge we have about contemporary society and the role we play within it. By this we do not mean any superficial knowledge of facts, such as what laws are in force or which institutions do what. The societal dimension of knowledge instead concerns the less palpable perception of which expectations we, as labor, have on society and what it really expects from us. These mutual expectations can be said to make up the individual's relation to society.

For large parts of the twentieth century, and especially the 1940s to the 1970s, this relation may be summed up in terms of a collective and very distinct social contract. The employee conscientiously took part in the mass production of the company in exchange for employment security and regular real wage increases. Through this the employee was able to make long-term investments in living quarters and a car, and participate in the mass consumption that was a prerequisite of mass production. In case of illness, retirement, unemployment, or similar, the employee's continued consumption was guaranteed by various general social security systems provided by the welfare state (Lipietz, 1992). Not only was the employee a prerequisite for the prosperity-creating growth in society, he was also the hub around which this entire society turned. The symbol here was of an industry worker in a big national company. The concrete, universal face of work was the industry worker. Thereby the individual had a clear and generally accepted image to relate to in his role as a worker.

Post-industrial society

Toward the end of the 1950s, however, a number of American scientific researchers started perceiving a structural upheaval of the labor market. At the beginning of the 1900s, the labor market had gone through a change of that proportion, and now, it seemed, one was faced with yet another. The upheaval at the start of the 1900s had consisted in industry growing to employ larger numbers of people than in agriculture.

In the 1950s, the industry sector was still the largest industry, but now it was instead a certain category of workers that grew in scope. White-collar workers became increasingly important for the economy of companies and society alike. By white-collar workers was meant something else than the indirect workforce, that is, bureaucrats on various levels, whose work it is to administer the actual workforce. Instead, one was speaking of the knowledge-wielding workforce (Cortada, 1998). It consists of everything from secretaries and teachers to academics and developers, in other words all those who have as their task to deal with, convey, generate, and implement knowledge. Other scientific researchers saw in this phenomenon the emergence of a new society, a knowledge society.

A knowledge society. Characteristic of a knowledge society is precisely that the handling, agency, generation, and implementation of knowledge rather than, for instance, capital goods are the value-generating processes in society. In contrast to industrial society where the social status and role of the individual in society were determined by her relation to the process of physical production, the social status and role of the individual in this society are determined by her relation to the process of knowledge production. This means that the knowledge society has a social structure that is different from that of industrial society. Some scientific researchers hence came to speak of a post-industrial society (Touraine, 1971).

In his classic study, *The Coming of Post-Industrial Society*, Bell (1973) claimed that post-industrial society is not merely a knowledge society in the sense that the number of employees in the knowledge sector increases. Education, knowledge, and merits are becoming more important at all levels of working life. Society is becoming more meritocratic. Teachers, engineers, technicians, and scientists form a social class of their own, a knowledge class. By class is here intended a social grouping shaped as a consequence of a common relation to production. Production is, in other words, the common denominator and consists of separate individuals. The knowledge class is hence a socio-economic class. The reason for this, according to Bell, is that science and production technology are more interlaced than previously seen in history. Technology is driven by theoretical knowledge rather than practical knowledge as was previously the case. Bell imagined that in the future state-financed scientific research would define and organize production in service of public rather than of private ownership. We have since been able to conclude, however, that the interlacing of knowledge and production also, perhaps even primarily, may result in the opposite: science financed by private interest and ruled by the production demands.

The fact that science and theoretical knowledge have become increasingly important is, according to Bell, because society in general and production in particular have become ever more complex and less lucid. This is also the starting point of Robert Reich (1992) when he, in the spirit of Bell, analyzes the labor market before the approaching twenty-first century. Reich is not only an academic (professor at Harvard), he has also been the secretary of labor in the Clinton administration. His analysis of the contemporary and future labor market has also had a resounding impact. According to Reich it is no longer possible to isolate and define products, companies, or economies with regard to their origin, affiliation, or nationality. It is, for example, meaningless, even deceptive, to speak of an independent Swedish product, a Swedish company, or a Swedish economy. Products, production, and companies instead form part of a global economy without national boundaries. In this borderless world, knowledge, technologies, and information develop and move relatively unrestricted in relation to one another. The only thing not moving as unrestrictedly is labor. We therefore, according to Reich, face a situation where, on one side, economies integrating and developing regardless of cultural, national, and institutional limitations stand in opposition to the other side where human beings are stuck in these very limitations. This relation of opposites is substituting the traditional opposition between labor and capital in the industrial society.

Just like Bell, Reich warns that the new antagonism may generate new socio-economic classes. And as in Bell's vision, it is the knowledge-generating, or symbol-handling, workforce that will be the victorious class. Furthermore, both Bell and Reich claim that the symbol-handling professions will be surrounded by simpler, mechanical service tasks performed primarily by women and ethnic minorities. These jobs are place-dependent and have to adjust to the demands of the knowledge-generating workforce. In addition to these "job types," which are both growing in number, there are also a number of continuously decreasing routine production jobs. These jobs are subject to harsh rationalization pressure and continually threatened by automation and outsourcing.

An information society. For Reich as well as for Bell, the contemporary and future knowledge society concerns knowledge as both the primary object of work and as a demand on the workforce. But at the same time, by assigning the central role in production to knowledge, the condition for both is that the economy is inseparably connected to the human being as producer, consumer, and sovereign decision maker. The development of computer technology, however, has made such preconceived ideas superfluous. Not so that the computer has come to substitute the human being in these functions – rather, it has completely disconnected the economy from these functions. When computers are connected into a global network that is not used for communication only, but also to produce and even analyze the information that is being communicated, we need to speak of an information society rather than a knowledge society.

Once again, it is not a question of a fully automated system. The world economy is no mechanical piano. But computerization, or perhaps rather the development and the integration of various systems that has been made possible through computerization, results in communication and transactions today being conducted on a global level, in real time, and to a previously unsurpassed extent. When this computer-served network has become sufficiently extensive, efficient, and exploited, its conditions, possibilities, and limitations will come to determine the communication and transactions conducted by virtue of its existence. Then we will have what Manuel Castells (1998) calls a network society.

A network society. In a global network for information, Castells does not only include the Internet, teleconnections, and mass media, but also the "hubs" and "nodes" where information is gathered, sent on, or processed. These may be made up of companies, institutions, or offices, but also of individuals. Companies are using the network in different ways. The simplest way is of course distributing information about the company, its products, and services. But the network also allows companies to vary their business range. Ventures may be local or global, on a large or small scale, all according to need and demand. As opposed to factories and warehouses, there is no need for extensive investment, buildup, or shutdown. The network can also be used for interaction between the separate parties of the business process (suppliers, customers, personnel). Furthermore, the network provides the opportunity to allocate resources in a flexible way. Through various techniques such as outsourcing, insourcing, intrapreneuring, franchising, subcontracted manufacturing, bulk purchasing, clearance sales, or strategic alliances, the resources can be optimally put to use. The network also allows companies the strategic opportunity to expose their brand and to adapt products to market niches or even to individual customers (Castells, 2001).

Finally, the companies may, like everybody else, use the network for economic transactions. The network has linked together the stock market exchanges of the world into a global market, free of national regulation or cultural and temporal limitations. But not only has the network linked together already existing markets, it has also developed them. By virtue of the network, transaction costs on the market have dropped considerably. This has attracted even more investors to the network, generating additional transactions. The market can thus mobilize previously unexploited investment sources such as private savings. And as investment through the network is growing, information obtained through the same network is also becoming the single most important basis for decision making on further investment. The market is becoming self-contained. Consequently, traditional intermediaries and gatekeepers in the shape of brokers, analysts, and investment trusts are being circumvented, making the market even more available. When investors as well as investment sources are decentralized in this manner, the strategies of investors will increasingly come to vary. The more self-contained the market, the more rapid the pace of transactions will be. As everyone gets information from the network, they will always have the same information and be able to react equally fast to changes (Castells, 2001).

As Robert Reich and Daniel Bell before him, Castells claims that the new network society will lead to social polarization. But in contrast to Reich and Bell, he means that this polarization will concern those who have access to the network versus those who stand outside it. There are of course social differences even between those with access to the network. There are the new elites, participating in crucial decision making in the hubs and nodes of the network. But there are also all those small savers and borrowers who only try to keep their personal economy above water but lack any real influence. Outside the network we find the marginalized. They have no importance whatsoever for the network. They are dwellers of metropolis inner-city ghettos, sparsely populated areas, and parts of the developing world. They make up "the fourth world" and risk sinking into what Castells (1998) describes as social black holes without opportunities or hope of changing their situation.

A risk society. The globalized society is, in other words, both a segregated and unforgiving society. On the one hand it contains a large number of people all over the world whose lives are dependent on the expanding economic order. The lives of these people, in that sense, share the same conditions, the same starting points, and the same direction. On the other hand, the global society is dotted by a large group of people left outside, and whose lives are completely devoid of the opportunities offered by the economic order: people who consequently have totally different conditions, other starting points, and whose lives to a large extent lack direction. The positive consequences of the evermore-efficient economic order are reserved exclusively for the first group of people. The only things truly common to both groups are the negative consequences.

The German sociologist Ulrich Beck (1999) attempts to identify three such negative consequences. It is, firstly, the globally manifest economic consequences of modern life. Although these normally hit the second group harder, they are nothing that the former group cannot steer entirely clear of. Pollution of air and soil and the greenhouse effect affect both rich and poor. The second global consequence is poverty. Through unemployment, bankruptcies, and stock market busts, the global economy distributes poverty seemingly as indifferently and arbitrarily as it distributes riches. Even though the welfare states of the West still offer a certain measure of protection against poverty, this is still a tangible threat for all those who are not already suffering from it. And although one may be protected from poverty as such, it is impossible to protect oneself from the various social consequences of poverty. Growing masses of economic refugees, xenophobia, criminality, drug abuse, and social misery create social tensions and spread insecurity and instability in the social organism. It also taxes the welfare system, which is having an increasingly hard time to live up to its original goal as a common resource. The third consequence is the global occurrence of organized, even militarized, criminal, and subversive groups. In common for militant anarchists, organized crime, and fundamental terrorists is not primarily that they constitute a threat to the economic order they abuse or oppose. However, they may constitute a serious impediment to social development, the safety of human beings, and their opportunities for making a living in general.

When society is no longer concerned with distributing wealth, but rather with distributing risk among its citizens, we are on our way to a risk society. This transition, according to Beck (1992), does not imply a raised awareness of the flipside of modern society only. Above all, it implies that modern society produces negative consequences, such as environmental damage, social exclusion, and ill health, to an ever-wider extent. Consequently, society is forced to organize itself accordingly and allot a growing amount of resources to prevent, administer, and deal with these consequences. Modern society is, in that sense, becoming increasingly reflexive (Beck, 1994). In contrast to early modern society, built by, so to speak, conquering the world and nature "outside itself," the contemporary "late-modern" society is developed increasingly through its various attempts at handling and controlling its own inner dynamic. This has been likened by Anthony Giddens (1990) to trying to ride Jagannath, the Hindu god of war, destroying everything in his path.

The risk society is also characterized by a new principle of distribution. Where the early modern society of labor distributed the riches of society selectively and according to socio-economic class delineations, the late-modern risk society distributes the risks of society more or less equally between all citizens. Although the reasons are to be found at a comprehensive system level, their consequences are found at the individual level. According to Beck (1992), the radioactive downfall from Chernobyl cared neither for national nor class boundaries. Since the risks and insecurity in society are the only things in common for citizens of a risk society, this means that society is becoming ever more "individualized." The major reason for this, however, is not environmental damage, but the changes to and globalization of the labor market (Beck, 1992). Just as Reich and Castells, Beck expresses the disconnection of the global economic order from its national and cultural roots. It has hereby also freed itself from humanity, perhaps not in general, but from the concrete individuals. A sign of this, according to Beck, is the ability of the economy to grow through the destruction of work opportunities. Although cut-downs and streamlining do not infallibly lead companies to success, they still point out the relative independence of the economy from the labor force. As a consequence of automations and outsourcing to low-income countries, the economy will hence successively shed job opportunities. Just like industrial development once saved society from slavery, the development in information technology will save it from full employment (Beck, 2000).

We may here see how all these social analyses in one way or another lay claim to speak for the fundamental principles of contemporary society, and where it is heading. However, this is done from slightly different angles and with quite different foci. In the term knowledge society, emphasis is put on knowledge and service as the objects of work and production. The terms information society and network society, on the other hand, focus rather on technology as the conveyor of information. In the risk society, however, focus is on the common and crystallizing flipside of society.

In spite of these differences, there are also striking similarities in the analyses. They all make pronouncements about fundamental changes in society and all claim that the traditional industrial social order is fading, partially or totally. The analyses consequently deal with the new emerging social logic. As for this logic, the analyses are also surprisingly concordant. Of primary interest to us here, however, is the significance accorded to work in the new social order.

The altered significance of work

Perhaps the most distinct conclusion in the separate analyses is that the economy is or is being disconnected from work. Economic growth and the creation of wealth in post-industrial society no longer require the substantial and stable army of professional workers that once constituted the basis of the growth of industrial society. Aided by information technology and various microeconomic strategies, companies are able not only to rationalize activities in order to make them considerably more efficient than before, they are also able to distribute and redistribute their resources between and among themselves on a global scale, and this with a scope and speed that the local sluggish labor force cannot adapt to. Large portions of the labor force are hence risking redundancy.

Consequently, the industrial and economic development that earlier seemed stable and foreseeable to the individual now appears unforeseeable and unstable. Techniques and organizations are becoming more complex and less understandable. The yardsticks are growing in number and becoming more difficult to read correctly. Knowledge is increasing, becoming more differentiated and qualified. Society is expanding and going global along with the growing number of information channels. Cultures, lifestyles, and values mix and develop.

The few studies on the topic point to the same thing. In an extensive study of value changes in Europe and the USA it is claimed that society is displaying an increasing fragmentation, becoming more heterogeneous (Ester, Halman, and de Moor, 1994). This concerns, not least, values relating to working life. The same wide conclusion was drawn in a survey of American working life conducted for the US army (National Research Council, 1999). It was there stated that the labor force is becoming more heterogeneous with respect to gender, ethnicity, education, and immigration status. Also, the traditional demarcation lines within working life, between different organizational positions, professions, and experiences, are becoming more blurred. Lastly, the researchers were able to conclude that employees arranged and organized their work in many different ways, resulting in a multiplication of working conditions.

The pace of these changes is also increasing. Companies are being reorganized, developed, changing focus, cutting down, rationalizing, restructuring, and merging. Goals are modified, attitudes changed, standpoints revised, numbers adjusted, commitments moderated, and expectations muted. Conditions are changing and decisions are continuously being reviewed. What was previously regarded as true and certain in this light seems more ambiguous, ambivalent, provisional, and uncertain. Over all, the global society seems to lack a fixed point of reference. There is no place, no perspective, no absolute knowledge, or value basis from which to approach the world without presumptions. Nor is it possible to agree once and for all on a standard or on what the standard ought to be. Instead we have to try and reach agreement with those concerned. Furthermore, it has to be done continuously, as everything is in flux. There are, in other words, no common or evident frames of reference, and consequently neither is there a society-spanning context to adapt to.

When society in general and working life in particular no longer are comprehensible and stable, but instead appear confused and blurred, the conditions for a social contract also cease to exist. Instead of being included as a functional part of the whole, the individual is left on her own. In such a situation, the individual herself has to formulate her questions and search for the answers: pave and fight her own way forward. It is no longer possible to blame one's past, one's disability or lack of knowledge. Neither is it possible to expect intervention from a higher level – God, the state, or the union. Instead, it is up to the individual to change, make the best of the situation, and acquire the knowledge necessary (Ester *et al.*, 1994; Halman, 1995).

This is also obvious in several Swedish and international surveys of work-related values. People are increasingly referring to their inner motives and values when asked to explain their actions (Zanders, 1994). These motives and values are also becoming increasingly differentiated. In a number of surveys of Swedish youth and various professional groups, researchers notice that people not only differentiate between instrumental and expressive motives; they also differentiate between separate expressive motives, for instance, social relations, self-realization, and altruism (Hagström and Gamberale, 1995; Hagström and Kjellberg, 2000, 2007). An important reason for this development is assumed to be the raised demands on autonomy in working life (Mortimer and Lorence, 1979). The more unsettled and confused conditions are in working life, the more the individual has to navigate according to his inner compass.

That common perceptions about the development of society also affect individual ideas about work was obvious in our surveys of consultants, system developers, and staffing nurses. They were all highly conscious of the expectations imposed on them by contemporary society. And whether they felt encouraged or scared by the development, they were all convinced that their working conditions were an expression of the change that was underway in society, and that it was up to them to make the best of the situation. This manifested itself, that is, through their constant comparisons of their own conditions with the more traditional conditions at large companies, authorities, or county councils. Sometimes this gave them a feeling of being "with the times," of being prosperous and even innovative. Seeing themselves as belonging to the successful workforce of the future not only gave them self-esteem, it also gave meaning to work.

> the principle is that I want to feel that when I finish a project or get something done in a company, I am more prepared. My market value is higher then, than what it was before. (Consultant)
>
> you can't sit still and wait to be given information, because he who is inactive has to go. In a way it is rather cruel, but that's the way it is. Someone who doesn't realize opportunities and makes sure to develop his competence has to go. (System developer)

There was, however, nothing meaningful pointing to a social community outside the individual job. The quotes instead point to a reality independent of the individual, characterized by development and change. Furthermore, they refer to work as an opening and a road into this reality. More specifically, work offers an opportunity – for those who dare providing for themselves, taking responsibility, and dealing with the situation – to follow or even ride the development. It offers to the individual only a possibility to profit from it and, in the best case, to gain personal satisfaction.

In conclusion, we imply that our relationship to work is decided not only at work but in relation to society as a whole. Further, we distinguish a new relationship in the making. Our relationship to work has traditionally been decided by the large, cemented institutions of industrial society, primarily trade unions, large companies, and the welfare state. These convey a strong feeling of being a participant in something bigger. As an individual worker one is a small cog in a gigantic wheel, generating growth and distributing wealth to all human beings in society. Against a similar backdrop the individual's work becomes a common concern to society. Everybody gets, so to speak, the same image of the relationship to work. And not only does this enable collective solutions, common values, and long-term engagements; it also puts the individual job into a larger context and gives it meaning beyond itself.

The new work life, however, is characterized by heterogeneity, fickleness, and individualization. Here, our relationship to work is decided by new technology, global markets, and short-term engagements. There is no community to fall back on. Instead, the prevailing feeling is one of loneliness and vulnerability to the arbitrariness of development and the market. The new work life also seems to have a hard time maintaining a common system of norms regarding work. All ways are good except for the bad ones. Hence, work life is becoming a personal project of development, alternatively of survival, rather than a collective resource and community.

The Existential Knowledge Demands

If work is no longer a collective resource for prosperity and community, but an individual tool for personal development or survival, not only does it entail a new social contract between the individual and society, it also means that the individual will have a new relationship to herself. We may call this the existential dimension of knowledge. By this, we imply primarily the image we have of ourselves and the expectations we impose on ourselves as labor. To a great degree, the traditional worker identity was shaped through collective resistance to the communal conditions of traditional work. Characteristic for large parts of the flexible work, however, is, as seen, that it lacks communal conditions. Communal knowledge, if such a thing exists, is not knowledge of concrete conditions or a certain kind of information. Instead it is, as has already been pointed out, knowledge about how to extract, handle, and use new knowledge. It is learning itself that is the communal condition of work. The question is then how a common consciousness and a stable identity may be formulated around something as individual and hazy as learning. In order to give an answer we will have to look a little closer at this learning and what it consists of.

Supercomplexity and metacognition

The telecommuting professionals we surveyed were constantly confronted with complex demands (Hanson, 2004 p. 60). To a certain extent, this was a consequence of the unpredictability of their work. New information, new tasks, and requests could arrive at very short notice and in need of quick responses. They always had to be prepared to reset mentally and to change their plans. To an even larger extent, this was the result of their work tasks.

> It's a little unclear from the side of the employer what it is that they want, and this depends on that they don't really know it themselves. They can make a suggestion. Then our project leader questions it. "Is it really this you want? You really should take a look at this." And this is how it's revised all along. (Telecommuting professional employee)

These demands include the capability to interpret the perspectives of other persons in order to perform insufficiently or vaguely specified work tasks. The consultants' work tasks were perhaps even more complex in a more personal sense. They had to navigate in the context of changing external conditions in the market in which they tried to maintain their self-identities and find social and societal connections on their own. This last type of demands do not only refer to strictly cognitive ones related to, for example, greater amount of information, mental overload, etc., but rather challenges in personal terms. Barnett (1999) claims that in order to function in today's reality we also need to master "supercomplexity," a competence to relate different perspectives to one another. Such a relativization of the individual social context and knowledge perspective leads to a realization, a kind of learning that not only confirms our frames of reference but also reconfigures them. This learning hence does not reduce the complexity of the world, but contributes to it.

These knowledge demands can be said to be of a higher order, and are therefore called metacognitive, in order to distinguish them from the "ordinary" intellectual knowledge demands concerning the relation to symbolic information, the act of interpreting and processing it by, for instance, analyzing it in terms of context, patterns, causes, and consequences. The metacognitive knowledge demands hence concern the ability to relate to oneself as an actor, to conduct oneself in and adapt to various contexts. Thus, if anything, they amount to a demand for self-reflection.

The process of acquiring a capability to handle such metacognitive demands can be related to emerging inconsistencies in a person's value system, beliefs, or moral standards. This may promote new perspectives when the person tries to make sense of the conflicting experiences. Moreover, such processes seem to be of a transformative character, promoted by critical reflections of taking-for-granted assumptions regarding values, norms, praxis, and life conditions, as described in critical traditions in adult education theory and research. Examples are Paulo Freire's emancipating pedagogy applied in the developing world (Freire, 1970) and the transformative learning theory initiated by Jack Mezirow in the 1970s, inspired by, for example, the women's liberation movement in the United States of America (Mezirow, 2000, 2003).

Transformations of such a character can be described as a kind of active reorganizing internalization process, from what earlier was conceived as outside less-reflected conditions toward what become inside reflected concerns on a higher complexity level. This, in turn, makes people more capable of internal overview, orient themselves, and act in dissolving external regulations. Such relativizing, or transformative learning, requires us to rise above the everyday practical frames of reference. But trying to do this is a little like lifting oneself by the hair. Distancing oneself from one perspective invariably means taking a new one. In adult developmental psychology, inspired by and the further developing of Piaget's theory of cognitive development (Piaget, 1977, 1982), this perspective has been described in somewhat different terms as, for example, "post-conventional" (Kohlberg, 1969; Kohlberg and Armon, 1984), "post-formal" (Sinnott, 1994, 2003), and "self-transforming" (Kegan, 1994, 2003) perspectives or frames of reference.

This is a process, or perhaps even a possibility to, by personal will and force, move between different perspectives and frames of reference (Hagström, 2003). This is also a possibility demanding continuous work. It is, in Barnett's words, not only work requiring learning; learning also requires a job. The metacognitive perspective in these terms enables interactions between persons whose frameworks are conflicting. In an overview of research (Amiot et al., 2007) the authors suggest that the competence to coordinate and integrate different social identities moves from fragmentation and differentiation toward an increased integration of this diversity. Transformations in such directions may be triggered by major changes, for example, political-cultural ones, immigrations, life transitions, and organizational mergers. Active coping and social support from significant others have been found to be important in such phases of change.

Moreover, a need for similar transformative changes has been underlined in organizational and leadership theory and research (Fischer, Rooke, and Torbert, 2001, Rooke and Torbert, 2005). Contrasting forces in an organization, such as between decentralization and centralization, or individual autonomy and social integration, can be regarded in "both–and" rather than an "either–or" perspective. They can be considered as necessary mutual parts in a process, increasing the potential of a positive dynamic, rather than contradictions that should be fought against (Sànches-Runde and Pettigrew, 2003; see also Hagström, Backström, and Göransson, 2009).

Demands on being able to move between different frames of reference do not concern the changing conditions of given tasks only, but also the continuous changes of work tasks, workplaces, and employers. A person moving like this in the traditional work life is a problem, and was earlier called a drifter. In the new work life, the drifter is something of a model. While yesterday's drifters were people who simply could not adapt to the framework of the workplace, today's drifters seem to be people furthering their career by transcending the framework. This ability to move in and between many different contexts also forms the core of what has come to be called employability.

Employability and entrepreneurship

Employability became a household word already in the 1960s. Back then it was used mainly in a socio-medical context about the ability of a person to gain and to stay in employment. As time went on, however, it came to mean the possibilities to match the abilities of the labor force to the new and changing demands of the work life. At the beginning of the 1990s the concept was central to the employment strategies of the OECD and the EU. The reason for this was not to be found in the then relatively high unemployment primarily, but in the decreasing competitiveness of the Western economies. The problem was not a lack of job opportunities, but one of competence. In other words, competence was expected to generate job opportunities rather than the other way round (Garsten and Jacobson, 2004).

Putting in concrete form what competence is needed for has proved difficult. This is, as has already been pointed out, not the least because the demands are both growing and changing. For instance, in the field of computer technology and programming, knowledge for a while developed so quickly that the education available was constantly out of date. Then when the stock market value of technology shares started falling in March 2000, the labor market demands for this knowledge fell as quickly. As the knowledge demands are not easily specified, responsibility is left to the individual who, under the banners of lifelong learning, continuous learning, and new learning, is expected to adapt his knowledge independently to the demands of the labor market. Representatives and institutions in the work life instead spend their time trying to teach people to assume this responsibility. And since such an assumption of responsibility to a large extent depends on the active participation of individuals, it cannot be forced, nor taught. Although job centers can threaten to discontinue allowances or offer the unemployed courses in starting up their own businesses, this kind of learning is about conveying a certain attitude, or a personal way of relating to work.

This attitude is best summarized in the concept of entrepreneurship. According to a classic leadership text on the topic it entailed that people, whether inside or outside organizations, are "in business for themselves" (Moss Kanter, 1989). Although entrepreneurship is an intrinsic part of the economy, economic theory, traditionally, has found the concept hard to deal with. The reason for this is that economic theories often are abstract and general to the point that the practically oriented entrepreneurship falls outside the theoretical framework. This was also the reason why Joseph Schumpeter originally formulated his classic theory of entrepreneurship as innovation. The economy developed, according to Schumpeter, exactly because of the departure of the entrepreneur from economic stability. By identifying, exploiting, and putting to use deficiencies, loopholes, or differences in an otherwise balanced economic order, the entrepreneur breaks it up, thus favoring a new order. Consequently, the entrepreneur is not subordinate to the conventional, static, and theoretical economic knowledge at any given opportunity. Instead, the entrepreneur generates new knowledge (Swedberg, 2000).

One prerequisite for the actions of the entrepreneur is, however, detailed knowledge of the practical conditions of the economy. The entrepreneur must at all times intimate and remain in contact with the financial, technical, logistic, and market aspects of the economy in order to notice and benefit from opportunities. In other words, the entrepreneur needs to be in possession of far-reaching practical knowledge of his area (Swedberg, 2000, p. 10). But what specific practical knowledge are we talking about? Naturally, one needs the necessary technical knowledge. But this is not what creates a business opportunity. Here, what is needed is the ability to create a business relationship. A business relationship is a social relationship. We could therefore define entrepreneurship as the creation of business opportunities through the establishment of new relationships between different groupings (Burt, 2000; Granovetter, 2000) – typically, the relationship between those who have something to sell and those who may consider buying it – but other relationships also have a role to play.

In an interesting case study of strawberry vendors in Venezuela, Monica Lindh de Montoya (2000) describes Freddy the strawberry man's continuous work establishing, maintaining, and using the relationships with private customers, restaurants, ice-cream stands, the bank, growers, purchasers, competitors, partners, friends, and family. Freddy was solicitous about and proud of the trust he enjoyed from everyone he did business with. But even though he liked dealing with people, social causes were not his driving force. He did not hesitate to break agreements when the stores so demanded. Nor did he hesitate to resume relationships if it meant new business opportunities. Freddy was a natural part of the social life in the different groups he did business with, but was not included in any one of them. Nevertheless, it did not mean that he was self-sufficient and true to himself only. He let others use him if it meant gaining access to and being accepted by people and groups with whom he saw a business opportunity. Even though he was an independent actor, he was simultaneously completely dependent on his surroundings. Freddy was a true entrepreneur.

Autonomy

As noticed, the new work life demands employability, and in order to be employable one has to be able to adapt to and move between different frames of reference. Against a backdrop of the often-limited scope of action of the individual in traditional working life, these demands may be interpreted as an opportunity, or even a demand, for autonomy. When the opportunity to move between different frames of reference arises, the individual is no longer limited to any one specified perspective, context, or place. She may, like Freddy the strawberry man, move in whichever direction she wants, settle wherever she wants, and leave whenever she wants. She gains a certain independence that is impossible within one frame of reference.

But in order for the individual to be independent, she is required to move purposefully between the various contexts. It is, in other words, required of her to take her direction from a wider plan, a plan which, in itself, is independent of the touchdowns in which it is manifest. The only one able to formulate such a plan is the individual herself. In the sense and to the extent that the individual allows herself to be guided by a personally formulated plan of this model, we are able to say that she is independent, relative to the different contexts in which she is moving. She is, thereby, an autonomous individual.

The new work life is full of people aspiring to autonomy in this sense. They only choose jobs that interest them. They change jobs when a better opportunity comes along. They use their work to realize themselves and have high demands for independence. They are hungry for success, determined, often well educated, and they feel no loyalty toward their employer beyond what has been specified in the contract of employment (Sennett, 1998).

In our studies, we have been in contact with such people: e.g. consultants, self-employed, system developers, and freelance journalists. They often described how they accepted a job or started an educational program for conventional reasons (a good salary, career path, working conditions, prestige, or parental expectations) but how they were not happy with it, how they broke free in order to try something else or to start their own business. Common for them is the feeling that they, in making these choices, followed an inner, very tangible will, rather than the expectations of others. In other words, it concerned an adaptation of work to the individual's goals in life.

> if I can continue to cultivate this role, that's the razor's edge for me. If I realize that I can't be active in this role, if market conditions are bad or if I can't get results from what I'm doing, then I'll have to start thinking about whether I want to change my position within [the company] or if I have to leave [the company] in order to continue cultivating this role. (System developer)

Anthony Giddens (1991) has described how life in the late-modern society has become a personal project for the individual. Other people, activities, and institutions are consciously chosen and exploited in order to further this project. These people, activities, and institutions may play a more or less central role for the life project of an individual, but they will always be subordinate to the project as such. Primarily, the individual identifies not with them, but with the project (Beck-Gernsheim, 1996). This shift from various "outer" common projects to the personal project implies not only a shift in the object of identification, but also a shift in engagement and loyalty. An individual may hence make a life project from her professional career, and in that sense identify with and commit to work. Identification and commitment, however, result from and are limited to the possibilities of the job to further the individual career. If the job cannot live up to these expectations in the adequate areas, the individual will quite simply change jobs, workplaces, employers, job forms, or attitude. Many employers cite this independence of the "new generations" as a reason for or legitimizing of increased flexibility and looser contracts of employment.

Is there a place for morals?

This shift of identification and commitment from outside to inner objects has also been documented by scientific researchers. In a series of studies, probably the most comprehensive of its kind, Ronald Inglehart, the American political scientist, tries to substantiate these changes on a global level. In a comparison between up to 43 countries around the world, he tries to prove that the economic and political development comes hand in hand with certain cultural values. For example, industrialization is linked to materialist values, that is, values ranking money and physical security at the top. Industrialization combined with highly developed welfare state systems of security, such as those developed in the West after the Second World War, however, leads to values looking beyond materialism. Hence, pronouncedly post-materialist values have developed in the United States, Western Europe, and especially in Scandinavia. These values rank freedom, self-realization, and quality of life above anything else (Inglehart, 1990). In a later study, he claims that his shift in values only forms part of a more substantial cultural change, which he calls post-modernization. By post-modernization is meant increased secularization, an intensifying focus on the individual, and a downward slide in the trust of authorities, and then not only in the shape of institutional representatives, such as politicians, teachers, and the police, but also in the form of science, technology, and reason (Inglehart, 1997).

In a revised version of the modernization theory Inglehart and Welzel (2005) argue that socio-economic development and cultural change influence the establishing and strengthening of democracy, framing these lines of reasoning in a human developmental perspective. Different lines of change such as toward democracy, socio-economic development, and rising emphasis of self-expression are considered as "working together." More recently Inglehart claims that the trend toward post-materialistic values can be regarded as only one aspect of an even broader shift from survival to self-expression values (Inglehart, 2007).

Inglehart argues that these changes can be summarized in two basic dimensions, namely one traditional/secular-rational dimension and one survival/self-expression dimension. Similar dimensions have been presented by Schwartz (2007). Based on data from 73 countries he presents three bipolar dimensions: embeddedness versus autonomy referring to the extent to which people are embedded in their groups; hierarchy versus egalitarianism, concerning the extent to which people are engaged in collective efforts to maintain society; and mastery versus harmony, referring to the extent to which natural and social worlds are regarded as good as it is or necessary to change. But he approaches the concept of value more deductively, defining its general characteristics in terms of, for example, desirable goals and standards motivating and evaluating actions, forming a preference, a hierarchy, or a system of priorities. Values are regarded as mutually related in terms of their similarity–difference in a consistent circular structure.

These value changes and ways of conceiving values as guiding actions and judging events in terms of desirability, for example, preferences toward autonomy or social integration, bring to the fore moral issues, such as the responsibility for others versus oneself. Moreover, if it is the case that we, to a larger extent than before, are choosing the objects we identify with and commit to, we will also be making demands on these objects to "be good" and represent values in harmony with our own. In order for us to identify with and commit to a job it will have to enjoy a subjective moral dignity. If we regard our lives as morally just in any sense, we simply cannot, with our credibility intact, identify with and commit to a job in conflict with these morals. Work, hence, always entails moral considerations.

These considerations will be noticed only when the job or the working conditions come to conflict with personal values. This may be the case already in the actual choice of work. The decision to choose or not to choose a job or a particular type of work may even be so obvious that the individual does not consider it an act of conscious moral consideration. Moral considerations may also be the result of social conditions in the workplace. This is something we noticed in almost all our surveys. They could manifest themselves, for instance, as social tension in the workplace. At the national energy authorities, where we surveyed telecommuting professional employees, there was a certain tension, if not a conflict, between those who regarded their work as the protection of the environment and of a society of sustainable development on the one hand, and those who simply saw themselves as neutral employees and energy system experts. In our study of staffing nurses, we detected this conflict on a more individual level as a result of the organizational conditions of work. The nurses would describe, for instance, how they had chosen to leave traditional care work, and instead chose, in this context a relatively new phenomenon, offering care in the shape of a clearly defined commitment, limited responsibility, and on a commercial basis. At the same time, they made their choice "from outside," aided by a professional education dedicated to care as unconditional commitment, personal engagement, and on an economically disinterested, altruistic basis. There is, in other words, something in the conditions of a staffing nurse that collides with the ethical principles of care, as specified in her education and in social traditions.

STAFFING NURSE: I don't know, I don't really know what to think. I haven't made up my mind about what to think. Because at the same time as the County Council is short of money and their personnel is being worn out, they use loads of resources for staffing companies. Perhaps one should rather invest this money in good personnel care, make sure the wards are well staffed and that the wages are good. Because of course it is better if you have stable personnel that can be educated and that give continuity.

INTERVIEWER: Do you personally have any moral scruples about working in the staffing industry?

STAFFING NURSE: Actually, yes. I do. I'm not against private alternatives, but at the same time I want there to be care for everyone. Now, with private care, you notice that they can select the good patients, while the County Council has to deal with the heavy and difficult things. They are sucking the County Council dry with these economic companies. I don't know what will happen in the future. I mean, staffing companies are a great alternative now, but for how long?

The conflict is even tangible in the actual work and the way in which it is performed.

STAFFING NURSE: Some colleagues keep a distance to the patients. I don't think that's a good quality. But now I can see that I have become the same. Because I chose it myself, but also because of the arrangements at work, the fact that I'll only be there for a shorter time.

INTERVIEWER: Is this something that scares you?
STAFFING NURSE: Yes, absolutely. It's definitely not a good quality. Definitely not.

As we can see, this is something quite different from the Lutheran work ethic, which, according to Max Weber, was the basis of traditional industrial society. The Protestant work ethic is a kind of duty moral, forming part of our backbone, and which we obey without questioning. Taking a conscious stance to work itself is not part of this ethic. Instead, it requires us to do our duty, as collectively specified. The new individualized work ethic, however, is rather a kind of moral of consequence, demanding continuous consideration and inner deliberation. It requires the individual to take a conscious stance on work, its goals, purpose, and function, and to compare this with her personal life project. The newfound interest companies take in ethics may also be understood, to an extent, as an attempt at presenting themselves as legitimate objects of identification in this process.

Exit or voice

The fact that the personal attitude to work is not without reservations, but the object of continuous deliberation, shows that the right to say "no" is always reserved. Such discontentment may in principle manifest itself in two ways: either by leaving work or by protesting against it. These two strategies are usually, in the classic terminology of Albert Hirschman, called exit and voice respectively (Hirschman, 1970).

By exit is meant the departure from one job, to the benefit of another. This is the rational reaction to discontentment when there are competing alternatives one may easily change over to, the way it is supposed to be in a functioning labor market. The reaction requires further that discontentment is immediate, obvious, easily remedied, that the individual is sovereign in her decision, and that she has no particular relationship to what she is leaving, or, as economists usually express it, that the decision maker is rational, the information complete, and the costs of transaction negligible. Exit, in other words, is embodied in the perfect consumer. According to Hirschman, exit is also the strategy traditionally quoted and favored by economists.

Voice, on the other hand, means that one argues and tries to change or resist what one is displeased with. It is a strategy people use when they, in one way or another, are dependent on that which they are displeased with. It is also a strategy implying a hope of improvement. But it may just as well mean that there are no real alternatives on the horizon. Furthermore, it is a strategy that is employed when decline, and consciousness of it, is gradually intensifying. The use of voice does not alter opportunities for, at a later occasion, using exit, while exit excludes all further possibilities of voice (Hirschman, 1970, p. 37). Voice, according to Hirschman, is the political strategy.

Our relation to work has traditionally been of the kind that we have to regard as a relation of dependence. Not only have we identified with our work and our position on the labor market by means of trade, industry, and class consciousness, but our entire welfare system is also constructed around it. In Sweden, the social policy of redistribution, labor legislation, as well as the dominant political dimension is built on the idea that we have a stable relation to work. Consequently, we are tied to our jobs in more ways than through our independent choices. The reaction on discontentment traditionally expected in working life is hence that we make our voices heard, with the purpose of changing the source of discontent (voice). The ways of influencing and changing work are also thoroughly institutionalized, through various forms of trade union representation, co-determination, trade union influence, and democratic leadership.

In our studies, however, exit was the closest at hand. Even though the interviewees did not hesitate to protest, they were not willing to compromise too much with their demands. The current workplace did not represent a long-term commitment (Allvin, 2004). If they did not see their opportunities realized within a reasonable future, they did not hesitate to change workplaces (see above for quotes under "Autonomy"). Prospects for influencing the workplace were, by many, seen as futile anyway. Staying, in a situation like this, implies renouncing oneself, described as the worst alternative of all – not because one was then forced to compromise one's demands, risking worse conditions, but because one was risking becoming dependent and getting stuck.

> If I stay at the ward, I'll obviously get more knowledge within the area of neurosurgery. But in five or ten years I won't be able to act on the market any more. Then I'll know neurosurgery only. Then I'll be standing here all the time, adapting to my employer. (Staffing nurse)

In his book *The Corrosion of Character*, Richard Sennett (1998) describes the difference between the traditional and flexible work life as the difference between long-term and short-term undertakings. Traditional working life was distinguished by greater endurance. The reason for this was the mutual dependence of employer and employee. According to Sennett, this mutuality no longer exists. The consequence is increased restlessness – and ruthlessness. There is no use in staying in a relationship and in being loyal. Staying is instead identical to losing the ability to control one's fate. A common destiny does not exist. She who stays is risking being left behind.

> The modern culture of risk is peculiar in that failure to move is taken as a sign of failure, stability seeming almost a living death. The destination therefore matters less than the act of departure. Immense social and economic forces shape the insistence on departure: the disordering of institutions, the system of flexible production – material realities themselves setting out to sea. To stay put is to be left out. (p. 87)

Sennett describes a number of people who, in one way or another, have been knocked about or humiliated in their encounters with flexible work. Common for all of them is that they have lost their faith in the future. They dwell on the past, regret not having quit in time, are bitter at life, or worried that they have neglected their children. The absence of a future makes them feel lost. They have been left outside. The moral of the book is also that the flexible work life is tearing apart what opportunities people have of establishing a stable identity, as flexible work lacks the socially located, long-term, character-building undertakings, which are the very preconditions of all social identification. If traditional working life was a common concern that we could all unite around, flexible work life is a social centrifuge tearing us apart and sucking the juice out of us all.

Flexible work is breaking up communal action. Even though it often encourages work in groups, teams, or projects, all participants are highly conscious of the fact that it is as an individual one will gain access and legitimacy, advance, or, in the worst case, be kicked out of the group. Team spirit in the work life, as already stated above and as Sennett also points out, is nothing but a social game. Work is not done collectively, only in different formations. The fact that the individual to an increasing extent regards herself as independent in relation to her work is hence perhaps rather due to that work no longer offering a collective with which to build solidarity. Independence is then not primarily a requirement of the job, but a reaction to the social fragmentation of flexible work.

Sennett (2006) has elaborated his thoughts further regarding the values and practices holding individual and institutions together – culture in that sense – that he regards as seriously threatened by the norms of the new economy. He argues that the flexible world of work related to the cutting edge of the economy (high technology, global finance, and new service firms) gains, for example, short-term thinking, not regretting anything, and accepting superficial human relations. Although this sector is only a small part of the economy, it has, he claims, exerted a strong normative and moral guidance for the economy as a whole. He argues that this negatively influences people's sense of a "narrative movement" (a continuity of their selves), their sense of usefulness (contributing with something of importance for others), and their "craftsmanship" (to do something well for its own sake).

These conclusions about threatening negative consequences seem to be in accordance with earlier considerations regarding unemployment (Jahoda, 1979, 1981). Negative psychosocial consequences of unemployment some decades ago, when emerging welfare systems decreased the worst forms of material losses, were mainly found to be associated with other losses. These losses represented so-called latent functions provided by paid employment, functions that often were hard to replace among the unemployed outside the traditional labor market. These functions concerned regular time structures, social contacts beyond the family sphere, collective goals, social status/identity in terms of a societal position (god or not), and regular activity. Thus, negative consequences of being outside the labor market in the 1970s seem to resemble consequences of being inside the new work life some decades later, both referring to basic aspects of people's autonomy and social–societal integration. In both cases the problems appear as related to lack of external regulations and structures as well as competence to internal regulation of one's actions in those contexts and conditions.

Some Concluding Considerations

In this chapter we have tried to account for the knowledge demands with which the flexibilization of work confronts people. We have shown that entering and function in working life is not only a question of knowledge and skills related to the work tasks in a strict sense, it also includes socializing people into a larger pattern of values and social relations. This concerns skills, knowledge, and competence being not only individually but also

The New Work Life and the Dimensions of Knowledge 121

socially rooted, being able to relate to other people, to society, and to oneself. This perspective justified our focus on the four broad dimensions of knowledge and new demands in work life.

Each dimension has then been related to increasing and partly new demands: cognitive ones related to, for example, lacking time and space for reflection and demanding capacity of meta-learning; social demands related to, for example, conflicting demands in the human service sector, inclusion–exclusion in social networks, and to the need for trust and psychological contracts; societal demands related to, for example, low integration in the society when lacking a general social contract between the individual and society; existential demands concerning, for example, continuous learning and making sense in a life course perspective.

The cognitive demands concern the competence to search, identify, value, and summarize increasing, more far-reaching, varying, and accessible flow of information, to make sense of and use it. The social demands, in turn, are no longer a question of unreflected skills one is being socialized into but more conscious ways of "playing the social game," manipulative or not. Such increasing demands of making sense of the information flow and navigate socially are not tied to a given workplace or even industry. Instead they are personal, directed to the individual. The consequences may be that the labor force as a collective is fragmented and reduced to self-propelling individuals.

It is relevant to raise the question whether this has increased the space of actions of the individuals or if this rather has resulted in the workplaces and the industries increasingly guarding themselves for the possibilities of individuals' "wrong decisions," as claimed by Bauman (2000). Such guarding tendencies can be found in new systems of controlling individual performances, in corporate cultures guiding their visions, values, and actions, in new identity discourses encouraging them to develop their employability, being, for example, entrepreneurs, as well as in thinking of their independence in terms of consumption in the market rather than in moral or political terms (du Gay, 1996).

Such tendencies point in many ways to a situation characterized by socially isolated individuals in a demanding, competitive, and unfriendly market. However, in a broader and a more long-term perspective the picture appears to point in more diverse directions. The tendencies outlined in the chapter indicate that the more dissolved the boundaries, the higher the demands related to the societal and existential knowledge dimensions. This, in turn, can be related to a prolonged socialization and personal developmental process during adult life. The individual has to act individually on a long-term basis as well as integrating in social–societal contexts, in both cases without clear external guidance by traditional boundaries, rules, norms, and values.

Thus, demands concern both individual autonomy (referring to the cognitive and existential dimensions) and social integration (referring to the social and societal dimensions). Potential opportunities provided by the new conditions can be associated with individual aspects such as people's life courses, career patterns, and biographies as well as to social aspects such as social roles, group affiliations, and role models. Individualization in that sense "does not mean the destruction or reduction of people's connectivity, but more individual freedom to connect and disconnect as they choose, making social networks more diverse, flexible, modular, and elective" (Welzel, 2007, p. 174). The problem to integrate into the society in an, at least partly, individualistic way is not a new socialization characteristic. What is new is that utilizing these possibilities seems to demand individuals' integration of societal and existential knowledge in more autonomous ways than before.

Post-materialistic values seem to capture individual fulfillment and social integrative value elements, guiding people's actions in more self-directed ways than before. Whether this captures the integration of existential and societal dimensions on a metacognitive level, complex enough to master the new knowledge demands, would be an interesting issue for further research. However, such changes, whether or not they are driven by intergenerational value shifts or adult lifespan development, seem to progress slowly and are not necessarily in correspondence with the need of the faster progressing, global, technologically and economically driven flexibility demands.

Part of the problems related to new knowledge demands may reflect such gaps and anomalies in a transition phase toward new and more flexible boundaries of work. At the same time the dissolving traditional boundaries increase interactions between people with different or even contrasting experience and frameworks. As outlined in this chapter, this may promote new perspectives providing individually as well as socially related skills, knowledge, and competence to utilize not only possible space of action in work but also space of development in life, individually and collectively.

4

The Place of Work in Life

Analyzing the unparalleled growth of the West in the post-war years, the French economist Michel Aglietta (1979) specifically emphasized the importance of the American lifestyle consumption. The export of American-style mass consumption gave production an outlet for its mass-produced goods and lifted the national economies from the ruins of the Second World War. Aglietta called the symbiotic balance between mass production and mass consumption the "Fordist" compromise. Originally, the term is from the Italian Marxist Antonio Gramsci, and refers to the American welfare capitalism, personified by Henry Ford. Ford was one of the very first industrialists to realize the necessity of creating his own markets. In 1914, a year after opening the first automated automobile factory, he offered his workers five dollars and an eight-hour working day. Not only did he, hereby, offer the workers generous (at the time) compensation for the monotonous toil in the factories. He also gave them the opportunity to take part in the consumption of what they produced. He also encouraged them to save their money, to think long-term, and to plan their consumption. He also employed a smaller contingent of moral advisors for this purpose (Lee, 1993, p. 78).

Ford's pioneering attempts to turn workers into reliable consumers were still rather limited. Instead, they would be implemented much more extensively and successfully by the welfare state during the 1930s. Inspired by, for instance, John Maynard Keynes' general theory of employment (1936) the Western welfare states practiced a policy of stabilization, balancing the higher profit demands of the employers with the wage increase demands of the employees. The welfare state took responsibility for maintaining demand through substantial public consumption, subsidized loans, and other general social insurance systems, guaranteeing the continual

---

Work Without Boundaries: Psychological Perspectives on the New Working Life, First Edition. Michael Allvin, Gunnar Aronsson, Tom Hagström, Gunn Johansson, and Ulf Lundberg.
© 2011 John Wiley & Sons, Ltd. Published 2011 by John Wiley & Sons, Ltd.

consumption of the workers in case of illness, retirement, unemployment, etc. (Lipietz, 1992). Through mass production of standardized housing and advantageous loans for buying them, the welfare state contributed to the shaping of the individual household into an independent economic unit with "the home of one's own" as the investment for the future. Around this and the car, as a necessary means of transportation between the home and the workplace, a common pattern of consumption then developed, binding the worker and making him dependent on a permanent job and regular real wage increases (Aglietta, 1979).

At the center of this society-spanning compromise stood "the conscientious worker" (Ambjörnsson, 1989). By virtue of his professional knowledge and his work ethic, the worker generated the material wealth everyone surrounded themselves with at the same time as his sense of duty and order constituted a guarantee for industrial peace, social stability, and the just distribution of welfare. All other roles in society were in one way or another derived from this role. Political engagement took place in collective form and was channeled primarily through various class-specific institutions – in Sweden dominated by the workers' movement in all its guises. The worker was also a man and men always worked. His family role was hence limited to that of breadwinner, absent during working hours. Housing was strictly class-specific, and the worker socially connected to the local community. Even consumption was class-specific. Overall, consumption was surrounded by the moral norms of work. Material wealth was only for those who had done their share of honest work, or who had undeservedly been prevented from work by illness, injury, or age. Furthermore, all consumption which did not, directly or indirectly, contribute to work or the reproduction of labor (i.e., to travel to and from work, recreation, or family care) was regarded with suspicion.

During the 1970s, however, the Fordist or Keynesian compromise between companies, unions, and the welfare state was torn apart. Companies were rationalizing and increasingly turning to the international world of business. The economy was in crisis and unemployment grew. The unions and the welfare state became subject to a crisis of legitimacy. The 1970s was a time of upheaval. In the 1980s it was clear that something had been lost, but no one was really able to say what this was, or what had replaced it. The term post-Fordism was coined by French and British researchers to signify what has risen or what is rising out of the wreckage of Fordism. As a current academic topic of discussion, post-Fordism is certainly not new, but there is still no consensus about what it stands for

(Mahon, 1994). The only instance of agreement seems to be the significantly increased scope and influence of market forces in society.

What post-Fordism shows is that the industrial conditions of production no longer form a common social ground for everyone to relate to and position oneself in. Hence, the traditional basis for the establishment of a collective identity is also gone. Although some still cling to the idea of themselves or their parents as "workers," this is an increasingly hollow identity carrying less and less meaning.

When common roles in society are disappearing, the social arenas with which they have been associated – work and leisure – are also being undermined. The separation of work and leisure is, of course, still a common concern for most of us. But it is not as clear a pattern in society as a whole. More and more people are working flexitime, irregular hours, or completely lack regulated working hours. An increasing number of people also have the opportunity to work from home or while traveling. At the same time, the availability of services has increased beyond belief. Certain services are available around the clock. Others, not least by means of the Internet, have become part of our home environment. Modern technology also makes us available whenever and wherever. The workplace in turn offers the personnel an increasing number of opportunities to satisfy various personal needs. All of this contributes to the border between work and leisure being broken up. This "break-up" is the topic of the current chapter.

In this chapter, we claim that the changing roles at work and in society in general tend to substitute an individually negotiated order for the traditional division of life into work and leisure. When the individual is forced to assume increased responsibility, it is up to her to maintain the distinction between work and leisure. The consequence of this individual assumption of responsibility is that the difference between work and leisure loses a lot of its universal applicability.

In order to show how we are thinking, we will first give a brief account of the research on the relation between work and leisure. Characteristic of this research is firstly that it describes this relation as one between two relatively homogeneous and clearly separate life spheres. Second, research has been consistently occupied with confirming a small number of fundamental relations between the two spheres. Early research, for instance, made great efforts to state whether the mental and social consequences of work were copied or compensated during leisure time, while later research has rather tried to determine whether conflict or balance in the relation between work and life outside it affects the health and well-being of the individual.

Third, recent research has introduced more sophisticated ways of describing the basis for and the character of coping strategies that workers use in order to handle demands and goals associated with the two domains.

In the following passage, we will try to show that life outside work is not as independent and homogeneous as research presupposes. In the two previous chapters we have already claimed that the organization of work in different ways is striving to become increasingly flexible, and that the individual hence has to assume increased responsibility for the work of others as well as for their own. The more flexible the organization of work, the more blurred is the separation of work from life outside work. But it is not only the "deregulation" of work that is contributing to this blurriness. Life outside work is being deregulated, too, or perhaps we should say "de-traditionalized." Here, as well, the individual is forced to take greater responsibility for her life. The individual is here given a wider responsibility through, for example, the spread of the customer and consumer role in society by the fact that even moral and political standpoints to an increasing extent are being shaped in this mold, and through the fact that family life and child-rearing to a larger extent are turning into a question of negotiation and strategic choices.

The consequence of this "double deregulation" is that the border between work and all other life loses much of its universality. Instead, it is up to the individual to establish and maintain her own delineations. By way of conclusion, we therefore, with the help of our personal research among other things, will show how, in which ways, and according to which principles it may be done – and what this, in turn, may mean for the perception of conflict and balance, respectively, in the relation between work and life outside it.

Separate Spheres

Throughout the twentieth century, social science ideas have altered regarding how work and life outside it are related to one another. The various ideas have usually taken as their starting point that these are two entirely separate spheres, and this idea has been reinforced by the common equation of "life outside work" with "family life."

With this state of things as a backdrop, various models have been suggested as to how work and the private sphere, and then primarily family life, are related to and influence one another. Early research dealt with three different models, which may be called *segmentation*, *spillover*, and *compensation* (see for instance overviews by O'Driscoll, 1996; Parker, 1981).

According to the segmentation model (Figure 4.1), work and life outside it exist largely in parallel and without affecting each other (Blood and Wolfe, 1960; Piotrkowski, 1979). Work life satisfied primarily material needs, while it was in life outside it that social and, above all, emotional needs could be fulfilled (Gardiner, 1997). This was not just a way of describing the actual state of affairs, it was also emphasized as desirable. In an industrial society offering fragmented, strictly specialized, and often physically demanding jobs to a large portion of the workforce, a clear delineation was needed. Respect for the individual's free choice demanded that life outside the hard work be regulated or influenced as little as possible by conditions in working life. Home became the private sphere where the individual could relax and feel protected from the demands and expectations of the outside world.

Already at an early stage, however, it was realized that work and leisure time had to be viewed in a more comprehensive perspective. This is, not the least, the case if work is of a kind making great demands on the worker, requiring part of the leisure time to be reserved for recovery. The spillover model (Figure 4.2) therefore claims that difficulties in one sphere tend to taint the other one. More generally, it is assumed that the boundaries between different life spheres are permeable and that experiences and attitudes within one area – for example work life – affect attitudes and behavior within another – for instance family life. This means that the actual content of working life, the character of work, would influence the course of life outside it.

Positive and negative influence has been demonstrated in both directions. Great care has been devoted to showing how practitioners of free and academic jobs more than workers participate in activities of varying character (Karasek, 1979). However, negative or unwanted transfer from working life to other life domains has manifested itself in the clearest

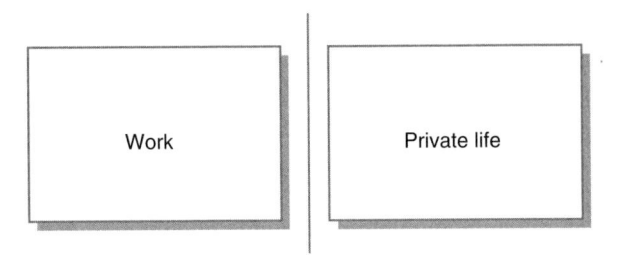

Figure 4.1 Segmentation

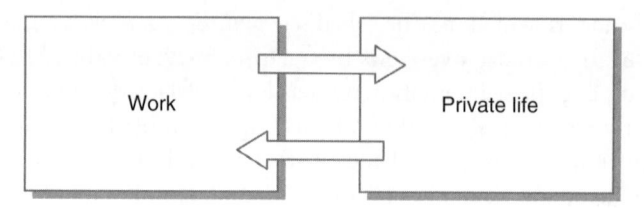

Figure 4.2 Spillover

manner (Frankenhaeuser *et al.*, 1989; Johansson and Aronsson, 1991; Meissner, 1971). Various ideas were put forward by, among others, Wilensky (1960) about conclusions to be drawn on the societal level. He suggested that monotonous, fragmented jobs ought to be linked to compensation, either in the form of interesting, creative, and developing leisure time activities or to substantially improved economic compensation. This compensation model (Figure 4.3) hence implies that defects in one domain may be compensated for and balanced by the content of the other.

Of the separate views expressed in industrial society, it is above all mainly the models of spillover and compensation that have been influential in the long run. One example is the demand-control model launched by Karasek and Theorell (1990), who, among other things, claim that high mental demands at work, in combination with a wide scope of action, lead to personal and professional development and to more energy to participate in leisure activities demanding coordination with others, such as club activities and non-profit work (Karasek, 1979).

It is interesting to note that in a time when women's employment outside the home was not a widespread phenomenon, the scientific discussion usually spoke of work and leisure. The prototype of the working man was exactly that, a man, and housework did not enter the model. Since then

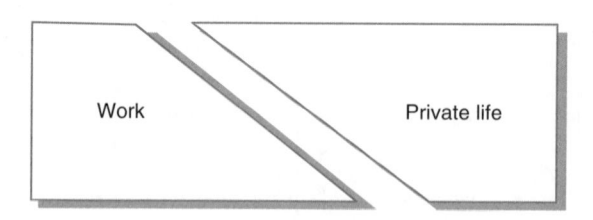

Figure 4.3 Compensation

women's occupation in gainful employment has grown substantially and the participation of men in childcare and housework has also increased, As we will see, discussions nowadays have to a large extent changed the focus to work and family.

Competing Spheres

While the labor market, the labor force, and working life have seen their characters changed, other views have simultaneously come into focus through research. One of them is called the conflict or competition model which was formed from the idea that every individual has only a limited amount of time and energy that the different life spheres have to share. If demands are high in all spheres and no adjustment or redistribution is possible then they will come into conflict with one another leading to role overload (Zedeck and Mosier, 1990).

Conflict theory also seems the most common starting point for research that has focused on the interplay between work life and family life. The consequences of such conflicts have been examined by, among others, Michael Frone (Frone, 2003; Frone, Russel, and Barnes, 1996). Using a specific scale for measuring the degree of conflict between work and family life, Frone has studied the impact of conflict and balance between the two domains. A general feature – found also in other studies (Kreiner, Hollensbe, and Sheep, 2009; Kylin, 2007) – has been that the tendency of work life to interfere with family life is reported more often than an interference in the other direction. Further, the results indicate that symptoms of depression are more commonly featured in a situation where family life is encroaching on work than the other way round. In a situation like that, when family life is disrupting work life, the risk of imperfect work performance is, not unexpectedly, larger. As soon as a conflict was reported, regardless of its direction, thoughts about changing jobs were also more common, as was absenteeism for domestic reasons (Frone, 2003).

In Northern Europe, especially in Scandinavia, social and family policy has been geared toward leveling the ground for working parents, trying to reach a balance between work life and family life. In other parts of the world, efforts are often made on an organizational level, in the shape of "family friendly organizational arrangements." Included are flexible working hours and work schedules, possibilities of part-time work, telecommuting, childcare arrangements, and the like (see, for example, overview by Eby *et al.*, 2005). The results of these efforts are to some extent relevant in this context.

In published evaluations, the starting point is usually the perspective of the organization while the focus is the effect of the family friendly measures on co-workers' attitudes and commitment to work. Scandura and Lankau (1997), for example, found that women who were able to work flexitime reported deeper commitment to and satisfaction with their work than those with fixed working hours. Another study (Goff, Mount, and Jamison, 1990) showed that employees who had access to and actually used employer-organized childcare experienced less conflict between work life and family life. There is also partial support that family friendly personnel programs are linked to higher levels of organizational performance and success. These and similar appraisals suggest that the support and desire of the employer to assist employees and co-workers with family support contributions is rewarded with work satisfaction, positive attitudes to the employer and workplace, and better work performance. At the same time, measures of this kind are still relatively rare. In most cases the employer is more willing to invest in various forms of stress management programs than in measures targeted specifically toward eliminating the cause of stress.

Coping with Boundaries

Establishing the character and sources of work–family conflict and family–work conflict is essential and useful. However, in order to investigate problematic conflicts further and to reach a better balance it is useful to change perspective somewhat, from the domains themselves to the border and boundaries between them.

Recent research on work–family interaction has become increasingly concerned with the blurring of boundaries between these two domains. With such perspectives, boundary and border theories have become relevant. Boundary theory may be described as a cognitive theory of social classification that focuses on the transitioning between roles (Ashforth, Kreiner, and Fugate, 2000). Border theory (Clark, 2000) is more specifically devoted to the work and family domains. Both approaches describe and analyze the ways in which individuals deal with the interaction and integration of life domains and the mechanisms by which various levels of work–family integration affect individual well-being. In an effort to achieve "work–life balance," they give less emphasis to conflict and incompatibilities between domains and turn to the ways in which individuals construct, maintain, negotiate, and cross the "lines of demarcation" between work and family (Clark, 2000).

With the introduction of boundary/border theory into the study of work and family or work and home, the individual is viewed as an active agent rather than a passive reactor to external conditions. We are dealing with a process that has been described as: "One's work–home boundary, its features, and its ascribed meanings are crafted as an ongoing, 'situated' accomplishment, meaning they are negotiated and transformed through social interactions and practices among various actors over time" (Kreiner, Hollensbe, and Sheep, 2009). The way that people deal with this process is closely related to their personal values and, thus, the degree to which they are involved in the various life domains such as work and family.

The blurring of boundaries may take various forms. They may be *flexible* in the sense that the relative scope of the domains may vary somewhat over time. They may also be *permeable*, that is, elements belonging to one domain are allowed temporarily to enter the other domain. Flexibility and permeability have been studied in terms of time and space (Nippert-Eng, 1996). An example of flexible temporal boundaries would be when employees are allowed to adapt their work hours to their children's school hours. Flexible spatial boundaries would be where the same room is allocated for work during working hours and for private use at other times. Temporal permeability is present when, for instance, an employee is allowed to receive personal calls during working hours.

The struggle to cope with boundaries is particularly apparent under certain circumstances. Kreiner, Hollensbe, and Sheep (2009) studied Episcopal parish priests who work with a congregation of church members. Because of the intense demands that their occupation makes on their time, they represent an interesting case of work–home demands. In the sample studied the vast majority of priests were married and lived traditional family lives. In a two-step qualitative interview study four major "boundary work tactics" were identified: behavioral, temporal, physical, and communicative tactics.

Behavioral tactics include the social environment, people who may help or hinder the priest's attempts at work–home balance such as spouse, children, co-workers, and supervisors (e.g. spouse always answering phone calls at home). Behavioral strategies also included the use of technology, various ways of balancing the risk of work–home conflict due to constant availability against the benefits of desired integration and work–home balance. A kind of differential permeability was also part of behavioral tactics, for instance choosing which specific aspects of work–home life will or will not be permeable. The priests' *temporal tactics* were similar to those of many other occupations. Flexitime is an obvious facilitator of this tactic, but it may also include other ways of controlling and manipulating work time, and banking time from one domain to be used later. *Physical tactics* were essential, especially for those priests who lived on-site in church-owned rectories located close to the church. It might, for instance, lead to special garden arrangements (fence, gate, hedge, etc.) with the purpose of creating a physical barrier between work and home. Some priests simply chose to live farther away from the church. Finally, *communicative tactics* is the term describing how the priests dealt with boundaries by communicating to others – e.g. spouse, children, staff members, parishioners – their preferences regarding work–home boundaries.

Telecommuting is another interesting example of work where boundary strategies become quite visible. It is one of the work forms believed to offer a new opportunity, especially for working parents, to reach a better balance between work and family life. As part of our study of telecommuting professional employees, participants working from home for up to three days per week replied to questions regarding segmentation and integration between the two domains. In addition to questions about temporal and spatial integration, we included questions on the mental dimension. The responses showed that the boundaries, mentally and in terms of time, between family and work domains were usually experienced as blurred and largely overlapping. Perceived overlapping in terms of space, however, was limited and the boundaries usually clear (Hartig, Kylin, and Johansson, 2007; Kylin, 2007). An increased sense of negativity was experienced as the overlap in time and space grew. Hence, a certain break-up of boundaries was tolerated, but when it was perceived as extensive it became an encumbrance. It was also found that although a separate room for telework appeared to improve unwanted spatial overlap, it did not affect unwanted temporal or mental blurring.

As would be expected, individuals differ in the degree to which they prioritize work vs. family/home, and this in turn determines their coping strategies. Somech and Drach-Zahavy (2007) identified eight different coping styles used by employed parents to deal with work intrusion into family life. They named these styles *super at home, good enough at home, delegation at home, priorities at home, super at work, good enough at work, delegation at work,* and *priorities at work.* The labels suggest that the value that these employees attached to each of the two domains formed the basis for their priorities and coping strategies.

Mutually Favored Spheres

Lately, the spillover model of the relation between work and family roles has been expanded. There is a growing understanding that the mutual transfer between life spheres can be both positive and negative. Moving between several roles potentially makes life more interesting and meaningful. This is a reasonable idea provided that each individual has a reasonable number of roles to fill and that the roles are not too demanding.

Under such conditions, work life and private life may benefit each other through the transfer of positive energy between the spheres, or even through an increase in the accessible energy total. With multiple roles, the individual can benefit from social support, the opportunity to experience success in several areas, wider perspectives in general, and an enhanced and developed self-image. Such beneficial effects of multiple roles could potentially compensate for possible simultaneous drawbacks (Barnett and Hyde, 2001).

As concerns about the negative impact of multiple roles increased in society, so did awareness in scientific research. It was assumed that the double role of working women constituted a disadvantage leading to an increased risk of health problems. It was even claimed that this did not influence the woman alone, but perhaps also her husband and children. However, in countries where a sufficient portion of women stay at home so that comparisons with women in gainful employment have been possible these apprehensions were not confirmed. Earlier studies certainly showed that the mental health of women staying at home was somewhat poorer than that of women in gainful employment, but it was not always feasible to determine a connection: poor health might have led some women into choosing to become housewives or housework itself might have led to poorer health. Some studies showed that when this confounder was controlled there was no detectable difference at all (Baruch and Barnett, 1986; Repetti and Crosby, 1984). Other studies, reviewed by Repetti, Matthews, and Waldron (1989), showed that the overall health of women in gainful employment was generally better than that of housewives.

Despite extensive research, attempts to show that multiple roles constitute a disadvantage in terms of health have failed. Instead, it has been found that women going from housework to part-time work, or from part-time to full-time, improve their mental health and that moving in the opposite direction gives the opposite result (Wethington and Kessler, 1989). Furthermore, it has been found that men's mental health benefits equally from their roles as husband, parent, and worker (Barnett, Marshall, and Pleck, 1992). As regards middle-aged women, there are research results showing that women with multiple roles are just as healthy or healthier than those with fewer roles (Repetti et al., 1989). Waldron and Jacobs (1989) showed that work outside the home had a positive effect on the health of unmarried women as well as that of married African American women while it had no such effect on the health of white women in gainful employment. The picture is complicated by results implying that the connection between labor market status and health is age-dependent. Thus, results from an Australian study (Lee and Powers, 2002) show that for women between 40 and 45 years of age good health was related to three or more roles. For women between 18 and 23 years of age, and for those between 70 and 75, one role only meant the best possible health.

The mechanisms dictating the connection between health status and the number of social roles are not known in full, but it is assumed that social support is involved. Maintaining several roles increases the individual's opportunities for social support and for inclusion in social networks, and such social integration has been shown to be positively related to several health outcomes (see, e.g., review by Uchino, 2009).

We conclude that entertaining several roles need not necessarily be disadvantageous and that under certain circumstances it may even be beneficial. If, however, conflict arises between the work role and family role, there is a risk that this negatively affects work satisfaction, well-being, health, and productivity. To a larger extent than previously assumed, this is just as valid for men as for women – we will return to this point later.

New Conditions Outside Work Life: The Consumption Society

The break-up of traditional sets of rules and growing demands on individual responsibility have changed working life, as we have tried to show in the previous chapters. Maintaining the idea of a homogeneous sphere with a clear division of roles *outside* working life is an even more problematic undertaking. Society as a whole has changed considerably during the last 25 years with the largest changes taking place outside of the working life.

This has happened in many aspects and on several different levels. Of interest for us here are the new, transformed roles that have developed in society. By this we refer to new, different expectations on an individual, that is, expectations from society, from social environment, and, last but not least, from the individual herself.

The fact that society in this respect has become increasingly heterogeneous is obvious. In the post-war years, the traditional basis of social division into separate socio-economic classes, generated in the conflict between work and capital, has slowly but surely diminished in importance (Olin Wright, 1997; Pakulski and Waters, 1996; SOU, 1990). New social differences and tensions based, inter alia, on education, position, sex, ethnicity, age, and generation have become more important for our understanding of society, its groupings, identity formation, and social dynamic. But although other differences and tensions between people have become of more pressing concern, in certain cases overshadowing class, it does not mean that class differences have disappeared or that class tension is of no importance in today's society. Rather, it is the case that the various differences may not be equally relevant – they may not be simultaneously evident or they may not have an identical impact (McCall, 2001).

Different combinations also produce different results and in certain cases the effect is cumulative. Already in the 1960s, American scientific researchers claimed that African American women with a low standard of education were at an intersection of several subordinate logics. As the struggle for equality reaps effects, segregation, inequality, and "outsiderness" thus retreat to such points of logic (McCall, 2001, 2005). In Sweden, for instance, being a woman on the labor market is normally no disadvantage. However, being an immigrant woman may constitute one. Being an older, non-European immigrant woman is a definite disadvantage, and an older, non-European immigrant woman with neither education nor knowledge of languages will be regarded as an almost hopeless case for an employment officer.

Consequently, today's society has to be understood as a social field of tension, made up of a series of social differences and tensions or conflicts. Thus, deciding on the most relevant tensions for consideration becomes an empirical question. It need not be the case that the tension per se has become stronger. Rather, it has multiplied and spread. As the new tension spread, so did social heterogeneity, making it difficult to gain an overview of society. In order to make the problem more incisive, we could even say that society no longer has a fixed social structure, just a multitude of different perspectives.

But not only has the social map of society become more complicated. We also *relate* to it differently. In other words, even the role of the citizen has changed. The conscientious worker, described in the introduction, increasingly has to step back for the sovereign customer.

The sovereign customer

The breakthrough of the customer concept arrived with the neo-liberal wave sweeping over the Western world after the assumption of power by Margaret Thatcher in Great Britain and Ronald Reagan in the USA at the end of the 1970s and start of the 1980s, respectively (Keat and Abercrombie, 1991). This has made many anxious to dismiss the term as a case of ideological rhetoric. But even though the launching of the customer concept is a way of introducing a certain kind of social development, the concept nevertheless has something to say about the demands that society makes, and is increasingly expected to make, of us as citizens. Just like the customer, the citizen is now expected to act more independently, strategically, and self-interestedly than the conscientious worker.

The concept of the customer is not only established in the market and within private consumption. It has also conquered working life. In their attempts to increase efficiency and quality in activities and in order to measure up to the ever-tougher international competition, a growing number of companies developed into service organizations. The idea behind the service organization is that everyone within a company should be conscious of its customers, and their personal relationship to these customers. But this is not enough. All activities, even the individual results of work, are to be assessed, not according to established norms and goals of production, but according to their ability to satisfy the customers. Yet another step in this direction was the breaking down and transformation of the bureaucratic company organization into internal markets. Colleagues became each other's customers. Goods and services were sold and entered into different accounts within the same company. Line managers became the customers of personnel departments, registry units became the customers of archives, and everyone became a customer of computer and property departments. The marketization of internal organization, or the "intrapreneurialization" as it has also been called, may even lead to different units being encouraged to compete with each other, even to take in external tenders, so-called insourcing, in order to further increase competition.

We have discussed the above in the first chapter of the book. What is interesting in this context is not rationalization per se, but the pedagogical task it entails. Through systematic usage of the customer concept the individual employee is made conscious of the market and its mechanisms. Where the bureaucratic organization previously protected the employees by channeling, transforming, and moderating the signals of the market, the "post-bureaucratic" organization strives to bring these signals to the individual employee directly. But taking the signals of the market to the employee is not sufficient. Through his role as a customer in the internal market game of the company, and in the relationship with possible subcontractors, the employee himself is placed on the market.

This development was further accentuated during the 1990s when the wave of marketization reached the public sector. Politicians became "orderers," public sector employees became "performers," while students, parents, patients, clients, pensioners, taxpayers, municipality dwellers, travelers, electricity, and telephone subscribers became customers in a market of private, semi-private, or public services. Walks in the park, bus rides, refuse disposal, or vehicle testing are today activities that we also perform in our capacity as customers of the park administration, the bus operator, the refuse collector, and vehicle testing authorities, with all that this entails in the way of demands for service, valuing one's time, and receiving value for money.

New relations

Social life participation in the capacity as a customer also entails a different view of and relation to other citizens of society. In society, we normally meet and understand other citizens from a starting point of the role we believe ourselves to play. In our capacity as employees, we meet and understand others as performers of a job or a task. As customers, however, we meet them as vendors of a service we need at a specific moment. Thus, the action of paying one's ticket and traveling by bus, for instance, does not constitute an action of solidarity to facilitate or at least not complicate the bus driver's job. Instead, it is a situation of potential negotiation. Even if the ticket price is non-negotiable, the service we are buying may be. For the price we are paying we ought to have the right to a seat, kind treatment, a nice and clean bus, and arrival according to schedule. If the service does not measure up to our expectations, we have, in accordance with the logic of market relations, the right to demand our money back, complain, change bus operators, or regard it as a breach of contract and reserve the right to break the agreement. In this context, the bus driver is reduced to a counterpart in a negotiation, a counterpart expected to act as calculatedly, instrumentally, and self-interestedly as we do. Hence, for us as customers there is no need to take him or her into consideration, but only what he or she has to offer us.

We see here that the customer role is not a social role in the traditional sense. The customer role does not contain any of the mutuality required for all forms of social interaction. Rather, the customer concept is a metaphor for a relation in market terms. It specifies only the conditions of the relation in question, more specifically the conditions of the market in terms of supply and demand, buy and sell, win or lose.

Just as industrial society once shaped and offered the citizen a role based on the idea of the conscientious worker, post-industrial society is shaping and offering its citizens a new role modeled on the customer. As did the old citizen role, the new role speaks of what society expects from us. In this capacity it is also aiming forwards. Through the citizen role a certain social order and a certain society is created. The customer concept disconnects and distances us from the companies, organizations, or authorities we work for or in other ways depend on (Long, 1999). Increasing awareness of ourselves as independent and self-interested customers is meant to put pressure on companies, organizations, and authorities to become more efficient and, in the long run, more competitive. In spreading the customer concept, society not only teaches its citizens to manage as customers, it also uses them to create a market.

The Moral Supermarket

Although we are increasingly expected to act in society as customers in a market, it does not mean that we, in our capacity as citizens, are merely victims of this market. As customers, we do not merely choose what we want, but also what we wish to achieve. In other words, our considerations are not simply economic but also normative and moral. This means that we can exploit our customer choices to influence companies, organizations, and authorities.

Pari passu with growing internationalization, or even globalization, politically motivated consumption is also increasing. Political consumption implies that the consumer uses her free choice in the market for political purposes. In its simplest and most common form, it means that we, when shopping, choose to buy products, the producer, or idea that we, for some reason, wish to support. Probably the most common examples are biodynamically grown produce and locally manufactured articles. Everyday consumption, in this context, also assumes political meaning. But political consumption may also mean that we take purely political action by acting in our capacity as consumer. This, for instance, is what we do when we support disability interest organizations by buying their Christmas cards, or when we visit an event where the proceeds will be given to charity. A more radical method is, of course, simply to boycott certain goods, companies, or countries. Even more radical would be to encourage other consumers through consumer information or lobbying to do the same. This has developed into a political movement per se, a movement including everything from information campaigns, for example the establishment of various certificates and branding systems for goods, to spectacular actions carried out by Greenpeace or animal rights movements, and all the way to more or less subversive campaigns of disinformation by means of so-called culture jamming, adbusting, etc. (Klein, 2000; Micheletti, 2003).

What is interesting about political consumption is that the instantaneous, everyday, personal little choices we constantly make in our capacity as customers become moral actions, in certain cases with far-reaching political consequences. It works for us as competition on the market continuously levels differences between products. Thereby, the marginal cost of changing products becomes very small. And since it is so easy to change products, demands for individual engagement are not very large either. In certain cases, such as ethical funds, there is not even a need for a personal standpoint. Therefore, it is relatively simple to mobilize a large number of participants. In this way, these actions differ from the voluminous, collective, and ritual manifestations of industrial society, performed at specific, tailored occasions only, such as elections to parliament, May Day, union meetings, demonstrations, etc. Unlike traditional political action, political consumption is instantaneous and unprepared. But the same traits, which in an economic context are assets, in political contexts become more problematic. Although the addressee is clear, the message conveyed by the political gesture is more obscure. The message may be both capricious and contradictive. At the same time, it can only convey what the consumers like and do not like respectively, but not what ought to be done about it. Therefore, it is not always simple for companies to decipher and realize what these thousands of individual consumers want them to do. The gestures are also inconstant, dependent on trends and media exposure. They also tend to focus on symbolic issues and prominent brand names, such as McDonald's, Nike, and Coca-Cola, rather than the concrete processes behind these brands (Micheletti, 2003).

"The nomads of the present"

Nevertheless, we increasingly express our engagement and politics through personal choices and gestures. A large part of today's moral and political issues are vocalized in and by social movements based on immediate gestures in this vein. Examples include anti-globalization movements, animal rights activists, racist and anti-racist movements, solidarity movements, religious movements, and interest groups for various sexual minorities, environmental, and women's groups. Common for them all are the increased importance and consciousness of the symbolic content of the issues on whose behalf they act. Another common feature is that the movements not only, or not even primarily, are instrumental associations for reaching a given political or social goal. Participating in such a movement is rather a symbolic action and a goal in itself. By professing oneself an adherent of the movement, one is showing the world how one wants to live. The gesture, in other words, does not demand a transformation of the future, but a possibility to live one's message in the present. The Italian sociologist Alberto Melucci (1989) has also called these new social movements "the nomads of the present." As a consequence of this immediateness their organization is also different from traditional movements. They are not clearly defined and bureaucratic, but consist rather of "networks of networks" – in other words, locally rooted networks that also branch out globally. They are open to all who want to participate and are held together by association rather than by systems of rules. Participation is facilitated by ICT, it is usually a part-time commitment, and does not prevent participation in other movements (Melucci, 1989).

Interesting for us here are not the social movements in themselves, but the fact that they, through their exposure in media and their constant presence, are offering themselves as a moral choice for the individual. Together, these movements and the results they *soi-disant* want to achieve form something that can be likened to a society-spanning moral supermarket. The supply and plethora, the ways in which they present themselves, the ease with which one enters and leaves the movements or chooses between them, makes the moral and political stances of the individual increasingly similar to those of the consumer. We choose those issues that, at the moment, upset us, suit us, or just happen to come our way. We participate at a distance by informing ourselves, accepting certain attributes, and by donating money. In return for this we achieve a certain social consciousness, a provisional standpoint, and emotional stimulus. The widespread but low-intensity presence of these issues and social movements in our everyday lives means that we are today involved in a larger number of social and political projects than ever before. However, the sheer multiplicity and ease of access tend to equalize the differences between them. We are therefore not deeply engaged in any one issue for a very long time either. Perhaps the most important thing for our conscience is not the issue we are committed to at the moment, but rather that we are always committed to one of them.

The Market Aesthetic

The new citizenry role offered by the customer concept hence allows moral and political action in addition to economic action. However, as already stated, it is not a social role in the conventional sense as it leaves no space for mutual social interaction. Neither can it, therefore, create a stable social identity. On the other hand, it offers almost unlimited choices of individual representation. This is achieved, quite simply, by presenting the self as a product. The self is here given an aesthetic representation similar to the product aesthetic offered by the market.

As market competition tends to level the differences between goods and services they are endowed with various meanings, in order to be seen and to get a competitive edge – meanings that go beyond their immediate utility value. For example, there is today virtually no product or service lacking a conscious aesthetic design or image (Lury, 1996). Goods and services are not merely expensive–cheap, practical–impractical, good–bad. They are also beautiful–ugly, fun–boring, cool–corny, etc. Products and services are then not just something to use. They are also something to be read, interpreted, and understood. In other words, they constitute a system of signs, a kind of language (Baudrillard, [1968]1996).

But even if this system of signs is a universal medium through which messages may be transmitted we ought not to compare it to a language in the accepted sense. It is rather a code consisting of a collection of simple distinctions (Baudrillard, [1968]1996). These distinctions assert themselves between and within people. They explicate, systematize, codify, and confirm social differences in the form of class identity, status, sex, ethnicity, and age, as well as psychological and existential differences. They are directed to, and hence also enhance, desire at the expense of will. By speaking directly to desire, consumption also appeals to loss, absence, or the "empty" individual (Baudrillard, [1970]1998). It then offers to fill this void with new experiences and qualities. Consumption as a form of activity may therefore be regarded as an expression of the romantic desire to "be someone else," to try different identities (Campbell, 1989).

As consumption is always directed toward parts of the individual's life, parts that are also stereotypes, it cannot be claimed that it offers the consumer an identity. By virtue of its selective appeal, it is rather breaking up the individual into categories, derived from and suitable for individual products. Consumption hence meets the consumer as a collage of more or less disconnected associations (Jameson, 1991). Unlike an identity, which gives the individual a biographical context, these associations merely offer her a collection of images without a time linkage. They present themselves as spatial constellations only. When, for instance, Viking Line conveys the image of a man surrounded by beautiful women at a New Year's party on board one of the company's ships, there are no references to the work and/or the privations the man has had to endure in order to afford his cruise in the first place, that is, to what preceded the picture. Neither are there any references to what consequences his social companions will have for his marriage. A world purely consisting of such images is devoid of context and internal meaning. It comes across as fragmented. This disconnected stream of images, associations, and symbols is characteristic of a consumption society.

By consumption society we mean a society where individuals create and recreate their lives (their biography and their plans) with reference to consumption and its requirements, rather than, for example, the requirements of work. It is not just a question of getting material from the images, associations, and symbols conveyed by culture, but also of relating to the more practical conditions of consumption. Does one prefer shopping cash or credit, second hand or new, necessities or luxury, saving or borrowing, maintaining control or letting oneself go, etc. (Lunt and Livingstone in Lury, 1996). The fact that the individual creates and recreates herself also means that individual consumption takes place in accordance with criteria that, one way or another, mirror the individual's self-image. Social life, therefore, to a large extent circles around profiling, showing off, distinguishing, and promoting oneself. Thereby, the individual also becomes a product, an image, and a symbol giving rise to associations and conveying a message to the world around them. What is important then is not to relate to others, but to show an aesthetic surface for others to make associations around. This has traditionally been the lot of women. Today, however, we all live, men and women, in what Susan Faludi (2000) has described as an "ornamental culture." In a consumption society it is therefore not advertising alone that calls out for our attention. We are all sending more or less insistent signals to one another. Thus, everyone is contributing to the general stimulus overload pervading the consumption society.

Work aesthetic and consumption aesthetic

In our consumption society, according to Zygmunt Bauman (1998), even the common work aesthetic has been substituted by an individual consumption aesthetic. This means that work, traditionally possessing an ethical value, now is being valued according to its aesthetic qualities. From an ethical perspective, all jobs, however monotonous, physically destructive, and humiliating, are meaningful and important for human dignity. The work ethic plays down differences between jobs to the benefit of the equality implicit in *doing* work. The consumer aesthetic, on the other hand, emphasizes the differences between jobs and elevates certain jobs to a status as "interesting" or "fun." A good job is something that satisfies the individual's desires, and is hence, like consumption, something where one can let oneself go. A job that does not fulfill these criteria is, in so many words, "boring" and something we wish to avoid at any price. A job like that can never be the object of free choice, but will be performed out of necessity only. It is also primarily performed by people with limited opportunities for choice, such as low-qualified workers and immigrants.

In a consumption society, consequently, the roles of work and consumption are reversed. Consumption no longer takes place on the conditions of work. Instead work takes place on the conditions of consumption. We choose a job in the same way and according to the same criteria as we consume. These choices rather than the fact that we work, or even how we work, signal who we are and what we want to achieve in life. Hence, having an "interesting" and "fun" job signals not only our ambition and our interests, it also demonstrates our ability to choose. A "boring" job, on the other hand, signals only an inability to choose. In order not to be regarded as incompetent or, even worse, unimaginative we need to legitimize such jobs with arguments such as "I only do it for the money," "I can quit whenever I wish to," "working hours allow me to do what I really want," etc.

The New Family

Not even in the most private of all social spheres, the family, is the individual free from all the choices with which today's society confronts him. The family, too, has gone through a dramatic transformation. The bourgeois family taking shape in the nineteenth century acted as a buffer against working life. More exactly, the family included and harbored the conflict between the economic demands of industrialism and the human need for care and intimacy. The bourgeois family thus functioned as a relief system within industrialism.

From the point of view of society, the family was the obvious economic and administrative unit. The family, not the individual, was registered by society and acknowledged as citizen and counterpart. The American anthropologist George Peter Murdock (1949) claimed that the basic family form was the nuclear family – in other words a man, his wife, and their biological children – and that its tasks consisted of limiting and channeling human sexuality, and contributing to the reproduction of labor, and hence society. This meant that the family should be both a place for food, rest, and recovery from work, and an environment for childbirth and upbringing. Furthermore, the nuclear family facilitated the economic cooperation between genders through a division of labor based on the superior strength of men, and women's "disabling burden of pregnancy and care." As head of the family, the man was consequently the representative of the family in all formal external matters, and hence legally and economically responsible. The woman, on her part, was to handle the care for husband and children and the housework. She was tied to the home and hence lacked legal and economic rights independent of this sphere. By fitting the family into society in this manner, its shape and organization were registered in the body politic, leaving the marks of a given distribution of gender and age outside the nuclear family formation: the bourgeois patriarchy.

During the 1900s, however, these conditions successively changed toward increasing gender equality. From having given women certain basic political, legal, and administrative rights during the first half of the century, the welfare state increasingly started turning directly to the individual instead of the family. Not only did this mean that women and men received the same individual rights within the framework of the family. In certain cases, for instance in countries introducing laws on individual taxation and laws on free abortion, the state also expressly undermined the sovereignty of the family (Bäck-Wiklund, 2002). This was not just a politically motivated reformation of the family, but an administrative adaptation to the participation of women in paid work, since the immense welfare development of the post-war era gave women increased access to the labor market. In the Scandinavian countries this was due partially to the growing demand for labor in general and partially to the large number of "women's jobs" created within the growing public welfare sector. During the 1970s, Swedish women's rate of employment was approaching that of men and housework as well as work was, to an increasing extent, expected to be "on equal conditions" (Hirdman, 1990). Another factor directly contributing to the equality of the genders was the development and spread of reliable means of birth control in the mid-1960s. Through these, women gained control of their fertility and their lives as never before (Lewis, 2007). The direct consequence was that women to a larger extent chose to delay giving birth, with reference primarily to education and career. To a great extent, women also chose to have fewer children and more women than before chose to have no children at all (Hakim, 2000, 2003). Together with free abortion, adoption, and insemination techniques, this contributed to the disconnection of sexuality from conception and parenthood. Instead, the "freely floating" sexuality through various attitudes, styles, abilities, techniques, and preferences developed into a part of the social personality of the individual.

Through these and other changes, the individual has been brought forward as the basic constituent of society. This means that individuals, women as well as men, to a larger extent are forced to take responsibility for their own lives. It is no longer obvious that the family constitutes a protection, traditional or institutional, against society and life in general. It is just a form of social life (Beck and Beck-Gernsheim, 2002; Hartig, Johansson, and Kylin, 2003). The individual therefore has to choose, not only whether she is to start a family in the first place, but also what form it is to take and why. The disintegration of the family as an institution has, at the same time, given rise to a minor industry of experts on everything from child rearing to sex and social life at the individual's disposal. But in the end it is up to the individual, in conference with other members of the family, to decide how, if, and on what conditions the family is to be constructed. One consequence is that the individual today, despite the gigantic supply of information and role models on family building, probably is less prepared for the task than ever before in history (Lasch, 1977). Idealized images and crass reality are mixed in a variety of apparently contradictory ways. Grand, costly church weddings, extravagantly furnished baby rooms, expensive prams, and wardrobes full of fashionable baby clothes coexist with a growing divorce rate, abortions, planned Caesarean sections, and children's ever earlier and longer stay at kindergartens, youth centers, and other organized activities outside the family. We want the romance but we are not quite ready to pay the price (Beck and Beck-Gernsheim, 1995).

The single most important reason for this is probably that we no longer know what good the family is to us. Earlier on, the very question would have been absurd. Back then, starting a family was as obvious a part of life as baptism, confirmation, and death. Today, the question is rather a starting point of family life. How to live, socialize, bring up, and name one's children are not only questions deciding whom to start a family with, but questions for repeated discussion which will assist in ensuring that the parties grow together, turning them into a family. One could even say that the family is nothing but a forum for negotiation (Bäck-Wiklund, 2002).

The family as a forum for negotiation

According to the British sociologist Anthony Giddens (1992) the democratization of private life also shapes the new family. Similarly to democracy in society, the family is an open relationship that constantly needs to be reproduced in order to endure. In contrast to earlier days when the family concept was identical to marriage, an undertaking before God and until death did us part, it now implies a mutual undertaking before one another. The only thing holy in this undertaking is the unconditional free will, in other words, that the relationship is not sealed for traditional or other external reasons, but for its own sake only: "that is, on the basis of what each party can gain from a lasting relationship with the other, and maintained only insofar as the relationship, by both parties, is regarded as satisfying enough for them to wish to retain it" (Giddens, 1992).

The family is, hence, not just a forum for negotiation, it is, or perhaps rather ought to be, a forum for unconditional negotiation (Björnberg, 2004). However, negotiations do not only take place within "the relation proper" between the two parties. Negotiations are also conducted continuously in relation to the children, the home, and the surroundings. Ever larger numbers of children grow up in big cities and other socially heterogeneous environments. Where to go and who to see is therefore always an open question. The same goes for pre-schools and schools. School close-downs, private and independent schools, parent cooperation, local pedagogical principles and curricula, and the right to choose whichever school one wants have created a plethora of choices and demands for the family to consider. A larger and more intrusive media fights for the attention of the children, forcing the parents to take stances, make rules, and conduct still more negotiations. Innumerable leisure activities, organized or less organized, offer children pastimes and possible lifestyle careers as performers, artists, sportsmen/women, actors, etc. from an early age. Parents choose, plan, give rides, and coach children – depending on their own perceptions and ideals of the children's health, physique, morals, intelligence, status, and future economy. All of these preparations, consequently, concern not only what children and parents may feel is healthy and fun; it is also very much a question of thinking ahead and optimizing the children's opportunities in life. Children are the common project engaging, driving, and legitimizing the family as a whole. The enticing future also offers the possibilities of gene technology and reproductive medicine (Beck-Gernsheim, 2002).

But negotiation is not just a process where the parties agree and successively approach each other. It is also a source of frustration and conflict. Areas subject to negotiation are also the areas on which opinions differ. One of the most common topic areas is that of housework. Here, most surveys paint a picture of a relatively traditional division of labor between husband and wife. Men assume the responsibility of the breadwinner and women that of the homemaker (Ahrne and Roman, 1997; Berntsson, Krantz, and Lundberg, 2005). This does not necessarily mean, however, that women renounce their self-determination and fall back on tradition. In interviews both parties admit to their participation in the traditional division of labor with a certain sense of guilt (Elvin-Nowak, 1999). The household-related division of labor is also the area around which most arguments and everyday conflicts take place. Both parties obviously want something different. Perhaps this is made even more obvious in relation to the family as an idea. Women like to imagine it in terms of a spirit of "community," doing things together for the sake of conviviality. Men, on the other hand, imagine the family more in terms of the practical requirements for family life, such as housing, cars, household economy, etc. Even their relationships vis-à-vis children differ. For women, children are the center and high point of family life. Any ideas of life "beyond children" hardly exist. Men, however, think and plan for life beyond the children and even speak of the necessity of "surviving the childhood of the children" (Bäck-Wiklund, 2002). The German sociologists Ulrich Beck and Elisabeth Beck-Gernsheim (2002) claim that something rather like separate identities, future plans, and self-images lies behind these and other conflicts. Consequently, the problem facing the family consists not merely of the controversy with the traditional distribution of roles, but perhaps more that the parties are not successful in communicating, discussing, and unconditionally negotiating their separate identities, future plans, and self-images.

The network family

To be unqualified, free will also mean that nothing can be taken for granted, and that the relationship is open. Separation is, in other words, always present in the conditions of the relationship, as a threat or a possibility.

Separation is also a prerequisite, directly or indirectly, for several of the new forms of family presently developing. When divorced or separated parents remarry, new families are formed at the same time as the original family members scatter over a number of households. This gives rise to several interlinked family systems with the children as the common denominator. In this system's model, marriage and parenthood are effectively separated creating new loci and orders of negotiation between those already established (Lewis, 2007). Separations are also the cause of the high percentage of single parents. At the end of the 1990s almost 25 percent of the million or so Swedish families with children under the age of 18 consisted of a single parent (20 percent single mothers and 4 percent single fathers). Many single parents, however, regard their situation as a problem and many, before long, enter into new relationships. But a growing number settle into their role as single parents and learn to appreciate the freedom this situation can offer. As such they also contribute to the plethora of family patterns (Erera, 2001).

To sum up, we see that today's family is not necessarily – at least not in the long run – the safe haven where individuals may seek refuge and get respite from the demands and insecurity of the surrounding world. Not only are family boundaries more porous, allowing the demands of the outside world to follow the individual inside, but the family itself is also a source of demands and insecurity. The development toward shared parenthood and the break-up of traditional gender roles means that the organization of family life is no longer obvious. There are no rules for who is to do what, when, and how, making it the subject of still more negotiation. The social psychologist Lars Dencik (1996) has claimed that the family risks being overloaded with functions, especially emotional and social demands, at the same time as the possibilities to fulfill these functions are shrinking and becoming more problematic. In that sense, family life is no antithesis of working life; as pointed out by Arlie Hochschild (1997), it may even be the case that for a growing number, of the highly qualified in particular, it is the work life that gives life its stability, challenges, and satisfaction while the home is being "taylorized," family life is routine or just feels impossible, and is hence drained of all commitment. However, as we shall see, the development has not quite brought us there yet – at least not in a Scandinavian context (Kylin, 2007).

In this passage we have not discussed the new work life directly. Instead, we have wanted to sketch something of the new social context where work exists and to which it has to relate somehow. Just like working life, this context is characterized by heterogeneity, change, and de-traditionalization. The social roles we support have changed and multiplied. Traditional class division, previously the locus of most roles in life, has not been substituted or supplemented by roles based on education, organizational position, or profession only, but also based on gender, ethnicity, generation, and age. The traditional citizen role, embodied in the "conscientious worker," increasingly has to leave way for the role as customer and consumer. The customer role is asserting itself, not only in the work life, which thereby increasingly assumes the character of a market game, but it is also by virtue of the role as customer and consumer that we make individual choices according to our possibilities and preferences. It is a role in which we increasingly make moral and political decisions, relate to one another, choose jobs, start families, and determine the conditions of child raising. The growing use of the customer and consumer role has thus given the citizen role a partly new content.

Organizing Living

What, then, does all of this mean for the relation between work and life outside it? In previous chapters, we have described how the dismantling of the common boundaries of work results in the individual herself being expected to define, plan, and take responsibility for the execution of work to a larger extent than before. Consequently, she is faced with a multitude of decisions, which otherwise would not be her responsibility to make. Instead of doing her work the *right* way, she now needs to do it in the *best* way possible. When simultaneously faced with a series of similar decisions in life outside work – for example concerning pension savings investment, electricity distributors, insurance companies, delivery wards, pre-schools, schools, moral and political commitments – where the individual is expected to choose the best possible solution for herself and also to the benefit of others, an important distinction between work and life outside it is dissolving. The distinction between work and life outside work has not been drawn simply along the lines of working hours and workplace. It has also been drawn between separate activities and social principles. Work has traditionally been a place for technical, instrumental, and functional action, whereas home was the place of rest, care, and respect. Although things have not always worked this way in practice, the distinction still mirrors the essentially different expectations that, despite all, characterize the respective spheres. Thus, when both work and life outside it are now increasingly being incorporated into the instrumental logic of the market the differences between previously separate social roles are shrinking. Work and private life blend together. It therefore may be difficult for an outside observer to identify which parts of an individual's life are work and which are not. However, it does not prevent the individual herself from making such a distinction.

The highly qualified worker

In her book, *The Time Bind: When Work Becomes Home and Home Becomes Work* (1997), Arlie Hochschild describes how work for the highly qualified part of the labor force is becoming freer, more challenging, and absorbing. Highly qualified employees are also increasingly content at work and in their role at work. They feel more confident and appreciated in their work role than in their family role. The reason, according to Hochschild, is not that they are receiving ever more education and competence development in and for their jobs, but that it is the opposite for family life. People today, regardless of their level of education, are significantly less prepared for the strains of family life than what was the case thirty years ago. One result of this, according to Hochschild, is that work and family life tend to blend together and even assume each other's qualities.

This might come to pass by work simply invading private life. It may very well be the consequence of a conscious employer strategy. The active involvement of the employees' whole lives into work is not just a way to get more work done; it may also be a way of ensuring their commitment (Fleming and Spicer, 2004; Kunda, 1992) – perhaps what we primarily think of when we take work home with us. The most obvious example of this is when we work more, more often, not in the workplace only, and not just during office hours. In our study of telecommuters, it turned out that highly qualified professional employees and managers worked more and substantially more, respectively, than the rest of the personnel. They were also to a larger extent "connected" evenings and weekends (Allvin, 2001). A general theme among those interviewed was also that of difficulties to mentally "switch off" work. One manager, for instance, complained about all those calling her at home at least once a day to ask about various things, even though she was not working from home but ill with a high temperature. Another sign of work invading private life is when individual work tasks are integrated into normal family life. One "freely" working system developer described how simple and smooth it was to sneak work into family life with the help of a laptop (Allvin *et al.*, 1999, p. 13).

> It happens quite often that I take along the laptop and sit in front of the TV with the others. I can write programs or something like that. And then from time to time you glance at the TV. (System developer)

But when work and life outside it blend together it does not necessarily mean the invasion of private life by work only. When the boundaries are blurring, private life is also able to invade the work life. Many highly qualified jobs are becoming increasingly individualized and personal. For instance, most workplaces have a multitude of "personnel fostering" activities in addition to the common coffee breaks. Fitness activities, sponsor systems, pub evenings, workouts, residential courses, yoga sessions, various kinds of educational programs, parties, and celebrations enable the satisfaction of a string of private and social needs during paid working hours. At a staffing company which we studied, each new employee received a personal contact at the company. The introduction took place in the evening, at a restaurant, over a glass of wine. We have also noticed that cooperation in organizations lacking a clear hierarchical distribution of responsibility tends to be very individual-based. Social competence and personal chemistry are allowed to decide who works with whom, who gets responsibility, access, authority, and information. The advantages are obvious. Work flows more smoothly and becomes more efficient. However, the disadvantages are that the workers risk being drawn into intrigues and dependence with no real bearing on the actual work. The supposedly intimate relationship opens the door to personal conflict, sexual intrigue, and hidden agendas. Other people are excluded for unclear reasons or simply because they do not "fit in with the group." The absence of a clear framework also gives individuals great freedom to "run their own race," satisfy their personal needs, or occupy space at the expense of others. In the worst case, this is destructive both for the organization and for those working within it.

One, perhaps extreme, example of this, increasingly noticed but still rarely studied or successfully documented, is how people with serious social disorders exploit working life to satisfy their personal needs. Most well known of these are perhaps narcissism and psychopathic disorders. People with disorders of this type care less about work itself and busy themselves above all with the social game at the workplace. They manipulate people in their vicinity and play them against each other with the purpose of obtaining and achieving what they want, which ultimately is self-confirmation. People like this are notoriously difficult to identify as they often are very socially competent, even charming. Instead, they can be recognized by the chaos and conflicts they leave in their wake (Gustafson and Ritzer, 1995). In contrast to the limited space for action of bureaucratic organizations, today's flexible organizations with their demands for independence and contact creation give these people relatively sizable opportunities to freely maneuver and satisfy their personal and often subconscious needs (Babiak, 1995).

We see here how work and life outside it are blending as a result of the ongoing break-up of the traditional forms of work and private life. For example, work is no longer as firmly framed by time and place. Neither is it necessarily limited to a hierarchical and industrial production process, and nor does it exclusively preclude economic dependence. A large portion of working hours for highly qualified employees, for instance, is taken up in obtaining information and understanding about things they actually want to know about. Post-secondary educational choices are rarely exclusively strategic. The same goes for life outside work. It is no longer limited to evenings and weekends, nor does it take the home as its obvious focal point. The lack of traditional norms and fixed roles, as we have seen, dissolves family relations and reduces them to a collection of agreements between two or several independent individuals. Family life is not necessarily characterized by social intimacy, mutuality, and emotional recovery, but can instead at times be just as instrumentally and industrially organized as may be the case for working life. The same is valid for moral and political standpoints, which are often just as defined by calculation, self-interest, and economism as was participation in the work life.

New mechanisms of classification

Work and life outside it blending into each other does not, however, necessarily mean that they are completely mixed. When work and private life cannot be differentiated through their given forms, they are of course not as easily distinguished as two separate life spheres. Our interviewees (Allvin and Aronsson, 2000) did not fall back on traditional distinctions, but had other means of separating work from their private lives. These methods were, in form, most similar to individual techniques for structuring and classifying life. They could then be used and combined in various ways and for different purposes.

The most common and perhaps most obvious techniques that we have reported relate to traditional divisions of *time* and *place*. A more subtle way of differentiating between work and life outside it is to exploit what Mark Harvey (1999) has called their separate *time economies*. When working, one is normally paid for accumulated time or an agreed result. In the first case, an individual will work in principle with a continuous intensity, while work in the latter case becomes more intense the closer one gets to the end result or the deadline. Working hours, however, are in both cases limited and characterized by unchanged purpose and direction. Both also differ from the time economy of the household. The time economy of the household is not made up of fixed time units or a given result, but instead consists of different series of tasks, which, to some extent, may be performed in parallel. Cooking, dishwashing, laundry, tidying, and cleaning, etc., do not necessarily have to take place within fixed time frames or with a specific result. But for natural reasons they have to be done in a particular order. Household time lacks formal limits and follows a cyclical rather than linear order. In contrast to working hours, it is static, or perpetual (to be compared with Hannah Arendt's classic 1958 distinction between "manufacture" and "labor").

The point of the separate time economies is that the difference between them also becomes a differentiation between work and private life, or at least part of one. If one performs an activity in accordance with the economic logic of working hours, it is work. If, on the other hand, one performs it in agreement with the economic logic of the household, it is not. If one devotes oneself to a single activity for an extended period of time in order to get it "done," it is equal to work. And if one, after completing it, does nothing specific, but just busies oneself with "little everyday duties," one has switched time economies and hence also switched off from work. In other words, it is the very manner in which things get done that separates work from life outside it, and not whether it takes place at a certain time or in a certain place. Engagement in a non-profit organization, for instance, may be just as focused, organized, and separate from private life as a traditional job. The tasks one is responsible for as secretary of the tenant-owners' housing cooperative are separate from the various tasks of the household, even though they are performed at home, evenings, and weekends (Taylor, 2004).

Another way of classifying life, reminiscent of the time-economy method, is the use of *contrasting activities*. Several of our freelance journalist interviewees (Allvin and Aronsson, 2000) were unable to switch off work when they were at home or with the family. Work was still on their minds whether they wanted it or not. What they then did was to devote themselves to some other activity requiring their full attention, in order to "force out" thoughts of work. Common examples included working out at a gym or with aerobics, sailing, carpentering, or gardening. Those who were the most intensely devoted to work were also the ones to devote themselves the most intensely to leisure activities.

Other family members, for natural reasons, also often function as a divide. Work may start, for instance, when the children go to school or kindergarten and finish when they come home again. The same is valid for husband or wife. His or her working hours are allowed to direct the personal work. However, it does not necessarily mean that the couple works at the same time – sometimes the opposite may be the case.

> Earlier, my husband worked a lot more and back then we were almost at home in shifts. If I got back home when he was there he might ask: But, are you back already? In that case I can go to work. (Freelance journalist)

Another way may be to schedule certain social activities forcing a pause in work. A freelance journalist working at home told us that she and several colleagues in the same situation regularly had lunch at each other's house at a certain time every day. Thereby she received not only a much-needed break, but also a proper meal every day, something she would otherwise be sloppy with during intensive periods of work. Other such activities may be afternoon walks, jogs, visits to movie theaters or shopping expeditions.

In her book *Home and Work*, the American sociologist Christena Nippert-Eng (1996) describes how a number of smaller, at first glance insignificant, artifacts and rituals also may constitute important *symbolical markers*, helping us maintain the division between work and private life. One typical such artifact is the diary. Do we keep double diaries? Which kind of diary do we have, and what kind of information do we write down in it? It is, for instance, not uncommon to have separate diaries for work and private life. It is also not uncommon that the information in them does not overlap. Keys are another such symbolical artifact. One way of maintaining the distinction is by having separate key rings for home and work. One, perhaps more obvious, way is to have separate clothes and dress styles at and outside work respectively and, in connection with this, different rituals for dressing and changing. According to Nippert-Eng, even separate eating habits provide a means of maintaining the distinction, as does the reluctance to use private money or credit cards for work-related expenses. These examples fall under what Kreiner and his co-workers (2009) would label behavioral tactics.

ICT is, in itself, also used for maintaining the distinction between work and life outside it. The virtual room, whether we are then speaking of the personal computer, Internet, telecommunications, or even the "common living room" in the shape of the TV, may, like the physical room, divide existence into work and private life respectively. The personal computer, for instance, may be reserved for work, while surfing the Net and engaging in social media is not. Certain sites on the Internet are legitimate workplaces, whereas others most definitely are not. Telecommunications may during certain hours or situations also be earmarked for work while, on the other hand, watching TV instead is an activity precluding work. Several of the freelance journalists whom we interviewed did not have a specific office arranged either at home or outside it. Instead, the laptop served as office. Opening it and switching it on was then the same as entering the sphere of work, irrespective of where one actually was in all other senses of the word. The reason why information technology is able to function as a dividing line between work and private life is because it actually gives access to another room, a room opened by simply activating the technology in question. The actual technical artifact – the computer, telephone, or TV – here works as a symbolic border guard in exactly the same way as once did the time clock or factory gates. It allows for concentration and filters away disruptive elements by signaling "work" ("Be quiet, daddy is on the phone") or, in the case of the TV, "leisure."

Individual strategies and universal attitudes

This list of different mechanisms of classification is primarily intended to be illustrating, not exhaustive. Each has his or her own techniques or combinations of techniques, and ascribes different importance to them. The importance is, however, not so much in the techniques per se as in their use, or more specifically in their systematic use. It is, namely, upon fitting them into comprehensive strategies for classifying existence that the various techniques assume their concrete importance. These comprehensive strategies are individual and most often not entirely conscious. They are, however, not completely unlike each other. Taking their cue from their extensive studies of housework, the two work life researchers Alan Felstead and Nick Jewson (2000) claim that these strategies concern the drawing of boundaries either in the home or around it. Depending on how the borders are drawn, they then believe themselves capable of deriving various universal attitudes in the relation between work and life outside it. Strong internal borders in combination with weak external ones would point, for instance, to a prioritization of work at the expense of the home while weak internal borders in combination with strong external would imply the opposite.

According to Christena Nippert-Eng, the individual strategies of border-drawing are to be regarded as something rather like points on a continuum between two distinct and ideal-specific poles. These poles consist of, on the one hand, a categorical division of life and, on the other, an extreme integration of all the different parts of life. The British sociologist Catherine Hakim (2000) instead, in a study of considerable scope on women's attitudes to work, contrasts a home-centered attitude, in which one would rather not work at all but instead concentrate on home and family (something which about 20 percent of British women claim to agree to), with a work-centered attitude, in which one is deeply committed to work and the personal career (also approximately 20 percent). More than half the women fell somewhere in between, and were consequently moderately committed to work and wished to combine it with life outside it. In our study of freelancing journalists (Allvin and Aronsson, 2000) we arrived at a similar result. We also distinguish two separate attitudes: one purposefully focusing on work and the personal career, and one more holistic, striving to integrate work and life outside it within the framework of a well-organized and clearly delineated private life.

The difference between the two attitudes is perhaps best made clear if we pit them against each other, as we have done in Table 4.1. Examples are taken from our study of freelance journalists.

We see here how the organization of work becomes a way of marking off work and prioritizing in life. We also see that the traditional spheres, of work

Table 4.1 Characteristics of two separate attitudes towards work and life outside it (based on Allvin and Aronsson, 2003).

Focusing work	Integrating work and life outside it
Puts the job first.	Puts private life first.
Maintains a clear distinction between work and private life.	Exploits and develops means of combining work and private life.
Works only reluctantly at home.	Prefers working at home.
Works often close to deadlines and takes time off after finishing a project.	Generally sandwiches work tasks and private obligations.
Works for hours on end.	Willingly varies the working day with lunches, meetings, walks, and short rests.
Works regardless of hour, day, and occasion.	Works only reluctantly evenings and weekends.
Goes on holiday during low-season.	If there is a workplace outside the home one chooses to take Fridays off in order to have longer consecutive time off.
Plans their work, not their private life.	Plans work, private, and social life.
Private life is allowed to take up space left over from work.	Planning becomes a way of keeping work in check.
Participates in childcare and housework according to the principle of division of labour and shift work.	If there is a family and children, work will be determined by their times. Work starts when the family leaves home and ends when they return.
Remuneration is symbolically charged. It is also an acknowledgment and a status marker.	Remuneration is not particularly symbolically charged. It is just supposed to be liveable.
"Works up" money for various purposes.	Emphasizes the importance of negotiating reasonable time frames and conditions for an assignment.
Emphasizes the importance of constant development. Does not differentiate professional and personal development.	It is important to choose one's co-workers, to feel comfortable with one's colleagues.
The categorical division of work and private life is consequently practical and organizational rather than mental.	Work and private life are consequently clearly separate on a mental level, but practically and organizationally they are thoroughly integrated.

and life outside it respectively, in all things essential are being maintained. The difference is that they are not automatically assumed, neither are they universal in character. Everyone divides up existence and creates space for both spheres according to personal means and patterns. The practical organization of work hence also mirrors the personal attitude to it. By means of organizing and delineating work one demonstrates, in other words, how one wishes to live one's life. A categorical division of existence into work and life outside it may be, for example, an expression of work having become one's life project. Similarly, an organizational integration of work with life outside it may be a way of subordinating work to all other prioritized areas of life.

Conflict and Balance in Life

Even though the research in question believes itself capable of identifying a number of principal relations between work and life outside it, it is no easy task to distinguish the corresponding conflicts or experiences of balance. What one individual perceives as a conflict may be regarded differently by another individual, etc. From a starting point for the separate attitudes above we may assume, however, that conditions for balance as well as conflict result from the organization of work and life outside it, and how one, consequently, has chosen to live one's life. This was particularly clear among the freelance journalists we interviewed (Allvin and Aronsson, 2000) who to a large extent had chosen this work form in order to be able to control the relation between work and private life.

> First and foremost, I never work at home; I make a clear distinction between work and free time in that way. Work always comes first, so suppers and other leisure activities will have to happen when there is time to spare. Days might be long, usually starting around 9:30 and I'm rarely home before 9:00 p.m. Thank Heavens, work is scarce in July, so I generally get a bit of a summer holiday. (Freelance journalist)

For those who, like the freelancer in the quote above, purposefully focus on work, each disruption of the work process appears a conflict situation. Every time the family, household, friends, or the surroundings in general demand engagement, presence, or attention without the work process allowing it, conflict arises. Hochschild (1997) describes a mother who found it difficult to read fairy tales to her children as she was constantly thinking of all the emails awaiting her. The natural thing for her would have been to follow the rhythm of the work process and read the emails as they arrived. The demands of her children and her fairy-tale reading for her commitment and presence hence collided with the way in which she would like to organize her existence. She knew what she needed to do, but was prevented from doing it, resulting in her being frustrated and irritable.

For her, fairy-tale reading and other family duties came to require a bigger effort and more discipline and concentration than her work tasks. Family life, rather than work, was perceived as strenuous. Home and family duties hence tended to assume a more industrial character. Hochschild also speaks of a general Taylorization of family life and housework as a consequence of all the available fast food, frozen food, fashion clothing, pedagogical TV programs, computer and TV games, childcare and other organized activities outside the family, etc. Parents do less and less and play an ever-smaller role in the activities of the home. In this sense, family life and housework have, so to speak, been de-qualified and drained of the "professional knowledge" they once required. Tasks that have not been taken over by the increasing automation of the household are bought or "outsourced" to the food, toy, and entertainment industry (Hochschild, 1997).

The purpose of this Taylorization of family life and the household is, of course, to give parents the opportunity to devote themselves to or to recover after work. Modern consumer society also gives substantial support to parents who want to or have to focus on work. It gives parents the possibility of being flexible in relation to family life and the household. In other words, it enables "entering" and following work on its own conditions. Family life should not have to be an obstacle to the "flow" which Mihaly Csikszentmihalyhi (1990) believes to be the optimal relationship to work.

> I'm extremely disciplined and organized in my work. But of course I let the job rule even if it affects my private life. It often happens that I work weekends. I don't work with assignments like most of my freelancing colleagues. I find the stories, news only, and send them in. It also means that I in no way depend on colleagues or others for my work performance. I do exactly as I please. (Freelance journalist)

Many of those whom we interviewed had absorbing jobs and simply raced on in life. Private life was either neglected or adapted and included in working life. For those purposefully focusing on work, such a flow is the closest one can get to a perceived balance between work and life outside it. Balance requires life outside work to be constantly adapted to work or even to promote it. In other words, balance here means the possibility to commit oneself fully, to be flexible and able to adapt to the demands of work.

This differs markedly from those who were striving to integrate work and life outside it into one whole. Here, balance had nothing to do with achieving flow, the goal was instead harmony.

> I work from home, which gives me the opportunity to organize my time so that I can do "other things" as well during the day. For instance, I write a few emails, then make the bed, read material for my next assignment, go out and play with the dog, start a bread dough, prepare sales, pick up the phone from time to time, check through old papers for new ideas, and so on. My days are a constant succession of private and work. I also move around the house, sit in front of the computer, then read on the veranda, phone from the bedroom. I love change. (Freelance journalist)

In the quote above, a freelance journalist describes how work is woven into and adapted to the various duties of everyday life. The change she claims to love is the change between the various tasks of private and working life. All these tasks are here neatly fitted into the whole of everyday existence. No single duty is allowed to take over. The balance here refers to the equilibrium she is continuously maintaining between all the separate duties. Balance hence requires the possibility to keep control of all the various parts of life, not letting any one part disrupt the carefully constructed whole. Planning is necessary and a way of keeping the work life in check.

When, in spite of everything, work forces its way in and takes up space it happens at the expense of other activities. One feels, for instance, that one cannot "be there" for the children or maintain necessary social relations with family and friends. Or, the perception is of the home falling into disrepair and of personal maintenance suffering. As the social relations in working life are relatively more important to those striving to integrate work and life outside it, conflicts with and between colleagues at work may be perceived as more disruptive. In other words, conflicts arise when the equilibrium of life's various parts is upset, leading one to feel stressed out and hounded.

However, the most serious reason for conflict is perhaps the economy. Integrating work and private life, as we have described it here, means that work has to be adapted to life outside it rather than the other way around. It is a compromise where the work life has to play second fiddle. Work life, however, tends to force itself on the individual through difficulties "picking up" jobs and a fluctuating or even dried-up economy. As long as one is young, possesses contacts, and the labor market is doing fine, one can always stay afloat. But as one grows older, contacts disappear one after the other and times are getting harder, work becomes a problem that is increasingly in conflict with one's needs and the life one wants to live. This was expressed by journalists in our study (Allvin and Aronsson, 2000).

> At the moment I'm quite worried. I'm turning 60 this autumn and have too few assignments by far. Many of my employers have retired, I have to look for new ones and it's not that simple. I actually don't know how to find a reasonable assignment to commit myself to and earn my living from. I do a lot of non-profit work and am not unemployed in that sense, but often lack an income.
>
> I'm trying to send out feelers, find new assignments, but have only succeeded in getting shorter assignments here and there in the last year. I've consciously approached networks in my district in order to find jobs there. I've had results, but not enough.
>
> One possibility is starting to draw pension at age 61, but my pension is very small even if I manage to keep going until 65, so in reality I have no choice.
>
> I have to work with things that engage me. I don't want to be an employee. So I continue the way I've been doing since the start of the 80s. (Freelance journalist)

What is perceived as conflict and balance in the relation between work and life outside it may, as we have seen, depend on one's attitude to work. In our interviews, we have been able to identify two reasonably universal such attitudes. On the one hand, we have those purposefully focusing on work and allowing private life to adapt itself accordingly. On the other hand there are those who instead are trying to integrate work and life outside it within the framework of a more holistic view of existence (see Table 4.2). The meaning of the balance between the two life spheres here varies between the feeling of flow and harmony. Conflicts, in turn, follow from disruptions of these feelings.

Table 4.2

	Focusing work	*Integrating work and private life*
Balance	When work is in flow.	When existence is harmonious.
Conflict	When private life hampers the work process.	When work forces its way in and upsets the equilibrium in life.

An Individual Matter

In this chapter, we have attempted to show that the separation of work and life outside it, to a high degree, is an urgent matter for most of us. Research usually characterizes this division as a distinction between two relatively separate life spheres – work and family or alternatively the workplace and home. At work, one is subjected to the laws of technology and economics. There, as a small cogwheel in the great machinery, one participates in the material reproduction of society. In the family, by contrast, the ruling laws are social and moral. One also takes care of others, gains an outlet for personal preferences, and gives meaning to existence. On the whole, this is also a reasonable division of life, provided that the two domains are physically separated and dominated by different activities. Further, it is a reasonable division as long as these conditions, in all things essential, are common for the majority of society. But when work no longer allows itself to be limited in time and space, when the laws of technology and economics spread throughout society, and when family life is more often occupied with logistics, negotiations, and strategic choices the division is no longer as evident.

From having been a common norm of society, the division of work and private life has increasingly become an individual matter. Those who have "free" jobs hence need to organize more than their work alone. He or she will also have to organize the relation between work and life outside it. Consequently, the relation does not assume a fixed and universal form, but instead results from individual negotiations with other family members, pre-school, school, co-workers, colleagues, managers, the specific conditions of various activities, etc., and, not the least, with oneself, individual possibilities, and preferences. Even when we, in various surveys, distinguish a relatively widespread pattern, we ought not to take it as a given order, but more as the empirical result of a collection of negotiations of this kind.

5

Work Life, Stress, and the New Ill Health

Toward the end of the nineteenth century, a new type of illness was observed in Western Europe and the USA. Symptoms varied from sleeplessness and anxiety to pressure over the chest and temples. The varying list of symptoms baffled contemporaries almost as much as the lack of physiological and material causes. The only common denominator was a "pathological loss of energy" and an inability to work. At the same time, the stricken did not belong to the categories that normally suffered privations at work. Instead they were businesspersons, professionals, professional employees, and students. A merchant described his troubles:

> I work from 8 o'clock in the morning until 10 o'clock at night. I can hardly take any time to eat; usually I eat on my feet, and then it is cold tasteless food. By 10 o'clock in the evening I'm so tired that I have trouble finding the strength to close my books. During the night the day's events whirl through my head so that it isn't until early morning that I can enjoy my rest. When I rise, I am deathly tired and must drink a few glasses of brandy in order to be fit for work again. (Quoted in Johannisson, 2006, p. 5)

The paralyzing tiredness he described is mental rather than physical, and it was also interpreted by contemporaries as symptoms of psychological, intellectual, and emotional overexertion. In 1869, the American physician George Beard formulated the diagnosis "neurasthenia" for the drop in nervous energy resulting from mental exhaustion. The diagnosis functioned as a generic term for a wealth of symptoms – Beard himself mentioned about eighty (Johannisson, 2006). At the outset, the diagnosis was not linked to work primarily, but rather to the dramatic transformation experienced by Western society in the decades before the turn of the

---

Work Without Boundaries: Psychological Perspectives on the New Working Life, First Edition. Michael Allvin, Gunnar Aronsson, Tom Hagström, Gunn Johansson, and Ulf Lundberg.
© 2011 John Wiley & Sons, Ltd. Published 2011 by John Wiley & Sons, Ltd.

century. Industrialization, the expanding capital market, and massive urbanization smashed the agrarian social order into pieces and distributed work, wealth, and status according to new patterns. Moreover, the transformation was accompanied by intensive discussion about modern society and the unnatural, reprehensible, and harmful life it offered.

Modern life also entailed what Georg Simmel (1903) described as an "intensification of nervous life" due to "the quick and continuous succession of external and internal impressions." The big cities flooded their inhabitants with consumer goods, experiences, and sensations. Anonymous money was flowing to an extent and in a manner unparalleled in history. New technology made society independent of the limitations of nature. Electricity turned the night into day. The railroad and automobile shortened traveling while the telegraph and telephone completely dissolved distances. Above all, there was a bustle, tempo, and changeability that agrarian society lacked completely. That all these impressions and unforeseeable conditions were unnatural, posing a serious strain on intellectual and emotional life, seemed obvious. In a 1901 contribution to *The Journal of Mental Science*, Dr. Symes Thompson cautioned:

> We must see many whose nervous system will go to pieces unless they can be taken away from stress in which they are living, whether that be on the stock exchange or in any other professional occupation where the nineteenth-century pressure is great. (Quoted in Johannisson, 2006, p. 3)

The "stress" to which Dr. Thomson is here referring concerns the detrimental effect of the contemporary intense pressure on the "nervous system," a pressure which is particularly felt in certain "professional activities," or, more precisely, activities at the epicenter of change, or the "front line" as we would call it today. Dr. Thomson himself mentions stockbrokers, which implies that market forces already at that time were a powerful contributor to the stress.

The stress thus concerned the relationship between, on the one hand, the changing and increasing demands of society and working life and, on the other hand, the overexertion and nervous exhaustion that follow from human inability to cope with these demands. During the decades around the turn of the twentieth century, this relationship was, to a large extent, understood in the context of a romantic critique of modernity. It was described as the natural resistance of the body against the unnatural demands of the contemporary period. The body was the place in which the destructive forces of modern society could be seriously observed and studied. Nowhere was the conflict between human biological reactions and the technical and economic demands of modern society as tangible as here.

However, as industrial expansion continued and the modern welfare society gradually took shape a couple of decades into the twentieth century, the critique of modernity lost momentum and was disconnected from the medically defined problematic. The diagnosis for neurasthenia was dismissed and the many symptoms hidden inside various intra-scientific special areas, such as professional medicine, immunology, and psychiatry (Johannisson, 2006). Instead, interpretational preference was assumed by industrial science. Exhaustion was here understood as a warning sign that the limit of human working capacity had been exceeded. The human being was regarded as an engine producing labor. Exhaustion, like the regulatory mechanism in a piece of machinery, simply regulated the body's labor.

Around the turn of the twentieth century, industrial science was also aiming at, through scientific methods, examining the conditions of exhaustion in order to enable the optimization of the body's labor. This self-assumed assignment, however, was not aimed merely at increasing industrial productivity; it also concerned the reformation of work itself. By adapting the work tasks and the working day to the physiological capacity of the body and by introducing breaks and days of rest it was believed that labor could be administered better, that professional injuries could be reduced, and even that contemporary hostile class conflict could be reconciled and remedied (Rabinbach, 1990).

Common for both the modernity-critical and the professional-scientific understandings of stress is the idea of a disharmony or imbalance between the human capacity and various external demands. The symptoms of tiredness we experience, mental as well as physical, are then an expression of the exhaustion and overexertion that follow from the attempts to fulfill these demands. The imbalance arises when external demands increase or otherwise change. It is thus not the individual who causes the resulting imbalance, but, quite on the contrary, the human capacity is instead portrayed as the fixed point and the yardstick with which external changes may be measured and assessed. Only when contrasted with the natural human constitution are the social changes and their consequences visible.

If one then, additionally, extrapolates the changing demands, one thereby seems to distinguish a potential or real context in which human existence could be, or even has been, in harmony with its surroundings. In the late nineteenth-century critique of modernity there were, for instance, references to pre-modern pastoral life, an era in which it was possible to gain a comprehensive overview of social life and when changes were cyclical and predictable. In early twentieth-century industrial science references are not to a real, if romanticized, historical context, but instead to a potential union of the motoric capacity of human beings with the demands of industrial machinery. The imbalance is hence regarded as a historical anomaly or a disruption of a potentially harmonious system. It is, in other words, a problem which it is not only possible but also imperative to take measures against.

Many of the conditions that were observed around the turn of the twentieth century may also be seen today. We perceive ourselves today, like before, as living in a time of accelerating expectations. These are expectations engulfing us from every possible angle, not only in the work life. It is as if time itself is running faster. At the same time, we are living in a world of new and changing conditions. The new economy as well as the new technology turns familiar ideas and procedures upside down. The world is expanding and borders dissolving. Life opportunities on offer are obvious to all but available to only a minority. The threats of existence, however, hit against everyone, without distinction. The greenhouse effect, international terrorism, pedophiles, resistant bacterial strains, pandemics, and tsunamis are all threats with which we had to learn to live.

Now, as during the turn of the twentieth century, psychological problems are on the increase. Since the mid-1980s, reports of tiredness, insomnia, worrying, and anxiety have increased markedly in Europe and North America. The problems also seem to be relatively universal, even though there are differences in scope between men and women, young and old people, employed and unemployed, and highly qualified and unqualified professional groups. More women, more young people, more of those not in gainful employment, and more workers with low-level qualifications claim to "feel bad" (a term which has become the new way of describing insufficient mental well-being without calling it "psychological problems," which has a more clinical ring) but the increase affects all groups. One consistent trend is that the increase in mental problems is greater in young people than in older people (WHO, 2006). Students, for instance, feel significantly worse than retired people (Hallsten, Lundberg, and Waldenström, 2005). In affluent countries like Sweden, Norway, and The Netherlands absenteeism due to illness has also increased dramatically during the second half of the 1990s and reached a peak in the beginning of the 2000s. Like the psychological problems, the increase is most significant among the young although this was taken from a previously very low level. Also, sick leave for diagnosed psychological reasons has shown the most rapid increase (Lidwall, Marklund, and Skogman Thoursie, 2005). Since then, there has been a decrease in sick leave, not because people have become healthier but, as in Sweden, rather due to new legislation and more restricted criteria for economic compensation during sick leave.

Just like during the turn of the twentieth century, the explanation offered for these problems is overexertion and exhaustion due to an inability to cope with the increasing and changing demands of the surrounding world. The relationship of the human being to her surroundings is still discussed in terms of balance and imbalance, natural and unnatural. We are also trying to understand the imbalance by referring to a distant harmonious state. In our case, this is an evolutionarily primordial scene in which the human being roamed freely over the savannah and, successively, acquired all the characteristics which ten thousand years later cause her trouble in the encounter with modern society. What sets this apart from perceptions around the turn of the twentieth century, however, is that we now have a carefully worked-out term for the relation at hand, a term incorporating individual problems as well as external demands, namely stress.

However, not all workers suffer from stress in modern work life. For many, the new and more flexible and less regulated forms of work have positive effects in terms of more influence, responsibility, and variation, which within reasonable limits contribute to greater mental, social, and economic resources, psychological well-being, and health. As a consequence, socioeconomic health differences in many societies have increased.

Stress as a Social Problem and Research Area

The various characteristics of what we now know as stress were already in place in the context of the far-reaching social transformation underway at the end of the nineteenth century. But even though the fundamental traits were already established, it does not mean that stress existed as a term and common phenomenon. It only took shape during the 1930s and 1940s and then as a purely physiological phenomenon. Most basic literature on stress also tends to refer to its origins in medicine. Subsequently, however, the term has been used in a variety of manners within a whole string of areas.

The fact that the term and the first theoretical models were formulated within the area of medicine also does not take away from the fact that these referred and still refer to the relationship of the individual vis-à-vis his environment. What has emphasized the term and given it its larger meaning is the body of social problems the term has claimed to explain. Stress is consequently not a mere intra-scientific explanatory model for certain specific psychological and physiological conditions. It is also an answer to a series of questions society has been confronted with and still is confronting. The various roles and shifts of meaning the term has experienced and still is experiencing may therefore be seen as adjustments to the historically specific problems and questions contemporary society was facing.

War and economic depression

The term stress was formulated in an era when the great social transformations in the Western world around the turn of the twentieth century were already over. Society was back on track and slowly regaining speed. Growth and wealth were steadily increasing at the same time as the vision of a future welfare society was taking shape. Nevertheless, this does not mean the contemporary world and the future seemed bright – quite on the contrary – inequalities in Western society were widespread. The insufficient buying power of the vast majority gave rise to a gigantic problem of product disposal with resulting stagnation and economic depression. In combination with international discontent it set the scene for the Second World War. The scope and horrific consequences of the problem hit individuals with the same implacability as a natural disaster. The psychological reactions displayed by human beings were therefore not primarily attributed to a self-assumed overexertion, but rather to the fact that their external and internal life quite literally had been smashed to pieces.

It was also the interest in the most primitive reactions of human beings to life-threatening circumstances that was the origin of stress research. According to the source of inspiration and forerunner of stress research, Walter Cannon (1914), human beings react to these threats physically and instinctively. When we become afraid or angry the body mobilizes itself to flee or defend itself (*fight or flight response*). When the Hungarian-born but Canadian-based physiologist Hans Selye first formulated the concept of stress in the mid-1930s nobody really took notice. This was partly due to the fact that he did not publish anything on the matter; he simply discussed it in his lectures. His colleagues also found the concept confusing and not user friendly. However, it was not necessarily an obstacle to fame. The reason for the indifference to Selye's theory was rather to be found in the fact that Canada in the 1930s did not experience the same life-threatening conditions as in other countries, and stress did not pose a tangible social problem yet. But ten years later, after the end of the Second World War, when Selye published his theory of stress (1956), the concept, for the very same reasons previously ignored, won immense attention (Cooper and Dewe, 2004).

Selye described stress as a *General Adaptation Syndrome* and claimed that it was a series of loosely connected reactions to life-threatening external events (Selye, 1956). Further, he believed the reactions to be developed in three different phases – alarm, resistance, and exhaustion – resulting in a successive depletion of the *adaptive energy* of the individual, a depletion which, in the worst case, could lead to death. The critique from the scientific community was not late in the coming. What was it, really, that the term "stress" described? What is the difference between a specific and a general reaction? What is needed to trigger a reaction of alarm? What is adaptive energy? Selye was not content with the concept, either, and several times thought to abandon it. Contributory to the general confusion was also the fact that Selye, due to his Hungarian background, had not fully understood the semantic difference between "stress" and "strain," that is, between the load a body is subjected to and the consequent resulting strain felt in the body. What he had in mind was actually the latter (Levi, 2002).

Nevertheless, neither the intra-scientific controversy around the term nor the fact that Selye based it on animal experiments only could prevent the spread of the term. By that time, the usage of the stress term and its penetration of popular consciousness were no longer in Selye's hands or even in those of the scientific community. The term had stirred the hearts of the general public, and not least the military, who had incorporated the term into their language and everyday explanations. Stress became a term of the times (Hobfoll, 1998).

Wealth and welfare

Having entered popular consciousness as a result of the collective experiences of depression and ensuing world war, the stress term quickly found its way into the everyday life of the post-war era. Despite the "cold war" between East and West, life during the "golden years" of the 1950s and 1960s did not cause any serious strain to most people, at least not of the life-threatening kind. As it turned out, however, this proved no obstacle to the continued usage and development of the term. People in general and medical science in particular had found, in the term "stress," an explanation why human beings fell ill, and it was an explanation they were determined to exploit. Instead of economic ruin, starvation, and shelling attacks, they merely had to adapt to the stress-filled events and to transform them "downward" into approaching the everyday context of middle-class life. During the 1950s and 1960s stress research also developed around so-called life events.

By life event is meant a separate event in the personal or social environment of an individual which, in one way or another, changes her life. The American researchers Thomas Holmes and Richard Rahe (1967) developed a scale, the *Social Readjustment Rating Scale*, measuring how many and how serious events an individual was faced with during a specific period of time. Each event was allotted a number of points with regard to the time and energy necessary for adaptation in relation to "marriage" defined as 50 points. The ratings were made by a representative group of people. The points for the events an individual had been faced with during this specific time frame were added up to a *Life Change Unit Score*. The life events and their ratings might vary from "Christmas feast" (12 units), "change of living quarters" (20 units), "pregnancy" (40 units), "losing one's job" (47 units), "divorce" (73 units) to "decease of husband or wife" (100 units). The scale, as seen, does not take into account the positive or negative character of events, but measures the resources required to adapt to a new situation. In several studies it was found that a higher life event score was linked to an increased risk of cardiovascular disease, such as sudden cardiac death. In later studies it has been found that negative and unexpected events have a larger impact on the health risks. The scientific journalist Alvin Toffler (1970) also brought attention to the research around life events and health risks when he, at the end of the 1960s, described how various trends in society resulted in an accelerated pace of changes within areas such as production, consumption, economics, social relations, and geographical mobility. On the whole, however, life event research and the scale that was being used perhaps more than anything else bear witness to the anticipation of a change from the relatively calm and predictable life most people still led in the 1950s and 1960s. It was also in relation to that life and that type of problem that the term stress was given its context.

Bearing this type of problem in mind, it is perhaps inexplicable that, toward the end of the 1960s, the explanation for the origins of various stress symptoms shifted from separate events in the surrounding world to the separate ways an individual has of understanding and coping with these events. Associated with this shift is, first and foremost, the American psychologist Richard Lazarus. He understood stress in terms of unique external or internal demands, which the individual appraises as straining or exceeding her resources. The thought is here that the individual herself, consciously or subconsciously, makes an appraisal of the demands imposed on her, comparing them with what resources she has at her disposal for coping with them. Stress reactions arise when the individual, in her appraisal, arrives at the conclusion that the demands are so great that the resources will not suffice. What is interesting is that the individual not only interprets and appraises the situation, but also tries to respond to and master it. Lazarus assumes that we humans do not just react passively to the situation we are facing, but that we manipulate it in the hope of arriving at a suitable strategy for dealing with it (Lazarus, 1981). In a more recent model of stress, the Cognitive Activation Theory of Stress (CATS) by Ursin and Eriksen (2004), more strict and formal logistic definitions of the stress concepts have been proposed. For example, "helplessness" is defined as the perceived lack of association between the individual's coping resources and the outcome of the threatening situation and "hopelessness" is defined as the individual's feeling that any attempt to cope with a stressful situation will fail. "Helplessness" and "hopelessness" will induce chronic stress and lead to mental and physical health problems according to well-known pathophysiological mechanisms described below. Expectancy of a positive outcome of a stressful situation ("I will manage"), on the other hand, will induce short-term activation followed by relaxation, a situation that will not induce stress-related disorders but, on the contrary, rather strengthens the individual's coping resources.

This certainly appears plausible and in line with how we believe ourselves to react to problematic and troublesome situations. However, the plausibility also follows from us probably thinking about a different type of situation than those that originally made the stress concept a preferred explanation to various social problems. Characteristic of the situations we imagine are, first, that they are ambiguous and may be interpreted in several ways. Second, they are shaped within a social context. We define them communally and they assume their meaning in and through a social process. Third, the situation does not simply lead to a reflexive and intuitive reaction on our part. Instead, it is a situation which may be dealt with in several different ways. And that is not enough; the way in which we deal with it will give rise to a new situation, which has to be interpreted, evaluated, and dealt with. The way in which we deal with the current situation hence has repercussions for our opportunities to deal with successive situations, situations which we at first may not be able to gain a comprehensive overview of. One typical example of such a situation is a divorce. The parties involved usually view the issue at hand in completely different ways and, in addition, disagree about which is the right way. Furthermore, it is an extended process in which both parties say and do things that completely change conditions for any further development. In the end, neither of them is able to say how it all started or how to put a stop to it all.

This means that the way in which we interpret and deal with a difficult situation, alone or in company with others, will have an impact not only on ourselves and our further actions, but also on our surroundings. Lazarus was also, at an early stage, involved in studies of the impact of stress in a larger social context. He studied, for instance, the impact of stress on the ability to perform qualified tasks (Lazarus and Eriksen, 1952) on recovery after medical treatment (Cohen and Lazarus, 1973) and the possibilities of dealing with stress at the workplace (Lazarus, 1991). These situations were all of a completely different kind from the potentially life-threatening situations Cannon and Selye employed in their experiments. In an acute life-threatening situation stress systems are activated which help the individual to cope and survive, whereas long-term mental stress induced by rumination and worrying may keep bodily systems activated for a long period of time and prevent rest and recovery. In response to chronic psychosocial stress, activation of physiological stress systems is harmful rather than protective and may induce various stress-related disorders.

Stress Models for the Work Life

Lazarus's research shows how the stress concept has adapted itself to the mainly social problems characterizing the industrial welfare society emerging after the Second World War. Outside the purely clinical sector the most acute consciousness of the problems was probably to be found within working life. During the entire twentieth century, industrial science tried to make activities more efficient by harmonizing the individual with the production process of which his work formed a part. Here, theories of the human being and his needs varied with the demands that production made of his work at that specific moment (Allvin, 1997). It was possible for the concept of stress to also link to these theories. In connection with the large organizations of the 1950s and 1960s, where gaining an overview was impossible, American researchers developed the idea of stress as a consequence of, for instance, role conflict, role ambiguity, and role overload (Kahn et al., 1964). Another model emphasized the necessity of the individual and his surroundings being fitted to one another (person–environment fit). Stress arose if the needs and their satisfaction, or the demands and the ability to deal with them, were not sufficiently suited to each other (Caplan, 1983).

Work environment and the good work: The demand-control model

In the Western world as a whole the enormous growth of the post-war years had taken place within the framework of a consensus between the parties of the labor market and a more or less pronounced welfare state. In countries like Sweden, this consensus was to a large extent developed on the initiative of the workers' movement. This meant that growth was used also for the development of work per se. In contrast to many other countries in the Western world, above all the Anglo-Saxon ones, where growth to a large extent was transformed into wage increases and private consumption, Sweden invested in development of considerable scope and the institutionalization of job centers, labor market measures, labor legislation, compensation systems, industrial safety, and welfare and working environments. One stage in the development was the expansion of the concept of working environment to include not just the physically and chemically affected environment, but also the social and mental environment. The wealth increase brought about by the post-war era hence came to be distributed almost exclusively through work. Consequently, the Swedish welfare was also shaped by work. It was in the workplace that welfare was to be displayed, politics generated, knowledge conveyed, values spread, individuals socialized, misfits rehabilitated, public health promoted, and democracy consolidated. Great effort was expended to make working conditions as good as possible. Sweden became the world leader in quality working environments (Allvin and Aronsson, 2003).

At the outset, the most important thing was for people to get a job with adequate remuneration and to make sure they did not suffer any harm at work. But in the 1960s and still more during the 1970s, the level of ambition was raised. It was not enough not to suffer any harm at the workplace if work at the same time was soul-destroying, deadly boring, and dumbing-down. In other words, it was not enough to distribute health and wealth. Work also had to give people an opportunity for development. In order to achieve this, developing jobs were needed. Consequently, industrial science in Sweden came to be more than a mere instrument of rationalization. It also developed into an instrument of the political will to create "the good work." One stress model formulated in accordance with that assignment implied that stress reactions arise not only as a consequence of demands that are too high in relation to the individual ability, that is, overstimulation, but also as a consequence of too low demands, that is, understimulation (Frankenhaeuser and Johansson, 1981). Examples of overstimulation include having too much to do, too high a work tempo, too difficult work tasks, or a conflict of demands. Examples of understimulation include overly monotonous and repetitive work tasks, where one is not able to put one's education, experience, or knowledge to use, where one finds no development, no new learning, and no variation.

Another stress model is the American Robert Karasek's demand-control model (Karasek, 1979). The model has since been further elaborated in cooperation with Töres Theorell at the Karolinska Institute, Sweden (Karasek and Theorell, 1990; Theorell, 2002, 2004, 2008a, 2008b). This model also points to the danger of over- and understimulation, but adds an activity dimension. According to the model, stress in the work life is not simply a question of high or low demands at work. The demands are also interacting with and moderated by the control one has, or lacks, of the performance of one's work or, differently phrased, by the extent of one's space for action and decision, the *job decision latitude*, at work (see Figure 5.1).

The space for action consists of two aspects: everyday democracy and the individual's competence to exert control (Theorell, 2002, 2004). The "everyday democracy," in turn, may be divided up into two aspects. The first is task control, concerning the possibilities to influence how work is to be performed, what is to be performed, when, in what sequence, etc. The second aspect concerns participation in decision making, where Theorell differentiates between different forms or levels of participation or influence. Examples of this include information from management to the employees or the other way round: consultations, negotiations, and decision making. Levels are seen as structures for creating conditions of fairness in the workplace. "Competence to exert control" of one's situation is developed before one starts a specific job and at the actual workplace. Competence to exert control implies, for example, that the employee is prepared and equipped to take control of unexpected situations at work.

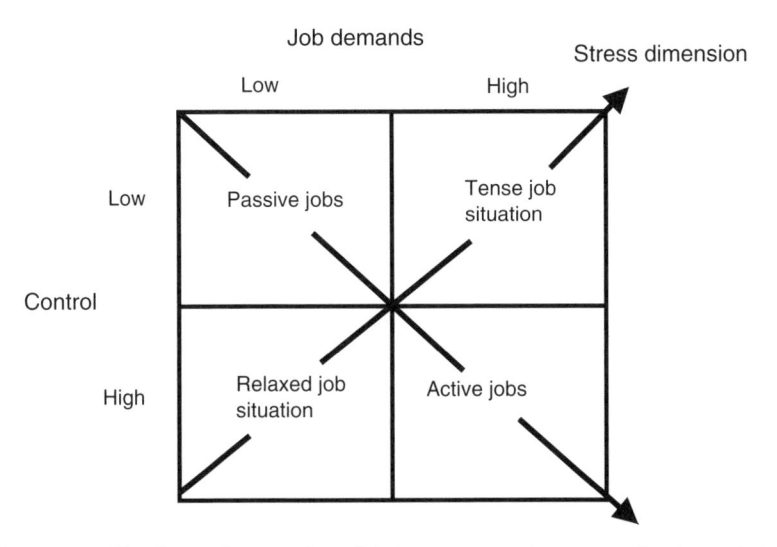

Figure 5.1 The demand-control model. (Source: Karasek, 1979. Used with permission of Administrative Science Quarterly © 1979 by Cornell University.)

An individual who has a high level of control (large space for action) is also able to deal with higher demands, not the least by being able to plan, influence, and delegate her work. The control dimension of this model also comprises variation, development, and learning. But more than that, the model also claims that whoever enjoys a high level of control will not only be able to deal with high demands, they will also be stimulated by them. For individuals with low levels of control (small space for action) the opposite is the case. As the employee lacks the space for dealing with high demands he or she will instead feel pressured by them. Lowering the demands, however, is not a solution. The result of work in a situation characterized by tension is an accumulation of tension in the worker. This may act as an impediment on the learning process in the long run. In a workplace where, for an extended period of time, one finds oneself in a situation of high demands and a low level of control it may be difficult to exploit an increase in space for action. In the psychology of learning, this has been interpreted, for instance, as "learned helplessness" (Seligman, 1975). The opposite is also true. At workplaces where, through a good balance of demands and control, one has been able to develop strategies for dealing with stress, one is also more likely to be able to cope better with times of trouble.

From a point of departure in this model, Karasek, Theorell, and others have shown that tense work situations are linked to an increased risk of cardiovascular disease (Johnson et al., 1996; Belkic et al., 2000). The model also explains why so many individuals in the lower ranks of organizations contract cardiovascular disease and other symptoms of stress, whereas the admittedly high demands higher up in the organizational hierarchy do not have the same effects on the individual.

The original demand-control model has also been elaborated to include a third variable – social support. When social support is included, the model expands from its emphasis on the individual's relation to her work and work tasks to include interaction and relations in the workplace. A third dimension crystallizes – isolation versus the collective (Johnson and Hall, 1988). Social support is no simple and theoretically pure concept. Certain facets of the concept, for instance, are related to participation in decision making. When the concept is linked to research tradition four separate meanings appear (Johnson and Hall, 1988), stretching from the individual to the collective level.

- Social support which meets fundamental human needs of comradeship and group belonging at work (requirements theory).
- Social support as a factor of socialization, which benefits an active action pattern (socialization theory).
- Social support as a resource for modifying the effect of the work load (resource theory).
- Social support which, on a structural level, protects the body of workers against more substantial demands and strains from the industrial system. Viewed from this perspective, social support is a basis for control, power, and identity in the body of workers (collective theory).

In the two last senses, the support may be viewed as an expression of collective control. Also, social support as a factor of socialization may be interpreted from a perspective of the collective. Professional knowledge, norms for relationships, and performances are then shifted to the individual and internalized in the cognitive and emotional structures regulating the action repertory of the individual. In this expanded model stress is hence related not only to the demands of work, but also to social structures.

It is no coincidence in countries like Sweden that the interest in health and influence control increased drastically during the 1970s and 1980s when there was a boom in concern for the collective influence of employees at work. The instigators of this development were the union organizations – not least the unions organizing the greater worker collectives. But the model was also acceptable to the employers who, in the increased influence of the employees, saw a means of reducing the individual's instrumental relation to his or her work as a prospect potentially benefiting production. During this time, the interplay of stress research on the one hand and democracy and influence research on the other was also intensified.

What is here of interest to us is that the model brings together contemporary political trends and the research around influence and control with the discoveries of stress research concerning the physiological and psychological limitations of human beings and their need for predictability and control. The psychobiological program of the individual has its granted space in the model, but the explanatory variables are primarily those of the social and material structures of organizations that may be viewed as an expression of power and relationships of domination.

But the model does not have a simply social and organizational perspective of stress. Above all, it explains stress in a certain type of job, namely jobs where control is so low as to allow space for significant changes through a reorganization of work, but not low enough for the workers to lack any form of commitment to their work. Such work we may find in many industries among lower officials and within relatively traditional bureaucratic organizations. Further, the model refers to a type of work in which an expansion of the space for action also entails greater control. The space for action is here not so great that an expansion of it instead leads to a perception of lesser control, which would rather be the case in the free jobs discussed in previous chapters. Finally, the model explains what in work is stressful with reference to the actual workplace. This requires that the work in question allows itself to be quite clearly delineated, both from the instability of the labor market and from life in general, which is not the case when working conditions are being deregulated and organizations are becoming more flexible.

The effort-reward-imbalance model

Demands, control, and social support are factors in the immediate surroundings. They also may be influenced to a relatively large extent through work-organizational measures. However, during the latter part of the 1980s, and still more during the 1990s, the social and political conditions for measures of this kind changed significantly. The neoliberal administrations of Margaret Thatcher and Ronald Reagan ruled Great Britain and the United States of America. In Sweden, the economic crisis of the 1990s upset the union initiative to organize the good work. Gradually, social engineering had to give way for the dynamic of the market. During the 1990s, unemployment grew, as did the differences in wage and employment conditions. Professional groups and individuals attractive to the labor market developed and negotiated advantageous conditions whereas the less attractive stagnated in wage terms and saw their conditions deteriorating. Labor market conditions and the individual employment contract, formal as well as informal, grew in importance in relation to the common organization at the workplace.

Against this backdrop, the "demand-control-support model" with its focus on the organization and influence of the workplace does not capture the new conditions. During the latter part of the 1990s another stress model caught the attention of industrial scientific research. The model in question is the so-called *effort-reward-imbalance* model, its originator is Johannes Siegrist (1996, 2008), and like the demand-control-support model it is a model developed for large-scale epidemiological studies. In simple terms, the model can be said to focus on what the job or professional role has to offer the individual. A large effort on the part of the individual has to lead to a corresponding reward on the part of the employer. An imbalance here increases the risk of ill health. Through work the individual is able to contribute with her performance and receive a reward. Work also entails social belonging. How these potentially positive conditions are realized depends on whether they are based on mutuality and fairness. The efforts of the individual at work are seen as part of a socially organized exchange process where society sets the reward. Rewards are, however, not merely material but also psychological and social. They are distributed through three different channels: money (material), appreciation (psychological), and status and career opportunities (social). Employment security may also be included in the model and then intersects all forms of reward. The similarities to research about psychological contracts and breaches of contract are evident. According to the model, a lack of mutuality and fairness regarding the individual's "costs" and "dividends," more specifically high costs and low dividends, is what creates the emotional strain which in turn may lead to ill health. A worse contract or a change for the worse in an existing contract may hence be a contributory cause of ill health.

In conformity with the demand-control-support model, the effort-reward-imbalance model is based on external conditions, but also includes various individual patterns of action and personality. One such pattern is "overcommitment," representing a marked result orientation in combination with a strong need to be liked and appreciated, sometimes also described as "performance-based self-esteem." Siegrist describes situations where great efforts on the part of the individual were triggered by an underestimation of the scope of the task and an overestimation of the personal ability combined with a strong underlying need for appreciation and praise.

A prerequisite of the effort-reward model seems to be that the individual exists in a market where she is expected to be able to choose or at least influence her conditions. She establishes relationships in the shape of informal social contracts. The model emphasizes individual motivation with strategic or instrumental acting as its basis. In this sense, the model has an individualist starting point but, through its subsequent focus on career and employment conditions, still goes beyond the immediate conditions of the individual at the workplace in order to find the explanations of individual stress and ill health. In doing this the model is a development and an adaptation to the increasingly market-oriented conditions of the new work life.

Illegitimate tasks as stressors and stress as offense to the self

We mentioned earlier in the chapter that role-related concepts had an important impact on work-life stress research in the 1960s when the work conditions and work environment questions began to attract attention. Concepts such as quantitative and qualitative over- and underload came to constitute important elements of the emerging work-oriented stress research. Role stress, role conflict, and subconstruct as role ambiguity and person–role conflicts were further concepts in the frame of reference emerging with researchers at the Institute for Social Research in Michigan. These role-related concepts did not have the same broad impact in work-life stress research as overload and underload had for analyses of the then dominant working environment problems in the industry. This is perhaps not surprising as Tayloristic organizational principles in general had the objective to reduce any ambiguity in the work, reduce complexity, and simplify the blue-collar work.

With roots in these concepts the Swiss researcher Norbert Semmer and his collaborators have developed the theory of illegitimate tasks and stress as offense to the self. According to Semmer the illegitimate task concept is a focused variant of the person–role conflict. We believe that the illegitimate task perspective covers aspects of work conditions that other stress theories do not address, and that the perspective has great explanatory power in a work life that is moving toward increasingly fluid and boundless working conditions and where demands for flexibility are high. It concerns above all one of the four boundaryless dimensions, namely the work task and its vertically and horizontally boundaries.

From a psychological point of view professional occupations are characterized by a close link between professional role and identity, and stress can be said to arise from the tension between these two aspects. New technologies and changes in the control system lead to changes in professional roles but also to the role of ambiguity as well as power and status shifts. Professional role implies what might be expected of the individual in the role but also what cannot be expected under normal circumstances or what the role occupant will regard as illegitimate tasks.

Semmer's theory focuses attention on tasks that do not belong to the "core" of the work role (Semmer et al., 2007, 2009). The theory, supported by empirical evidence, is that the stressors are valued differently depending on whether they belong to the profession's core tasks or not. In order to analyze and explain reasons for stress it is therefore necessary to draw attention to the existence of tasks outside the profession's core. Tasks are regarded as legitimate when they conform to standards of what can reasonably be expected from a role occupant, and they are perceived as illegitimate if they violate these standards. These kinds of task are conceived as offending one's professional identity, and thus the self (Semmer et al., 2009, p. 70). A task is therefore not illegitimate in itself. A job may be legitimate for a person in one occupation, but not for persons in another occupation. An individual may also perceive a task as legitimate in one situation but illegitimate in another. An example of this can be when a person is doing extra activities outside of what can be expected in the role, and this happens when someone is on sick leave. If the manager has a wider defined role than the subordinates and does not clarify the context, the employee can perceive the same task as illegitimate.

Illegitimate tasks should also be distinguished from extra-role performance that is done on the initiative of the role owner himself. In our studies, we could see examples of this type of voluntarily expansion of the work role. There could be many reasons for such voluntary work – the workers were inexperienced and did not know the acceptable standards for the work task or they were engaged in such tasks because they wanted to help work comrades.

The perspective thus brings forward that stress outcomes depend not only on the stressor in itself but are linked to the professional role and its boundaries and to the individual's identity and self-perception. The link between identity and role means that tasks that confirm the professionalism create pride and self-esteem while tasks outside the profession's core and non-professional role become a threat to identity and self-esteem. When people are commanded or in other softer forms assigned to tasks that are incompatible with their professional roles then those tasks become stressors and a threat to the individual identity. According to Semmer this can be seen as an offense to the self (Semmer *et al.*, 2009, p. 73).

The theory points out two categories of illegitimate tasks: unreasonable and unnecessary. Unreasonable tasks are outside the range of one's occupation. It can be incompatible with one's occupational status, like when beginners are assigned to tasks that are too difficult or when experts are assigned tasks far below their ability. The individual experiences this as not fair. An unnecessary task is defined as a task that should not have to be carried out.

The illegitimate task theory opens new ways of analyzing stress when turbulent changes alter occupational roles and tasks. Such alterations are carried out in Sweden, as in many other countries, through restructuring after the global financial crisis and recession, through privatization, and through new forms of governance such as New Public Management. It concerns occupational groups all over the labor market, but not least professional occupations that had their working conditions and jobs changed. There is a lack of broad descriptive studies of changes in professional work, but there are indications that professionals devote more of their working time to administrative tasks, documentation, and policy-related tasks outside the profession. These tasks have a potential for being perceived as illegitimate. What this development means for the strain and stress among professionals is not well studied. The illegitimate task perspective has intuitive application in professional work but its scope is broader and the theory may be useful for analyzing many situations where roles are changed and people are assigned new tasks.

Time pressure and commitment to work

But the 1990s were not characterized solely by individual employment contracts, changing conditions, and new possibilities on the labor market. It was also a time when technical and global changes increasingly started appearing as both unavoidable and socioeconomically necessary. It was no longer possible not to choose, or even pretend not to notice, information technology and globalization. Cut-downs on personnel, for purposes of enhancing competitiveness, increased the workload of remaining personnel. At the same time, the changing competence demands, time pressure, and overexertion in the work life were starting to be taken seriously. Psychological problems became more prevalent and spread to previously unaffected groups. The tempo in the work life accelerated. Highly qualified and motivated entrepreneurs and professional employees wore themselves out and "hit the wall," having worked too intensively for too long. These people lacked neither influence nor control in their work. They had appreciation and good conditions. Also, it was difficult to see the phenomenon as a problem of the working environment, or even as a collective problem at all, when it was the individuals who, of their own accord, pushed themselves to the brink of exhaustion. Far from everyone was hit, and apart from the time pressure and high demands the conditions of the sufferers were often quite different. Still, it was obviously a question of some kind of imbalance between the individual and his environment.

Research came to orient itself increasingly toward the human constitution and the capacity of the body. Although physical reactions have always had a place in the various stress models, explanations were not generally sought in the body. Instead, they were detected in the environment or the human attitude to this environment. But as the methods for identifying biological stress markers developed, primarily through more easily administered measurements of stress hormones in urine and the saliva, biological explanations once again rose in esteem. Before entering more deeply into the stress model commonly referred to in this context, we ought to say something general about the reactions of the body to stress.

Bodily reactions to stress

When we are subjected to stress, there are two systems in the body mainly controlling what happens. For both of these, activation originates in the brain. Mental processes in the cortex (perceived stress) signal to the hypothalamus, which is the stress "center" of the brain and which sends out signals to the body via nerves, the secretion of hormones, and the immune system. One system is the "sympathetic nervous system." This system sends signals from the brain to the adrenal medulla which responds by secreting the two stress hormones adrenaline and noradrenaline. These hormones quickly enter the blood circulation and affect other body functions, especially the cardiovascular system and the release of energy from the liver in the form of lipids and glucose. The other major system reacting to stress consists of the hypothalamo-pituitary adrenocortical system. The pituitary gland is stimulated to secrete an adrenocortical stimulating hormone (ACTH) which, via the blood circulation, promotes the secretion of cortisol from the adrenal cortex. Cortisol is a stress hormone that affects the metabolism in the cells and the functioning of the immune system. Cortisol levels in the blood are registered and regulated in various brain centra. In normal circumstances, this means that a feedback system continuously regulates the cortisol levels in relation to the demands of the environment. If these regulatory mechanisms are damaged or if their sensitivity is altered, cortisol levels may become too high or too low or not respond adequately to a challenge, which negatively affects the dynamic of the entire system. The result may be that the body is unable to activate the system in the case of an acute stress exposure, and is also unable to return to the original resting level once the stressful situation is over. This will compromise the individual's chances to cope with various demands and increase the risk of health problems.

The sympathetically activated adrenal medullary system of adrenaline and noradrenaline reacts very quickly, and the amount of adrenaline and noradrenaline in the blood may increase dramatically in less than a minute, while the pituitary adrenocortical system is much slower to react. The cortisol level of the blood peaks only about 30 minutes after stress exposure and cortisol is therefore of specific importance in adaptation to long-term stress. Adrenaline and noradrenaline are commonly regarded as the active defense reaction of the body (*fight or flight response*), while the cortisol reaction is regarded as a reaction to defeat or dejection (Henry, 1992; Frankenhaeuser, 1993; Sapolsky, [1998]2004) preparing the body for a more extended mobilization of energy. To sum up, the activation of these systems has as its purpose to mobilize energy in a situation of acute danger. The psychological and physiological reactions in a situation of chronic stress differ in many ways from those resulting from acute short-term stress. While acute stress, for instance, strengthens the immune system and certain memory functions, increases performance efficiency, and reduces the sensitivity to pain, long-term stress has the opposite effects. Stress hormones, which can be measured in blood, urine, and saliva, can be used as measures of individual stress level but also constitute a link between psychosocial stress and a number of health problems.

The balance between catabolic and anabolic processes. The activation of various biological stress reactions, such as increased heart rate, increased blood pressure, and the mobilization of energy in the form of lipids and glucose in the blood, allows the individual greater resources for coping with strains of different kinds, above all with those demanding physical effort. In conditions of stress the mobilization of resources primarily concerns resources already stored and available in the body. Creating extra nutrition for the cells of the body through the ingestion of food and subsequent digestion would simply take too long. Processes activated by stress may therefore be described as processes taxing bodily resources, or catabolic processes, and serve as a protection of various organs and functions in the body in connection with acute stress exposure. Contributory to these catabolic processes is primarily the secretion of stress hormones into the blood following signals from the brain.

These acute stress reactions are hence processes of vital importance but in order for them to function properly there is also a need for periods of rest and recovery. Between periods of acute mobilization, especially during sleep, the body goes through a process of growth, digestion, storing of resources, strengthening of the immune functions, healing and repair of damage, etc., that is, various anabolic processes, controlled for instance by sex hormones and growth hormones. Sleep has also been proposed to be of importance for consolidation of memories.

In order for the individual to function properly and for well-being, a reasonable long-term balance must be attained between activity and rest/recovery, that is, between catabolic and anabolic processes. The implication of this is that intensive activity, for example in the form of work, is not per se damaging for the body. Provided that the activity is followed by an adequate period of rest, humans and animals can be exposed to intense as well as to extended periods of stress without serious health consequences.

The allostatic stress model. This is also the realization on which the so-called allostatic stress model is built, formulated by the American researcher Bruce McEwen (1998). The allostatic stress model describes under which conditions our biological stress reactions may be good for our health and well-being, and under which circumstances these reactions may constitute a health risk. In conformity with other models it emphasizes the importance of adaptation. But in contrast with, for instance, the demand-control-support model it is not the environment and then particularly not the organizational environment that is to be adapted to the human being. Instead, the model assumes that the environment will be in constant flux and that human beings will continuously adapt themselves to their environment. Like the term homeostasis, allostasis refers to the idea of balance. However, in contrast to homeostasis, allostasis does not refer to a structural state, but to the process through which the body continuously adapts itself to the demands of the environment. It may be described as "the flexibility of the body giving rise to stability." The equilibrium achieved is therefore a balance over time, between activity and rest. In other words, the allostatic stress model is concerned with the individual's need for a natural rhythm in everyday life.

The adequate and healthy way of reacting to stress entails a quick activation of the various body systems that increase the individual's capability of dealing with a threatening situation. When the individual experiences stress, for instance, in the shape of excessive demands or a very high work pace, it influences, among other systems, the cardiovascular system. The heart rate and the blood pressure increase, and the blood is redistributed from the gastrointestinal system and from the skin to the working muscles, the heart, and the brain. Energy for the cells is released from the liver in the form of glucose and lipids. The production of anabolic hormones, such as sex hormones, decreases. Processes contributing to long-term growth and survival, such as healing, metabolism, growth, and reproduction, under circumstances like these have to stand back for the acute mobilization of energy. Furthermore, the coagulative ability of the blood increases and sensitivity to pain decreases at the same time as concentration is focused on the "acute threat" and certain memory systems are reinforced (Sapolsky, [1998]2004). Taken together, these "extraordinary" reactions contribute to the enhanced ability of the individual and the protection of the body. Muscles, the heart, and the brain receive more blood and nutrition. In the case of injury, blood loss will be minimal and the pain of an injury subdued.

These energy-mobilizing reactions are useful, above all, in the case of physical threat, but enhanced concentration powers and reinforced memory functions are advantageous also in the context of mental challenges. The individual is able to focus her full attention on the situation at hand and will better remember how she got into the situation, increasing the chances of avoiding similar "threat situations" in the future.

Reaction patterns like these are therefore believed to have been necessary for the survival of humans and animals, for their development and adaptation to new conditions during millions of years. One may assume that conditions during the earlier stages of human development were relatively stable for very long periods of time and that changes in the environment happened only gradually. Conditions like these have enabled a successive evolutionary adaptation, that is, individuals with the "right" traits have had the largest chance of survival and of passing on their genes to the next generation. Some human species have by evolution been driven out of competition and died out. Only Homo sapiens has survived to our days and come to dominate earth. However, during the last few thousand years, and especially during the most recent century, the changes confronting man are of his own making. The speed of change has also accelerated. Biologically speaking, today's human being is the same individual as one a hundred thousand years ago. The stress reactions mobilizing above all physical strength, however, are not always as well suited to their purpose in the society and work life of today where mental demands are more common than physical ones. The inadequate mobilization of resources to prepare for "battle" in response to psychosocial stress is considered to be a key factor in the relation between stress and health. But high physical demands may of course be found in today's society and work life as well, for example, when delivering a child, in construction work, or in healthcare jobs.

In order for the physiological systems to work at their optimum an acute activation requires a successive quick deactivation. As soon as the "threat" is over the body needs an opportunity for rest and recovery. For Stone Age man, the "threat" may have consisted of attack by wild animals or hostile human beings, a storm, or an intensive hunt for prey. Between these periods of acute stress one may assume existence to have been fairly calm. When the basic needs of food and shelter were fulfilled, time was probably spent eating, mating, resting, and sleeping. At that time, no artificial light was available except in terms of a fire, and humans had to adapt their activities to the presence of daylight. This means that during the dark period of the day our ancestors had to be rather inactive. Today, humans can be active 24 hours a day thanks to electric light and various means of communication. In today's work life, the "threat" may consist of not being able to finish a project on time, not having the time to write a report for a meeting, making a public speech, participating in a debate, perceiving a conflict between work and family responsibilities, caring for an injured or ill fellow being, or instructing and helping a co-worker, that is, demands that do not allow themselves to be resolved by a "fight or flight" response. The psychological strain of this stress is often also protracted in time and the individual is unable to switch off the exposure in the same way as in the case of physical threats or strains. Long-term high blood pressure, a high heart rate, high levels of blood lipids, increased coagulation, and stress hormones will in this case harm the body, the cardiovascular system in particular, instead of protecting the organism.

According to the allostatic model, ill health may occur in conditions of both over- and under-activity in the allostatic stress systems. Over-activity may occur when the individual is repeatedly exposed to stress while receiving too little time for rest and recovery between the exposures. An example of such a situation could be when a medical doctor at an emergency ward is obliged to take care of a stream of new patients with no time for rest in between, when fire-fighters and police repeatedly respond to emergencies, or when a teacher, apart from a number of demanding classes, also has to be personally engaged in the psychological and social conditions of the pupils outside the classroom and worry about cut-downs and reorganizations on his own part. If, in addition, time outside work is teeming with various demands, the allostatic load increases further still.

Over-activity in the stress systems may arise when the strain is of a long-term character or when the individual is unable to relax. This may be the case for people caring for a chronically ill relative, a commitment entailing constant activation. It may also relate to work tasks and responsibilities which cannot be dropped, as well as anxiety for future events. Such conditions result in an over-exposure to stress hormones, long-term increased blood pressure, and a high heart rate. Digestion will not function properly as the body is focused on action. Furthermore, the individual will experience insomnia due to high levels of adrenaline in the blood. She will sleep badly and wake up early. And as sleep is the most important recovery period, lack of sleep means the individual will have to mobilize more resources still in order to cope with the next day's work. This may be the start of a vicious circle potentially leading to a state of exhaustion.

Under certain circumstances the reactive ability of certain systems may decrease. The sensitivity of a system, for instance, may rise or fall depending on the upward or downward regulation of the receptors reacting to certain hormones. Insufficient mobilization of one particular system may entail compensatory overreactions in other systems, contributing to an imbalance between biological systems and ensuing health problems. For example, the balance may be upset between the activities of the sympathetic and parasympathetic systems. These systems have opposite effects on a number of functions. Increased activity in the sympathetic nervous system, for instance, increases the heart rate, while increased activity in the parasympathetic system will lower it. Under normal circumstances, cortisol keeps the immune system in control. If cortisol levels become abnormally low, there is a risk of the immune system becoming overactive, causing allergies or attacking healthy cells in the body, which is what happens in the case of autoimmune diseases such as type 1 diabetes, arthritis, and systemic lupus erythematosus (SLE). If cortisol levels instead are raised over an extended period of time the immune system is weakened and the risk of infection enlarged, sensitivity to insulin falls, and the production of sex hormones is hampered. Sheldon Cohen (2005, 2009) and his colleagues in a series of controlled experiments have demonstrated the effect of stress on susceptibility of upper respiratory infections. For example, individuals exposed to two years of stress were four times as likely to develop a common cold compared to individuals not exposed to stress when all participants had been exposed to the common cold virus. In addition to all this, fat storage is stimulated in the abdomen because of the large number of cortisol receptors located on the fat cells there. This fat is very mobile and may quickly enter the blood stream in the shape of free fatty acids, increasing the risk of cardiovascular disease. Furthermore, the insulin sensitivity of the cells falls, increasing the risk of type 2 diabetes.

The ability of the body to cope with intensive acute stress is quite adequate for a limited duration of time. One example is childbirth when stress hormones may increase tenfold or more compared to the usual level. For a healthy young woman a situation like this will not normally entail any risk of permanent health problems. Even in circumstances of purely mental challenges, such as public speaking before a large audience, the adrenaline values may rise to many times the base level. Normal office work usually raises the adrenaline level by approximately 50 to 100 percent compared to the corresponding resting level. This increase is modest compared to what takes place in the event of childbirth. However, the important difference is that the stress load at work is a daily occurrence, endured week after week, month after month, whereas childbirth is relatively short of duration and only takes place once or a few times in life. No individual would survive these extraordinarily high stress levels for an extended period of time. Supporting evidence also points to a long-term or chronic stress load being more of a problem today than short-term intensive stress, presuming that the short but intense period of stress is followed by a period of rest. Typical signs of emerging serious stress-related health problems are the occurrence of a number of symptoms at the same time, such as impaired performance, lack of motivation and problems to concentrate and stay focused, memory problems, diffuse pain in the body, sleeping problems, frequent or long-lasting infections, chest pain, palpitations, oversensitivity, and dizziness.

In this passage, we have discussed various stress models relating to the development of society and work life. The purpose of this has not been merely to give an introduction to stress as a concept and area of research, but also to show how the concept is constantly shaped and reshaped in connection with the historical and social context in which it is being used. The various stress models are therefore attempts at explaining and solving the problems society is facing. It also means that any one theory is not necessarily more right or true than the next. Rather, the theories are adapted to different realities. Explanations for stress and ill health appearing in bureaucratic organizations in the 1960s and 1970s focused on the organizational limitations of the actual workplace. In the 1990s, when differences in employment conditions increased and became more individual, conditions outside the workplace, personal abilities, and their relation to work came to play a greater role. Siegrist (1996) introduced the term "status control" in order to cover the intended external conditions, while Johnson and Hall (1988) discussed the need for developing a conceptual system, placing the interplay of individual and environment in a wider social context. These are the conditions addressed by the effort-reward-imbalance model. The more the economic, organizational, and technical development – with its growing element of market forces and demands always to be active and available – appears necessary, the more the focus of the problem is being shifted from the design of the environment to the individual's abilities to cope with the demands she is facing. Hereby, the allostatic model also comes to contribute to the explanation. The different stress models complement rather than substitute one another. In contrast to the shifting definitions of the concept of stress, the bodily responses to stress have remained the same for thousands of years in humans and animals.

The New Work Life as a Source of Stress

In this book we have discussed the new work life, its various aspects, and consequences. This has included the organization of work, knowledge, and learning as well as life outside work and its relation to work. Perhaps what is most controversial about this work life, and which we have not yet discussed, is to what extent it causes increased strain in people and to what extent it gives people greater opportunities to cope, develop, and prosper.

In large parts of Europe, people are accustomed to regarding working life as part of the well-organized society. The design and conditions of work are something which, to a large extent, is regulated by laws and agreements. Work is also not something we do just because we have to. In other words, the basis of work is not just economic but also political and moral. Work is, more specifically, the means by which the individual may contribute to the whole. It is a way for the individual to justify her existence in the eyes of society. Society, in turn, needs to offer the individual possibilities for work under reasonable conditions. This mutual undertaking is the basis of the often unspoken contract between the individual and society which, for a long time, has been a matter of course in countries with a developed welfare state. When companies and public organizations, to an increasing extent, are exposed to or are opening themselves to the influence of market forces, the conditions of work, however, change fundamentally. This, in turn, has a series of consequences for the demands imposed on the individual.

- When the demands of the market affect the design of work, the regulation of work becomes increasingly varied and flexible. This means that the individual, to a larger extent, personally has to determine when, where, how, with what, and with whom she has to work. The individual also has to take responsibility for, and the consequences of, her work. With the demand for independence, however, follows a greater insecurity for the individual regarding what and how much is expected of her. The consequence is often that she works significantly more than she would otherwise have done.
- When the individual increasingly has to design and determine her work by herself, the social relations and roles around work also become more unclear. People are then more confronted unconditionally with others at work. Among other things, this means that relations between people at work, and between work and life outside it, take on a more open, more ambivalent, and problematic character. All of this adds to the new, higher demands imposed on people today.
- When work to an increasing extent is being defined and motivated from the viewpoint of the logic of market forces, it will also be depoliticized and demoralized. Thereby, the social contract between the individual

and society is jeopardized. The way the individual motivates and identifies with her work is instead brusquely confronted with the fickle but relentless demands of the market. The individual consequently feels exposed and vulnerable.

We will observe these three consequences in due order on the following pages and will draw attention to the resulting augmented strain for the individual. At the same time it is important to keep in mind that more unregulated work offers new opportunities for people to develop their talents and abilities and, thus, for many individuals contribute to an occupational career, wealth, well-being, and health.

The freer the job, the harder it is to free oneself of work

When the conditions of work become more free and flexible, the result is not possibilities only, but also a pressure on the individual to work more. The pressure may of course originate in the individual's personal interest in and feeling for work. In our studies we have several examples of individuals, becoming so absorbed by work that they cannot relax. These are primarily people working in independent positions with great challenges and substantial rewards. There are consultants and developers who never switch their mobile phones off, and who carry their laptops everywhere. There are also staffing personnel who become so intoxicated by their success that they work virtually non-stop (Allvin, Jacobson, and Isaksson, 2003). An extreme example is the phenomenon of "karoshi" identified in Japan. This means that a person works more or less continuously without rest until he or she suddenly dies due to exhaustion (usually a heart attack). This happens to relatively young people who devote all their daily life to work and according to Japanese occupational health statistics the number of "karoshi deaths" has increased in recent years.

But the pressure may also come from outside. The deconstruction of the bureaucratic regulatory frameworks surrounding work, in the interest of a more flexible "post-bureaucratic" organization, is a conscious rationalization measure. The idea is to introduce the demands of the outside world to the employee. Consequently, the employee is not meant to work according to the rigid regulatory framework of the organization, but directed toward the market or its alter ego: the customer. Perhaps the most palpable consequence of this redirection is the increased time pressure on the individual as well as the required ability to deal with fast and recurring changes. Time is no longer a frame or yardstick for work – it is instead something to fight against, something to be vanquished. We have previously described this as the "time environment" of work (Allvin et al., 1999).

Yet another source of pressure, probably more common than is believed, is the personal insecurity of the individual. It concerns all those who, in one way or another, feel pressured to work more than what is formally demanded by the job. It may be due to a lack of personnel, threats of cut-downs, or redundancies. But it may also be due to a personal fear of being vulnerable, passed over, or outrun.

It is not unreasonable to believe that the source of the increasing pressure on the individual carries some significance as to the consequences of this augmented pressure. An individual who is driven by external demands to work a lot will probably sooner see his health impaired than someone driven by their own will to work. At the same time, those encountering the augmented pressure as an external demand may meet it together with others and, hence, find support among co-workers and colleagues. Those who are driven by their own insecurity, on the other hand, are left to their own means and probably see the others at work as a contributing factor to the growing demands.

The demands of the traditional work organization could be countered, to a large extent, with collective strategies. The Norwegian sociologist Sverre Lysgaard (1961) described the worker collective as a protecting buffer between the individual and what Lysgaard called the insatiable demands of the technical/economic system of the company. But when the collective is weakened, there is no longer any strong actor standing between the individual and the demands of the system. The result, as we repeatedly have pointed out in this book, is that the individual is forced to face these demands on their own. The question is to what extent the individual, with his limitations, is able to work out strategies for dealing with the increasingly hazy structures of time and space and to protect himself against excessive demands.

Within traditional work organization, the intensification of work takes place primarily within the time and space frameworks of the job. Overtime is regulated and economically compensated. In the new flexible work, however, the intensification is dealt with by the individual. The individual must hence develop her own personal strategies for responding to the augmented demands. New information technology dissolves or topples the traditional limits of work. The intensification of work is thus increasingly channeled through various individual strategies, compensating or exceeding the limits of the job or of the individual. Three separate types of compensatory or transcending strategies of this kind can be identified (Gustafsson, 2008).

Intensifying work within agreed working hours. The first and perhaps most common type of compensatory strategy is to, within the framework of the normal working hours and the workplace, work more and perform various extra tasks. Primarily, this involves speeding up the work pace – a possibility in many kinds of jobs, but of very limited feasibility in others, for instance, certain kinds of service production.

The next step is to cut down on lunch breaks, or even skip having lunch at all, and reduce meetings and time for reflection. Over the years a great many studies involving all types of work have been carried out across the world describing this type of intensification of work. In the fourth *European Working Conditions Survey* (European Foundation for the Improvement of Living and Working Conditions, 2007), the researchers constructed an index based on the two items "working at a very high speed" and "working to tight deadlines." The analyses showed considerable variation between countries, from the highest rank with more than 50 percent in Sweden, Denmark, Finland, Austria, Cyprus, Greece, and Slovenia, to less than 35 percent in Bulgaria, Latvia, Lithuania, and Poland. One of the clearest trends is that since the first survey was carried out in the beginning of the 1990s there has been a constant rise in the levels of perceived work intensity. This trend is valid for almost all countries in the former EU-15.

Transcending the time-related framing of work. If the first level of compensatory efforts within the time frame proves insufficient, the next and second level of compensatory strategy may be stretching or transcending the formal time frame of the job. One type concerns working more than the formally, or informally, agreed working hours. Finding good statistics of how this is done is difficult when considering the right to overtime compensation. Union sources claim that there has been a deregulation of scale, particularly among professional employee groups. Overtime compensation, for instance, has often been swapped for a week's annual holiday. The total amount of paid overtime appears relatively unchanged throughout the years in Sweden. On the other hand, there is no statistical material showing the development of unpaid overtime. However, as was shown in Chapter 2, it is much more common to be paid for overtime among employees in highly regulated work than in unregulated work. This situation has probably grown over a long period of time.

In one study, common characteristics in groups with a sizable share of unpaid overtime were identified (Aronsson, 1999). One such characteristic is that the work tasks are not managed in detail, or that they cannot be managed in detail with satisfactory results. Rather, the work is goal-directed with goal and result achievement as the main means of control. Work tasks of this kind have no clear work cycle coinciding with or possibility to coordinate mentally with the 9-to-5 schedule or the 40-hour working week. The work tasks of these professional groups are also characterized by the possibility of performing them better than well. There is no obvious point where the result has been achieved and is no longer possible to ameliorate, as is the case in the production of goods. Task quality is also a mirror of the person who performs the task. Good work gives a good service record and vice versa. Being identified with one's task in this manner surely contributes to one's job motivation and to the experience of professional identity and competence, but it also increases the vulnerability to changes, as in the possibilities of career advancement. In other words, work is organized so as to make it difficult to delegate to someone else.

Part of the picture is, as mentioned, that information technology has radically changed the possibility of transcending time and space. Professional jobs or office work tasks that cannot be completed during normal hours at the workplace are easily performed at home or somewhere else. The opportunities for working outside the ordinary workplace also depend on how much control the company or the worker has over working time. If we again look at the analyses in the fourth *European Working Conditions Survey* (European Foundation for the Improvement of Living and Working Conditions, 2007) and compare countries we find a large variation. In Nordic countries and in The Netherlands, workers can choose, to a much higher extent than in other European countries, to adapt working time to their needs. About 50 percent of the workers have the possibility to adapt working hours within certain limits or entirely, which is much higher than in all other groups of countries where work schedules are mostly set by the worker's company with no possibility for changes. These results demonstrate the boundarylessness in Swedish work life concerning the time dimension.

Transcending personal health limits – sickness presence. The third level of compensatory strategies stretches not only the limits of work, but also those of personal health. This manifests itself, for instance, in the phenomenon of "presence despite illness" (Aronsson, Gustafsson, and Dallner, 2000; Aronsson and Gustafsson, 2005a). "Presence despite illness" refers to the phenomenon of people going to work despite problems and ill health, which normally would require rest and absence due to illness. In a broad sense, sickness absence and sickness presence are both rooted in the same general cause: poor health. Sickness absence and sickness presence can be regarded as mutually exclusive alternatives of action in the case of illness and/or reduced work capacity. Since the first studies on sickness presence appeared about 10 years ago the research has increased rapidly and work-related as well as more individual determinants for sickness have been identified.

The first Swedish population study on sickness presenteeism was performed in 1997 (Aronsson, Gustafsson, and Dallner, 2000). Just over a third reported that they had gone to work two or more times during the previous year on occasions when they felt they should have taken sick leave because of their health. The highest level of sickness presenteeism seems to be among those in human service occupations (teachers, medical doctors, nurses, welfare workers, child minders, etc.). Workers in those sectors have a higher frequency of working when sick. One reason may be that workers in this type of work provide for the fundamental human needs of other people. There is a moral obligation to go to work in order to prevent those in need from being left without support. Physicians have been a popular occupational group for studies of sickness presence. A British study found that a large majority of the doctors had worked on some occasion when feeling ill. Low sickness absence acted as a potential health problem among medical doctors (McKevitt *et al.*, 1997). The most common reason for sickness presence was that there was no one else to do the job, which means that their absence would be unfair to their colleagues as patients had already been scheduled. Similar results have been obtained in other studies of physicians by McKevitt and Morgan (1997) and in a Norwegian study (Rosvold and Bjertness, 2001). These studies indicate the importance of value systems and third party relations.

The first wave of sickness presence research showed not surprisingly that poor health is a strong determinant for sickness presence but a hypothesis is that extensive sickness presence also may result in sickness absence and poorer health. That question has been the issue for some recent longitudinal studies, mainly performed in Nordic countries. Virtanen *et al.* (2003) investigated the health and sickness behavior of temporary and permanent employees in Finland. Individuals who went from temporary to permanent positions decreased their level of sickness presenteeism and increased their sickness absence. The reason seemed to be that those with temporary employment tried to qualify for permanent employment by keeping sickness absence low, which leads to their higher sickness presence. Kivimäki *et al.* (2005) also compared two groups (The Whitehall II Study) who were in poor health (due to heart attacks). One group had gone on sick leave while the second group continued to work as usual (sickness presenteeism). After controlling the risk factors, the heart attack risk for the group with sickness presenteeism behavior was doubled after the three-year follow-up. The conclusion was that an over-utilization of sickness presenteeism could lead to deteriorated health.

There are also two new Swedish prospective studies which show that sickness presenteeism has an impact on future general health and also on sickness absence in a follow-up period of three years. Sickness presence on more than five occasions during the baseline year was a statistically significant risk factor for future sick leave of more than 30 days. Two large samples were used, one female-dominated from the public sector and one male-dominated from the private sector (Bergström *et al.*, 2009a; Bergström *et al.*, 2009b).

An interesting and somewhat surprising finding in some recent studies is that sickness presence is more strongly associated with self-reported health than sickness absence (Caverley, Cunningham, and MacGregor, 2007; Aronsson, Gustafsson, and Mellner, 2010). This association is also stronger in groups with low replaceability – often highly educated workers – than in groups reporting replaceable work tasks. It is also stronger in economically constrained groups than in groups with a better economy.

A general conclusion is that sickness presence as a compensatory strategy when ill is related to the increased differentiation of new working life. The highly educated workers go to the job when ill because no one will or can do their tasks, low-paid workers go to the job when ill because they need the money, and temporary workers go to job when ill because they want to qualify for a safer employment.

Another form of compensation strategy is to take out holiday time instead of reporting sick. In one study, 30 percent report having done this (Aronsson and Gustafsson, 2005b). Professional groups have the most extensive use of holidays instead of sickness absence, that is, occupational groups enjoying relatively free jobs, such as social welfare secretaries and social psychologists (over 60 percent), civil engineers, computer specialists, journalists, economists, administrators, and personnel administrative officials are well represented.

Furthermore, when the individual assumes the role of boundary setter, her personal character traits will probably come to play a greater role. Self-esteem is, most probably, one such character trait. It may be divided into basic and performance-based self-esteem (Hallsten, Josephson, and Torgén, 2005; Johnson, 1997). Basic self-esteem is relatively stable and not as easily shaken by the demands of the environment. Performance-based self-esteem, however, requires continuous confirmation. One hypothesis is that people with performance-based self-esteem find it more difficult to defend themselves against excessive demands. The effects of this personal disposition may become particularly critical when the individual is subjected to incompatible demands or a substantial workload. Performance-based self-esteem hence becomes a risk factor for compensatory action strategies.

Yet another behavioral pattern of interest is the so-called workaholism. There are, however, no comprehensive studies comparing the constant supply of work in free jobs with workaholism. Nevertheless, we have in our studies been able to observe how people with a tendency toward workaholism not only work more than others, but also profess to a more pronounced imbalance between work and free time, which might point to work tending to transcend its traditional limits of time and space.

We have here described how the individual meets the increasing demands in her work by simply working more. In order to be able to do this, she develops various compensatory strategies for circumventing the traditional boundaries of work, primarily those limiting the hours and place of work. But many of the demands made by the new work life cannot be resolved by an intensification of work. These demands are of a completely different character.

Social conflicts in and outside the workplace

The more deregulated work becomes, the less formal are also the circumstances under which individuals interact in their work. When, in this way, cooperation is based on competence and person, rather than on function and position, social relations around work come to be more unconditional, complicated, and ambivalent. People put more of their personality into work. References to personal chemistry and social competence become important requirements for cooperation. Cooperation also becomes more emotionally charged. Thereby, it is also more unpredictable, uncontrollable, and demanding.

In combination with the raised demands on performance, social intercourse makes demands that, at times, may be difficult to live up to. It is no longer enough just to do one's job. Whether the individual wants to or not, she is drawn into the social relations surrounding work, its relationships of dependence, power games, and intrigues. Colleagues may be a support, but also may be a source of disappointment, conflicts, inhibitions, and violations, which add to rather than appease the demands of work.

In our studies we have observed conflicts not only between individuals in work groups, but also between different groups within a workplace. These are generally conflicts between those working under freer conditions and those whose work has a more traditional and structured form. It may, for instance, cause envy and distrust between telecommuting professional employees and administrative personnel left at the workplace (Allvin, 2001). It may also cause irritation and the freezing out of individuals who will not accept working overtime in a project group composed of people with different employment agreements. In both cases, the conflicts concerned are between people working in the same place but under different conditions.

Perhaps this is at its most obvious when both in- and outsourcing are mixed in one organization. In our study of staffing nurses we came across a situation where the local municipality was renting beds in one of the county council hospital wards (Allvin, Jacobson, and Isaksson, 2003). Working at this ward, therefore, apart from the regular county council personnel, was also a number of municipal employees. During vacation times, there were also staffing nurses from three different staffing companies at the ward. In one single ward, the personnel hence had five different employers and five different types of employment agreements. Staffing nurses, who had only recently passed their examinations, worked together with and could even be the supervisors of municipally employed colleagues with significantly longer experience but only half the wages. In situations like this the performance demands of work will tax the personnel. The mere intra-personnel social interaction and cooperation may be just as challenging. We ought, therefore, to be able to speak of "social stress."

Here, too, individuals develop different strategies for coping with these demands, strategies that have effects on themselves, the work group, and the company as a whole. One of these strategies we have previously spoken of as "social competence." Social competence is a strategy in the sense that the individual develops a distanced, technical, and perhaps even exaggeratedly pleasant attitude in response to the social demands of work. This attitude is a strategy for avoiding social demands without having to repudiate them directly. The individual socializes without interacting in the true sense of the word. For an individual to interact, she has to make a personal stance, which will draw her into relationships. In order to avoid this, she plays the social game and follows the social stream. She makes the right moves, says the right things, and outwardly seems to be committed. Under the surface, however, she is closed, distant, or just absent.

This is often a successful strategy. It is also a strategy practiced, from time to time, by everyone in modern society. Being forced to use it constantly may result, however, in the relativization of norms and emotions and, by extension, in the individual becoming socially overstrained and depressed (Forseth, 2005).

Another strategy is to form cliques and erect barriers against all outsiders. Through this strategy, a well-defined social zone is created – controlled and predictable at the same time as it reflects all new external demands. As long as the boundaries are maintained, this strategy does not need to entail any detrimental consequences for the health of its practitioners. In the long run, however, the strategy is untenable. When the boundaries finally collapse, the individual may feel violated and abandoned. Such excluding strategies are also probably perceived as frustrating, incomprehensible, and uncomfortable for those left outside or for those happening into conflict with the group in question.

Other strategies are isolation or any other kind of emotional dissociation practiced by the individual. Strategies of this kind often prove counter-productive, as they have repercussions on both work and the individual herself. Work motivation falls as the individual simultaneously becomes bitter and cynical (Astvik, 2003).

But the consequences of the deregulation of work touch not only the social relations at work. The border between work and life outside it is also breaking up as work is being deregulated. This means that work-related demands and expectations, to a larger extent than before, spill over into private life – and vice versa. At the same time, as seen in the previous chapter, life outside working life is becoming ever more complicated and demanding. The implications are that the individual personally needs to identify, evaluate, and classify the various demands. Fulfilling all demands is impossible; she needs to choose. And in addition, she needs to negotiate and compromise with work, family, and friends alike. Boundary regulation becomes an important skill.

Apart from all the separate demands placed on the individual, she also faces the problematic task of balancing all these demands so that no demand-maker becomes dissatisfied. Consequently, the individual needs to balance the demands of working life against the demands made by life outside work. The individual develops various strategies to maintain this balancing act. On a comprehensive level, we have divided these into strategies intending to create more space for work and strategies purporting to integrate work with life outside it.

The development of strategies intending to free up space for work may entail a lifestyle of working too much and having problems relaxing. These are also strategies that are flexible in relation to the increasing demands of work. Demands encroaching on work, however, are at a constant risk of coming into conflict with the demands of work, resulting in imbalance. The development of strategies intending to integrate work with life as a whole is, on the other hand, more flexible toward the demands of life outside work. Here, the source of conflict is instead the demands of working life, constantly threatening to result in imbalance. Nevertheless, in both cases the conflicts may be a cause of stress.

As we have seen, the result of deregulated flexible work is not an increased workload alone. The deregulated work also gives rise to increasing social demands and resulting conflicts. These are demands and conflicts in the relation between work and life outside it as well as in work itself. But the higher flexibility of working conditions does not complicate the relations of the individual with other people only. It also exposes the individual to herself, with consequences for her self-image, her possibilities, and her place in society.

Insecurity, precariousness, and alienation

In our studies of free jobs, we interviewed a great number of people who were very enthusiastic about their working conditions. They often expressed a seemingly unshakable self-esteem and appeared to regard themselves as the chosen ones: successful and at the forefront of development. They made no difference between themselves and the work they were doing. Their successes were for them simply a result of their personal competence and creativity. They also described the development of the job, the organization, or the industry as a natural side effect of their own personal development. Among these people we also occasionally encountered their opposites. They could be difficult to detect, as they had the same jobs, worked just as much, and were, at least on the surface, just as successful. On the other hand, they completely lacked the enthusiasm and self-confidence of their colleagues. They seemed to have no faith in themselves. For these people, words like competence, creativity, and personal development were not inspiring but threatening and full of demands.

Consequently, the same working conditions, which made some feel motivated and free, made others feel insecure and vulnerable. The self-assured enthusiasm of the colleagues rather increased their sense of insecurity and abandonment. A type of culture had even developed in certain workplaces, particularly among the younger employees, where questioning and doubt was close to a taboo. The feeling of not being able to, not being up to, or not having anything to contribute was therefore a feeling one had to keep to oneself (Allvin et al., 1998).

A similar sense of exposure existed also among those with temporary or precarious forms of employment. This sense of exposure is also most acutely perceived by those who did not choose such a work form voluntarily. For instance, journalists, forced into a freelance existence for family reasons or because they had been unable to get permanent employment, felt significantly worse and worried more about their economic and professional future than journalists who had personally made the choice to work as freelancers (Allvin and Aronsson, 2000).

Being in dire economic straits and worrying about one's personal economy is generally closely linked to ill health. In a study of the living conditions of temporary employees, it was found that the risk of ill health was several times larger among those frequently having to worry about their economy than among those rarely worried (Aronsson et al., 2005). This was also more tangible for the men concerned, although the difference between the sexes was not significant.

The study group was sharply polarized in terms of the extent to which they had been in a situation of economic emergency, which was the basis of a division into "very poor," "poor," and a so-called standard group, composed of people who never, or only once or twice, had found themselves in an economic emergency situation. An emergency situation could mean, for instance, having had to borrow money in order to cover one's expenses; something close to 60 percent of interviewees had been forced to do that. Approximately the same percentage had been unable to pay their bills on time, and close to 50 percent stated that they had had to dispense with things like TV and terminate newspaper subscriptions in order to manage their expenses. Men living in "economic emergency," that is, the "very poor," had a risk of mental ill health more than fifteen times higher than men belonging to the economic standard group. One explanation for the high level of ill health among these groups is that economic strain and economic emergency are closely related to insecurity and the lack of control over personal life – conditions which, within work-life research, are known to be extremely stress inducing.

The phenomenon is usually called "economic stress," and refers to stress that may result from worry about the economic and professional future (Starrin, Åslund, and Nilsson, 2009). Worry develops into stress when the future is unpredictable and the individual feels unable to influence it. Similar worries will always be an intrinsic part of temporary and precarious forms of employment, but the constant reorganizations, relocations, and company closures of the new work life mean that one cannot feel completely safe in permanent employment either. In spite of this, there are many who do not dare leaving their permanent employment for fear of not getting the work they want, or not getting a job at all. Instead, they stay on in jobs where they, perhaps, are unhappy. This kind of stress is constant and long lasting and, thus, contributes to stress-related disorders to a greater extent than short-term stress, which generally does not cause health problems.

Being locked-in. People in insecure temporary jobs may be called outsiders. Many want a permanent job instead of moving from one temporary job to another. Labor market mobility is too high in this group. But there are also a group of insiders who have too low mobility. When an individual feels that she is in the wrong occupation or the wrong workplace, but does not have the courage to quit, we may speak of being "locked-in" (Aronsson and Göransson, 1999; Aronsson, Dallner, and Gustafsson, 2000). When the feeling is of both situations being true, one may speak of being doubly locked-in. In the Swedish labor market, for instance, approximately 20 percent of the permanently employed may be included in the category of the doubly locked-in. An additional approximately 15 percent belong to the categories professional lock-in or workplace lock-in. The proportion of locked-ins is significantly higher among low-skilled blue-collar workers. There are also substantial differences between professional areas, mirroring educational background and class division. Within professional areas demanding longer educations – for example teaching, schools, technical, and computer activities – the proportion of locked-ins is significantly lower. There is also no difference between men and women. Lock-in is, above all, a question of social class and education. There is no comparative data from other countries but according to, for example, the report "Mobility in Europe" Sweden has a labor market with comparatively high mobility.

Locked-ins and doubly locked-ins, to an even higher extent, are exposed to continuous stress at work. More often than all other employees, permanently as well as temporarily employed, they report stomach problems, uneasiness, tiredness, and listlessness. Locked-in also means professional stagnation. The perception of those locked-in is of having significantly reduced opportunities for learning new things and developing at work. They also feel that their bosses do not give them support. What is the chicken or the egg in this situation, however, is difficult to say. Those finding themselves in an occupation they are not happy with probably take less of an interest in learning and competence development than people in a profession with which they are happy. This, in turn, may lead to a lesser degree of support and encouragement from managers and employers.

The fact that they are locked-in and finding it difficult to leave their jobs at the same time means that their opportunities to protest against their conditions are hampered. Thus, the personal attitude toward work becomes defensive. They do little or nothing in order to get out of their situation, neither have they actively protested against it.

There are not many studies of the connection between this kind of silence and ill health. However, it is reasonable to assume that the silence is linked not only to fear, but also to perceptions of powerlessness and the suppression of emotions. Fear undermines confidence and creativity (Argyris, 1986). People who are afraid lose their dignity, feel ashamed (perceive a lack of respect and esteem from others), and increase their defensive behavior. Feelings of shame, not admitted, lead to anger which, in turn, leads to additional feelings of shame. When such anger is suppressed, conflicts are left unresolved, and the individual is left in a state of emotional tension. A state like this will also result in the tensing of the individual's relations vis-à-vis her environment. Being unable to criticize and make one's voice heard was also found to be related to symptoms of ill health (Aronsson and Gustafsson, 1999; Aronsson, Gustafsson, and Dallner, 2000).

Loss of moral motivation

The locked-in problematic has become more palpable now that the influence of market forces has changed conditions in many workplaces. Such is the case for many within the public sector. Among the nurses in a Swedish study who, at the end of the 1990s and the first years of the next decade, left their permanent employment with the county council for the staffing industry there was, for example, significant discontent with the rationalizations and cut-downs resulting from the adjustment of the public care sector to more market-oriented conditions (Allvin, Jacobson, and Isaksson, 2003). The nurses described how their choice of profession and employer had originally been morally motivated. They had wanted to work with people within the public health care sector that earlier had been perhaps the prime object of national pride. Working within the public sector in general, and then in health care in particular, had not only been a means of entering the labor market for them, it had also been a question of ideals. They stood by something they believed in, something they felt was worth dedicating their working lives to.

When, subsequently, the far-reaching healthcare rationalization of the 1990s introduced market mechanisms into activities and let the economy push the moral commitment aside, the workload increased at the same time as contact was lost with the value basis of the job. This, of course, did not happen overnight. For a long time, they accepted the demands for efficiency, customer satisfaction, and extended work tasks as a necessary means of developing the healthcare industry. But when the means became a goal in themselves, and no gratitude for work was forthcoming, their work motivation was depleted. During the 1990s, health care in the public discourse was discussed almost exclusively in terms of inefficiency and snowballing costs. It was even described as part of the "economically draining sector." Working in health care no longer meant what it used to mean.

When the moral motive and the general legitimacy had been drained from work, only the increasing demands, heavier workload, shrunken resources, and hopeless wage development remained (Allvin, Jacobson, and Isaksson, 2003). It was under these circumstances that the health problems, fatigue depressions, sick leaves, and personnel turnover started to increase within the healthcare sector. For the nurses we interviewed, this was the backdrop against which they entered the staffing industry, making a personal promise never to return to the county council.

What these nurses describe is not primarily a work environment problem, although one may choose to see it as such; it is rather a redefinition of the professional role, resulting in certain working conditions coming to dominate work almost completely, in a way which previously had not been the case. To the extent that the workers also feel alien to the new professional role or that the new conditions do not even lend themselves to summary into a professional role, it also means that the social contract between the individual and society symbolized by work risks being broken. If this is the case, we ought rather to speak of a problematic of alienation. It is also not unreasonable to regard part of the problems of the public sector, for instance, discomfort in the surroundings and absenteeism among the personnel particularly within schools and health care, as an expression of alienation.

The New Ill Health

By way of introduction to this chapter, we gave a mood picture of working conditions and mental overexertion at the turn of the previous century and the contemporary debate about social transformation and health. One hundred years later, issues of work life, stress, and mental health are once again at the top of the scientific and political agenda. Two kinds of diagnoses dominate sickness absenteeism statistics in Europe – joint and muscle problems and mental ill health (European Survey of Living Conditions, 2006). Despite substantial improvements in the physical work environment, with fewer heavy lifts and better ergonomics, the extent of joint and muscular problems, such as neck, shoulder, and back pains, has not decreased. Latter-year research has shown mental stress to be a contributory cause in the development of these problems (Lundberg and Melin, 2002; Johansson et al., 2003; Lindgren, 2009). Lesser physical strain but greater mental demands may hence partially explain this state of affairs. We will regard the growing mental ill health primarily as connected to the conditions of the new work life. Evidently, this connection is not without its uncertainties. In many of the "new jobs," for instance, at call-centers, there may be taxing physical strain whereas stress in the form of quantitative overload is very much present in the "old jobs." We will, however, allow ourselves a generalization and call the mental part of ill health the new ill health.

Despite extensive research, it is difficult, on the basis of the previously presented stress models or of other existing theoretical models, to describe clearly, analyze, and explain the development of sickness absenteeism. The various models were not developed for the purpose of explaining absenteeism, but rather with the goal of explaining the connection between stress and illness. In many countries, research issues within the area of sickness absenteeism are also numerous: one concerns general explanatory factors of the large increase in absenteeism; another why individuals take sick leave; a third research issue concerns the relation between absenteeism and illness, etc. We will here not enter deeply into these questions or the problematic of sickness absenteeism research as a whole, but instead concentrate on a few of the phenomena we believe are connected with the conditions of the new work life. The following examples are from Sweden, where we are familiar with the conditions and reliable statistics are available, but we believe that similar conditions exist or will exist in many other countries. As the rules and regulations for sickness absence vary between countries, official statistics may look different in different countries. For example, it is unusual to be able to be on sick leave for long periods of time without losing your job. However, in Sweden it has until recently been possible to be on sick leave for more than a year.

Mental ill health

Since the 1980s, the general picture in Sweden, as well as in Europe as a whole, is one of a substantial increase in the mild mental ill health, particularly among young women. Illnesses concerning mental health represented at least 26 percent of long-term sickness absenteeism in the year 2000. From 1992 to 2002, which was a period of dramatic changes in Swedish working life, the number of illness-related absences of more than 60 days due to mental ill health increased approximately threefold. Psychiatric disorders and diseases of the musculoskeletal system during the period 1987 to 2005 were the most common diagnoses for early retirement pension. They together accounted for 65 percent of the total number of new cases during those years. The mental diseases increased in number between 1987 and 2004, while musculoskeletal disorders decreased. This development meant that the mental illnesses in 2005 for the first time were the leading cause for early retirement pension in Sweden.

In professional employee groups, the proportion of psychological diagnoses is even higher and more common than illness-related absences due to joint and muscular problems. Women are in general affected more than men, which in part may be due to the fact that women are more often found in the jobs most affected, for instance in professions with repetitive work tasks, and in emotionally taxing jobs within the healthcare sector and pre-school, and partly due to women still holding the main responsibility for unpaid duties in the home and with the children and, thus, having less opportunities to unwind and relax away from work.

Tiredness and sleeping disorders. The development of tiredness and sleeping disorders is a common class of symptoms of mental ill health, as it is also a sign of being subject to stress. If one is touched by these symptoms, there is, in all likelihood, also a lack of recovery and recreation in the background. These symptoms, through their connection with the anabolic and catabolic processes and the immune defense of the body, also may be seen as early warning signals and pre-stages of more severe physical and mental ill health. One example is the strong connection between sleeping disorders and burnout (Ekstedt, 2005), infections (Cohen *et al.*, 2009), and musculoskeletal disorders (Canivet *et al.*, 2008).

In the yearly Swedish Statistics Survey of Living Conditions (ULF), it is visible how tiredness and sleeping disorders have developed since the 1980s (Hallsten, Lundberg, and Waldenström, 2005). In the ULF material, not only the professionally active are included, but also those outside the labor market, as well as retirement pensioners, making it possible also to interpret the results in a wider societal perspective. The material may be divided into three time periods in order to mirror the turbulence shaking the Swedish labor market from the beginning of the 1990s.

- The first time period, between 1985 and 1989, we may call the 1980s survey. It provides a description of working life and society before the advent of the economic crisis and the high unemployment of the 1990s.
- The second gauging, between 1994 and 1997 (the 1990s survey), is conducted in the midst of Sweden's economic crisis, a crisis marked by unemployment, restructurings, cut-downs, and new management methods for work. The spirit of the time was characterized by an increasing discussion and perception of a lack of security and trust in society.
- The third period, between 1998 and 2001, we may call the turn of the century survey. In this time period, unemployment falls and Sweden experiences an economic recovery. At the same time, sickness absenteeism dramatically increases, above all the long-term absences.

We might expect the work-life turbulence of the 1990s to correspond with an increase in tiredness and sleeping disorders among the working population. Consequently, the trend ought to be one of increasing problems in the 1990s survey as compared to the 1980s survey, subsequently to plateau around the turn of the century when unemployment had fallen, cut-downs in the public sector decreased, and the social economy achieved a better balance.

These expectations, however, are disappointed. Instead, tiredness and sleeping disorders for the professionally active population between 20 and 65 years of age increased markedly throughout the time period. And as if that is not enough, there is also a significant and continuous increase among the professionally inactive of the same age. We may also see an increasing spread between the different groups. In the 1980s survey, the difference between the category reporting the least significant tiredness (no unemployment experience, 40–64 years of age) and that reporting the most (not employed, 40–64 years of age) is one of approximately 9 percentage units. In the turn of the century survey, the difference has more than doubled, to 20 percentage units. At the lowest percentage is now old age pensioners, with a level of 30 percent, and at the top we find the younger workforce, with experience of unemployment (55 percent). It is also in the latter group – younger people with unemployment experience – that we find the steepest increase of tiredness. Sleeping disorders, too, increase in a similar manner.

This association between mental health and a problematic labor market situation was also found in a recent study by Lager and Bremberg (2009). That study investigated the relation between national labor trends and young people's mental health as part of the WHO study, "Health Behavior in School-aged Children," in ten European countries between 1983 and 2005. A very strong correlation was found between increases in mental health problems among young people and the proportion of people not being part of the labor force.

Worry and anxiety. Stress is often also accompanied by some form of emotional reactions. These may vary between low-spiritedness and irritation to worry and anxiety. There is no established theoretical model explaining these reactions in the same way as biological ones. On the other hand, there is extensive research showing how conflict and ambivalence in social relations may lead to emotional as well as physiological reactions. In the work life these may concern uncertainties in the personal professional role, unfairness in the workplace, bad or non-existent leadership, mobbing or discrimination in the workplace, conflicts between work and private life, as well as unemployment and precarious employment conditions (Barling, Kelloway, and Frone, 2005).

Since the 1980s, the presence of worry and anxiety has developed in a similar way to tiredness and sleeping disorders (WHO, 2006; Hallsten,

Lundberg, and Waldenström, 2005). Worry and anxiety have increased in all social groups. Similarly to tiredness and sleeping disorders, the most substantial increase in worry is to be found in the younger age groups, especially among those between 15 and 25 years of age, and the smallest among old age pensioners. In contrast to tiredness and sleeping disorders, however, the spread of the groups is not increasing. On the contrary, it has decreased significantly. The curves instead convey the feeling that everyone feels the same worries and the same anxiety. This is also confirmed by a general increase for all social groups, an increase that does not seem to be immediately connected to conditions in the workplace. Students, for example, form the group in which the largest number report feelings of worry and anxiety. The development is the same as for schoolchildren.

How are, then, the results of these different surveys of tiredness, sleeping disorders, worry, and anxiety supposed to be interpreted and understood? First, the defaulting covariance between the changes in the work life on a macro level and the increasing problems on the individual level probably ought not to be interpreted to the effect of work-life conditions as being negligible. There is a wealth of scientifically proper surveys on the individual level, confirming the correspondence between working conditions, tiredness, and sleeping disorders, not the least within research conducted according to the demand-control-support model. Research also shows that approximately one-third of a Swedish group of long-term sickness absentees perceive their ill health and absenteeism as intrinsically linked to their working conditions (Göransson, Aronsson, and Melin, 2002). The proportion connecting their sickness absenteeism with both working conditions and private life is just as large. There is, however, great variance between people with different diagnoses. Those absent due to diagnosed burnout emphasize work as a contributory cause to a much higher extent than people absent due to diagnosed lung disease and cancer. Other studies have produced similar results. One should also keep in mind that human beings are quite resistant and adaptable, as well as the fact that it may take a long time until a moderate but chronic stress load manifests itself in palpable symptoms – sometimes as long as several years.

One reasonable interpretation of these results is that, apart from the work life, there are also other conditions, as yet not identified by work-life research, contributing to the severe increase in tiredness, sleeping disorders, worry, and anxiety. The most vulnerable group seems to be the middle-aged and elderly, falling outside the active workforce. This group also seems to be a group with many problems – economic problems, after-effects of previous positions in the work life, poor health, and having been excluded from work life because of ill health.

> There are not many studies on the situation of old age pensioners from a perspective of stress or to what extent they are touched by the after-effects of working life, which may shed light on these results. One interpretation might be that the old age pensioners, who have left occupational life behind, are not as sensitive as younger people to social changes. They are, to a higher extent, in control, both in and over their situation. (Aronsson, 1989, 2004)

A new prospective study based on the large cohort is very interesting in this context and gives a deepening understanding of the after-effects from work (Westerlund *et al.*, 2009). The researchers used yearly measurements of self-rated health in a varied French occupational cohort (GAZEL) and examined health from 7 years before retirement to 7 years after. Their findings suggest that the burden of ill health is substantially relieved by retirement for all workers apart from those with ideal working conditions. High physical and psychological job demands and low job satisfaction during the later years in work were associated with a steep increase in suboptimum health before retirement and increased benefit from retirement. Those with a low-risk profile of work-related factors had no such retirement-related improvement, which suggests that demanding and not satisfying work puts an extra burden on health, but that the effects are reversible.

Exhaustion syndrome or burnout. If we add a paralyzing physical and mental exhaustion to the tiredness, sleeping disorders, worry, and anxiety, the result is what is sometimes described as burnout. The term burnout was coined in the 1970s by American scientific researchers. At the beginning of the 1970s, the American medical doctor Herbert Freudenberger perceived a gradual depletion of energy and increasing depression among a number of those engaged in non-profit work with drug abusers at a clinic in New York. Around the same time, Christina Maslach was able to observe the same process among health care personnel in California. Independently of one another, they both called the symptom burnout, describing it as a severe loss of motivation. In contrast to being "merely" worn out from having worked too much during too long a period of time, burnout also involves (an extinct) personal engagement. It is not just a matter of working a lot; one is also trying to achieve something. This was also characteristic of the not-for-profit working personnel in New York and the healthcare personnel in California. They were driven in their work by an inner demand on themselves.

During the 1980s, the symptoms came to be associated with the jobs created within "the new economy," and were even given the nickname of "yuppie flu." Since then, the symptoms have primarily been linked to the ever-increasing demands facing people in the new work life. However, demands on work performance are not the only important factors in this context. Conflicts in the workplace and the feeling of having been treated unfairly are just as important causes. In one of the rare truly comprehensive studies in this area, Lennart Hallsten at the former Institute of Work-Life Research in Stockholm has also shown that people outside the labor market are affected by the symptoms to as high an extent as the gainfully employed. The unemployed were even the most severely hit category of all. Further, it was shown that family problems and private conflicts substantially increase the risk of burnout. The symptoms were also more frequent among the young, women, and professional employees (Hallsten, Lundberg, and Waldenström, 2005; Hallsten, Josephson, and Torgén, 2005).

It is difficult to separate the diagnosis of burnout from others with similar symptoms, for example, depression. In statistics of sickness absenteeism we may also detect significant increases in the number of depressions during the past 15 years. In work environment statistics, it is above all anxiety that is on the increase. In both cases, professional employees top the statistics and, again, women are the ones with the most severe problems. Common for them is also that they, in their work, "are in more or less intensive contact with other people, and that they during the 1990s were hit by repeated reorganizations and cut-downs" (Swedish National Board of Health and Welfare, 2003).

What we have called the new ill health is, above all, an increasing mental ill health, manifest also in physical problems, such as muscle pain, sleeping disorders, pounding heart, chest pain, indigestion, recurring infections, and memory disruptions. It is a kind of ill health that is taking ever more diffuse and emotional expression, which is therefore difficult to diagnose through conventional medical examinations, and which is consequently often described as "medically unexplained symptoms" or "subjective complaints." These symptoms seem to be caused by dysregulation of important physiological systems rather than by somatic diseases. The new ill health is related to work in the sense that it results in increasing sickness absenteeism from work. At the same time, it is not limited to those in gainful employment. The problem is just as serious for students, the unemployed, and other groups outside working life.

The New Ill Health, Work Environment, and the Possibility Space of Work

To conclude, the big question we are facing is how the new ill health really relates to the increased and transformed demands of the new work life. Of course, this is a question no one quite, as of yet, can answer. Rather, this is one of the questions work-life research will have to tackle during the next decade.

However, it does not mean that we know nothing of this question – quite on the contrary. There is extensive research where people on sick leave refer to their demanding working conditions. At the same time, people's need to give a rational explanation of their condition and the demands of the social insurance authorities for a legitimate diagnosis both contribute to the causal relations becoming blurry. The more diffuse the symptoms, the more credible it is that the individual will refer to a concrete cause of her ill health. A cancer diagnosis, for instance, is sufficiently unquestionable for it to remain legitimate under the searching glances of the surroundings and the social insurance office. A syndrome of exhaustion and depression, on the other hand, needs causes that are concrete and relatively close at hand in order for it to win legitimacy, in the eyes of the individual concerned as well as in those of others.

We also know that the new ill health is found also in groups outside working life. Some of these groups, for instance students, are even more stricken than groups within working life. Against this background, one might get the idea that the new ill health is unrelated to the new work life. But this need not be the case. As illustrated by the study by Lager and Bremberg (2009), conditions on the labor market in Europe seem to be strongly linked to changes in mental health among young people. One possible explanation is that an unsecure and rapidly changing labor market creates worry and uncertainty among students and people who are about to enter the labor market. This creates anticipation stress as it is likely to contrast with their expectations induced by information from authorities, school, and mass media that they are in a fortunate position where all kinds of educational and occupation opportunities are open to them. In reality, a large proportion of young people will lack higher education and/or occupational training necessary for being competitive on the labor market today. The new ill health is, in all probability, linked to increasing social demands, insecurity, and precariousness, or what we, in non-specific terms, have called social and economic stress. These causes of stress are not always attributable to individual factors at the workplace. In analogy with the new work life, they simply cannot be delineated and pinpointed to any one specific workplace or job. They concern the conditions of the labor market, the personal career, self-image, employability, private economy, the relation to life outside work, and personal interests alike and to an equal extent. In other words, for both the new ill health and the new work life, the borderline between the work of the individual and the social development in general is becoming increasingly porous. What is happening in society as a whole is also reflected in the individual's work, and vice versa.

Nevertheless it is difficult, perhaps even impossible, to isolate one or any number of causal relations between various diffuse and emotionally tinged symptoms on one side and different conditions for jobs that lack a clear and specified work environment in the shape of specified working hours, workplace, and work organization on the other. On the whole, the blurry borders are making it increasingly difficult to speak in any general terms about work and the work environment. Perhaps the case is quite simply that we cannot take "work" as a starting point for our research, believing that we are thus saying something generally true about the work environment and its health consequences. Perhaps we would do better to proceed from "the individual," her life situation, and the strategies she is employing to cope with it in order to explain her possible ill health.

Astvik (2003) described a series of strategies home help service personnel employ in their work, and which are expressed in their meeting with the clients of the home help service. These strategies may be rational or irrational, conscious or subconscious. Among other things, she describes the actions of the personnel both in terms of conscious mastery strategies (coping) and subconscious survival strategies (defense). In the same way, the strategies may be constructive or destructive. This does not imply a classification of the strategies as such, but a characterization of the consequences they entail for the relation to the clients, that is, the quality of their work. But we may also imagine such a classification with respect to personal well-being.

> On the one hand, the strategies where the individual care givers compensate through individual efforts which, in the longer perspective, may lead to exhaustion and an increased risk of exclusion from the profession through

long-term sickness absences and early retirement. On the other hand, there is the risk of the care givers protecting themselves by means of strategies that always seriously damage the quality of the services they are expected to perform. (Astvik, 2003, p. 53)

By strategies, we hence mean the ways in which the individual chooses to cope with his circumstances, in this case his working conditions. Which way he chooses does not depend on his working conditions alone, but also on how these relate to his personal situation. What is, in this context, interesting is that the individual, in his attempts to cope with his situation, adopts strategies that jeopardize his health. In some cases he is aware of this. In other cases, he chooses a harmful strategy because he cannot perceive of any other option. Sick leave, for instance, may be a last resort.

The individual's ability to act is determined by his concrete working conditions as well as by other conditions. To just as large an extent, if not more, it is, however, a question of his action repertory. In other words, it is a question of the individual's possibilities to choose other, more constructive strategies. Or, to take it from Amartya Sen (1999), it is a question of the individual's "possibility space."

The possibility space of the individual is limited by several factors. Apart from the obvious limitations, such as personnel cut-downs and limited resources, there are here also social and cultural limitations. The individual focus of the new organizational ideals and management instruments, at the expense of the collective, constitutes yet a limitation. Several studies have demonstrated the importance of collective strategies for the well-being of the individual, particularly in workplaces with heavy workloads (Länsisalmi, Peiro, and Kivimäki, 2000).

In conclusion, when an increasing amount of responsibility is delegated to the individual at the same time as the direction of work becomes ever more indirect and diffuse, we can see that the individual becomes the co-creator of his working conditions, like he never was before. This means that it is not only the working conditions, but also the individual's manner of coping with and relating to these conditions, which determine the quality of work and the individual's health alike. One conclusion we may draw from this is that a progressive work environment policy is not just a matter of developing the work environment. The individual's ability to cope with his conditions will also have to be developed in a manner constructive for all parties involved.

In this chapter, we have discussed different ways in which the new flexible working conditions may increase the strain on the individual. Although the immediate connection is far from obvious, we may discern new and growing ill health in society, ill health that, partially, has to do with the new work life. This gives a very negative and, to some extent, depressive picture of what is happening in society. We have chosen to focus on these negative aspects in view of the trend of increasing psychological problems, particularly among young people. However, the new ill health does not affect all people. On the contrary, some individuals are likely to benefit from the new working conditions.

The new working life means in many cases more influence and control, more responsibility and flexibility, and a stronger relation between effort and reward, conditions which according to the stress models described above are likely to reduce stress and create an active and stimulating work situation. However, only some workers usually highly educated and in high status positions with advanced social and communication skills and a strong basic self-esteem may benefit from these conditions. This means that health differences between individuals are likely to increase.

The health risks of stress should not be exaggerated. Most individuals can handle daily hassles and challenges without any signs of ill health or only temporary symptoms. Mental and physiological responses to stress activate processes which contribute to mobilize extra resources and protect vital functions. It is only when these responses are prolonged or frequently repeated that health problems appear according to the pathological processes described above. As pointed out earlier, rest and recovery, sleep in particular, between periods of stress are of significant importance to avoid negative health outcomes. Individuals who enjoy their work and are successful in working life are usually in a better position to recover efficiently when off from work. It is easier to unwind and relax after a stimulating and successful workday compared to a work situation characterized by uncertainty, worry, and distress. Negative emotions induce chronic activation of the stress systems and cause sleep disturbance. In conclusion, the new working life may start positive processes in some individuals and vicious circles in others and, thus, increase inequity in health in society.

Barbara Fredrickson (2003, 2004; Fredrickson and Branigan, 2005) has built a theory and performed a series of empirical studies that show that positive emotions seem to have a number of useful effects and consequences. There are effects that are clearly interesting in order to understand a changing world of work, where innovation, creativity, and initiative requiring interaction between people are growing. Positive emotions appear to have the ability to broaden people's thinking ability and temporarily coordinate thoughts and actions. The desire to test boundaries and to be creative and social as well as the desire for intellectual activities increase when people feel joy; this is also the case with physical and artistic behavior. Positive emotions also build up social, psychological, intellectual, and physical resources. Research on work-life conditions and how organizations can and should be designed, however, has hardly taken note of this knowledge about emotions, and this line of research on health promoting rather than health damaging factors is likely to receive increasing interest in future research.

6

Some Concluding Comments and Reflections

In this book, we have tried to provide a picture of what we have called the new work life. We have described various principles and techniques employed to make work more flexible, the knowledge and attitudes it requires of the individual and the relations to life outside work, and the types of stress and the ill health it may lead to. The effects of the companies' attempts to increase their flexibility entail different consequences in different sectors of the economy and for different groups in the labor force. Central actors, for instance, increase their flexibility and protect their power by spreading and distributing insecurity to subcontractors and temporary employees. The absence of boundaries or changed boundaries that we have discussed and which has provided the main theme of the book, is in many cases linked to the strict steering and regulation in other parts of the more and more internationalized economy. In the book we have been especially focused on two groups but the changed conditions influence the whole workforce. The first group is people working in the front of work organizational development, which to a rather high extent consists of well-educated people in highly skilled jobs. The second group consists of the class of workers in precarious employment characterized by a low level of certainty over job continuity and working hours, low level of protection against unemployment, and a low level of training on the job. That group is heterogeneous in many aspects but a common denominator is the precariousness and unpredictability.

We have discussed a series of different theories, concepts, empirical investigations, and our own examples. These have not always concerned the

---

Work Without Boundaries: Psychological Perspectives on the New Working Life, First Edition. Michael Allvin, Gunnar Aronsson, Tom Hagström, Gunn Johansson, and Ulf Lundberg.
© 2011 John Wiley & Sons, Ltd. Published 2011 by John Wiley & Sons, Ltd.

new work life directly; sometimes they have not concerned the work life at all. Nevertheless, they have in various ways been significant for or connected to one or a number of aspects of the area. The purpose of collecting them, in other words, has been "epistemographic": to chart and structure the knowledge area.

But we did not want simply to describe the area. We also wanted to discuss its possible meanings. And the meanings we have shown closer interest in are those emanating from a socio-psychological perspective. Through these, we feel able to distinguish certain comprehensive patterns in the new work life. They are all connected and one might very well speak of them as different aspects of one and the same phenomenon. In this concluding chapter we will summarize but also bring in some observations, comments, and reflections on coming forms of regulation.

The Deregulation of Working Life

One of these comprehensive patterns is the deregulation aimed at making work more flexible. This kind of deregulation means that the rules and norms that have traditionally defined and directed work, in various manners and to varying degrees, are now being softened up or simply abolished. Rules that were previously universal and non-conditional are becoming increasingly dependent on the individual and situation in question. We have seen examples of this concerning working hours. Many have so-called free working hours, and even larger numbers work flexitime. The same thing is valid for the workplace. Mobile jobs and telecommuting are only two names for work that no longer needs to be tied to one specific workplace but may be located and carried out where it suits the tasks or the person performing them. Also the work order, that is, the mode of procedure for work, in an increasing number of jobs is adapted to what the situation demands or to the preferences of the person performing it. And this is not only valid for goal-oriented jobs and projects but also for all tasks involving service and social relations. We may also see a deregulation of the cooperation, briefing, and delivery of work. Work is not always bound by the rules of the bureaucratic organization. Many are able to choose their co-workers, if only for certain tasks. And to an increasing extent, this takes place across department boundaries, even between companies and organizations. Going through formal channels in order to contact someone, within or outside the personal unit, is less often a necessity. Sometimes, this development is so far driven that the organization around work seems more like a network than anything else.

But it is not only the norms and rules surrounding work itself that are subject to deregulation. It is also the employment. The permanent employment with conditional tenure is more and more often substituted by various forms of temporary employments, temporary-hired personnel, and limited assignments. The companies are here aiming for flexibility by making the workforce exchangeable.

All of these deregulations also mean that the boundaries of work are becoming more porous. Work tends to spread into everyday life and the private person. At the same time, private life and the individual are forcing their way into working life. People bring their work home at the same time as they let their personal interests and needs direct their work. This is sometimes encouraged and then seen as an expression of personal engagement and creativity.

Simultaneously, the mixing of work and private life is facilitated by the ongoing deregulation of life outside work. Here, however, it is rather a question of a relatively widespread de-traditionalization of society. Our identity, our social roles, political and moral commitments, and our family life are becoming, to an ever-larger extent, subject to personal choice. This is also because of the effect of the deregulation that is taking place in the work life. The conditions of work are increasingly subject to individual choice.

The Individualization of Working Life

Another pattern is the individualization following when the individual herself has to define, plan, and carry out her work. The thought behind the deregulations is that the company is to become more flexible and able to adapt activities constantly to the demands of the surrounding world. It is therefore the individual's responsibility to bring about this continuous adaptation.

Although the deregulations mean that the individual is entrusted with a larger responsibility and sometimes also larger authority, or *empowerment*, this does not mean that she is given a blank check of action. The deregulation is almost always followed by new regulations. In contrast to the traditional regulations of working life, however, the new ones are not directed to the workforce as a collective, but directly to the individual.

The independence of the individual hence requires the internalization of the value systems and goals of the company. In order to leave the individual space for action and responsibility, the regulations assume the character of guidelines and practical attitudes. Instead of regulations we ought therefore, perhaps, to speak of different management techniques.

The consequence is that work makes new demands of the individual. In dealing with these demands new professional knowledge is developed. The miscellany of technical solutions, together with the fast pace of changes, means that it is not necessarily a merit to learn the skills of any one technique. This may instead form an obstacle to adaptation and thinking along new lines. Instead of specific technical knowledge, the ability to learn new things and to adapt is gaining in importance. At the same time, social relations are becoming more important in the work life. Hence, for this specific purpose, a series of techniques is being developed to manage them. While technical knowledge is becoming more abstract and universal, social knowledge is becoming more specific and technical. In both cases, however, they are becoming more person-specific and portable.

As a consequence, the individual is expected to be unattached and mobile in relation to her work. As conditions are constantly changing, no one is able to assume enduring responsibility for her. A job may disappear on short notice. It is therefore not enough simply to have a job. The important thing is instead to be able to get a new job at any time. Working life thus becomes a personal project, and the job a temporary meeting place, akin to a central station where people meet and interact on their way toward different destinations.

The Heterogenization of Working Life

A third pattern is the heterogenization, and also polarization, of the work life that this entails. We may see it in the separate working conditions, which we have respectively called flexibility through empowerment and flexibility through exchangeability. In the first case, working conditions are to a large extent dependent on the individual, and the individual is expected to make informed choices and take personal responsibility for them. In the second case, conditions are independent of the individual, and the individual is not expected to make any defining choices in her work, but only in relation to the undertaking as such, or more specifically whether she is to accept the assignment or not.

But we may also see a heterogenization of the individual's relationship to work, that is, to the role work plays in her life. To a very high degree, this is purely individual and dependent on the individual's abilities and opportunities. Nevertheless, we can distinguish two fundamental attitudes: one attitude where work is central and life outside work has to adapt to it, and one where work is integrated as part of a personal life context.

The same heterogenization also concerns the new ill health. Symptoms are diffuse and personal. Occurrence and spread in society also mean that they are difficult to link to any clear common conditions. People are hit in different ways, which may be dependent on separate working conditions and the individual constitution as well as on personal attitudes.

The New Inequality

All of this means that people in working life have less and less in common. New conditions break up the traditional collective in and around work. This also means that the collective differences are splintered into a whole string of smaller, even individual differences. New social categories emerge as various differences gain attention, for example, the difference between qualified and unqualified, and between those in demand on the labor market and those who are not. We may also notice differences between conditions and undertakings, independent of work, for instance between those with dependents and those who have only themselves to support, between those who are geographically mobile and those who are not, between the young and the older. We can also see differences between those who want to but cannot (the worn out), those who can but do not want to (the alienated), and those who both can and want to but are not allowed (the marginalized).

This inequality is one between various relatively temporary and relatively heterogeneous groups and between individuals. These groups and individuals do not necessarily have anything in common. Not even the inequality between them necessarily represents something that they have in common. Therefore, direct opposition between them is not a necessity either. Opposition, despite everything, is still a way of relating to one another. Opposition is something to mobilize around, to argue about, and, possibly, to bridge. It is something giving life identity and direction. What would, for instance, workers be without capitalists, and feminists without patriarchy?

The problem of the new inequality, however, is that many of the groups and individuals lack relations of this kind with one another.

Without a clear opponent it is difficult to channel inequality through resistance and struggle. And most inequalities are never channeled through resistance and struggle – they result only in frustration, illness, and disgrace.

New Strains and Symptoms

We have also tried to summarize the various strains caused by the changing demands of working life. These may be described as belonging to three different types. The first type of strain is the quantitatively and qualitatively increased workload. The rules for when, where, how, and with whom one is to carry out work have functioned traditionally as both a recommendation and as a buffer against unreasonable demands. The deregulation of the formal and informal system of rules hence results in some people working more than they otherwise would do. They, quite simply, work too much, for too long, and everywhere. The blurry boundaries and the recurring changes they entail mean that people are becoming more insecure about what is required of them. Therefore, they also do not know if they can live up to the demands. They cannot know when their work is done or whether what they have done is good enough. The difficulty to "switch off" from work, and the insecurity around what is actually expected of them, is a source of stress.

The second type of strain resulting from the changing demands of the work life is social. As the boundaries are blurring, social relations inside and outside work are also becoming more unclear. They are becoming less conventional and thereby less obvious. People are unable to relate to one another by virtue of their functions alone; they must also relate to each other as individuals. The consequence is that social relations are becoming more extensive, complicated, and unpredictable. However, it is not only social relations in the work that are becoming more important and demanding. The unclear boundaries of work also mean that the relationship to life outside work is becoming more recalcitrant. To the extent that work entails increasing social strains, at the same time as the opportunities for relaxing social relations with family and friends are decreasing, we may here detect yet another breeding ground for stress.

The third type of strain is the heightened insecurity brought by boundaryless working conditions. The very conditions some perceive as liberal and free will for others appear diffuse and demanding. For these people the blurry boundaries inspire only feelings of insecurity and vulnerability. And the more these undetermined boundaries of work are also linked to an individual assumption of responsibility for work, the more this insecurity will also entail a shrinking confidence on the job. This lack of confidence is a threat to the personal economic and professional development, and hence a cause of economic stress.

These strains are mirrored in what we have called the new ill health, that is, more specifically, the increasing mental ill health in the shape of tiredness, worry, anxiety, and depression. Similarly to the strains resulting from the new work life, the new ill health is diffuse and difficult to link to any individual factors of the work environment. It is not even limited to working life or to those in gainful employment. Students and the unemployed, for example, belong to the most seriously affected groups. Rather, the new ill health may be found among all those about to enter, those who feel the pressure of, or in other ways are dependent on the increasingly competitive labor market.

Is the rather dark picture we have painted the coming new brave working life or is it an expression of transition problems when workplaces are transformed by globalization, information technology, and the new flexible organization forms? Human beings are creative and adaptable and may develop their ability to cope with boundarylessness and develop supporting collective protecting structures. In addition to our observations on insecurity and stress there are also many examples on how people develop strategies that increase their control in and over their work.

Flexibility and Power in Times of Economic Recession

In the introductory chapter we described how the international economy had been liberalized and deregulated in recent decades and the interaction between this development and regulation at the national and the company level. There is more and more of a network economy with changing boundaries between firms. In the introductory chapter we also said that there is no sharp border between an old and a new working life. Today's national and international work life consists of a plethora of working regimes with increasing heterogeneity, differentiation, and polarization. This is how we perceive the relationship between the old and new work. When new industries, markets, companies, techniques, and forms of cooperation develop they change the premises for other industries, markets, and companies, forcing them to adjust to the new situation in various ways and to different degrees.

Restructuring is not a response to a temporary crisis anymore; it has become a permanent state. These continuing changes create new forms for management and work organization in the companies but the changes are also created by new management techniques and changes in the organization of work. The international financial crisis that began in 2008 was the first tough test of this network economy where organizational flexibility and restructuring had been key words. The crisis started with a crisis-like type of restructuring. A first observation was of the high speed of the crisis from the international financial system to the real economy and to different sectors, companies, and individuals. The speed confirms the strength of liberalization, international integration, and the dismantling of various borders. In both the economic system as a whole and within single companies, we could witness how the central and strong actors managed to create for them a flexible mechanism through which they could maintain control and locate the uncertainty and adverse consequences to other parts of the system or to the more peripheral parts of the network. When demand fell in manufacturing, the strong actors managed to distribute the negative effects more or less immediately to the major subcontractors, who quickly began to give notice to their staff about layoffs. The major subcontractors distributed in turn uncertainty to their subcontractors, which pushed the uncertainty even further out of the system's peripheral elements, and so forth. There is of course no systematic research on the effect of the acute crisis and the following economic recession yet, but the immediate impression is that flexibility and power are rather strongly interrelated.

Another aspect of flexibility that quickly came to be used in Sweden was reduction of the number of temporary jobs. This type of job contract has steadily increased in Sweden, as in many other countries, over the last 25 years. When the financial crisis spread to Sweden in autumn 2008 temporary employees were the first victims. Their contracts were not renewed and they gradually lost their jobs when the contract time expired. During the first year of the crisis, the companies used the numerical flexibility and distributed uncertainty and problems to the individuals who formed the reserve army of the companies. The size of the reserve army varies across industries. Outside the core of permanent employees the companies often have a protective buffer of workers on temporary contracts, representing an average of about 15 percent of the total workforce in Sweden. However, the economic recession was so extensive that reduction of these fixed-term contracts was not enough and after some months the companies also started to discharge workers in the core groups.

The recession also activated another aspect of flexibility, namely, shorter working hours. In many manufacturing industries, especially within the car industry, the parties came to an agreement about what is called "business cyclic adapted working hours," which means that the working hours were reduced during the economic recession. This flexibility measure concerned primarily workers in the direct production of commodities – not corporate officers.

In the innermost core of large companies and in the banking system from where the crisis emanated very little or nothing happened concerning reward systems and benefits. Both national and international policy initiatives, with the aim to regulate and introduce restrictions in the bonus systems and other problematic factors, seem to meet strong resistance within the system itself.

As was said above, there is still no systematic research on the effects of the financial crisis and the recession, but there have been many demonstrations and illustrations of power through flexibility. The flexible company seems to have power to distribute the uncertainty in order to protect its own business. The modern network economy has not changed the old truth that powerlessness is to be in a position of dependence – more than ever this seems to be the basic condition for individuals as well as companies and a strong mechanism for polarization between individuals as well as among companies.

Future – Trust or New Forms and Fields for External Regulation?

In this book we have described two separate ways for achieving flexibility in an organization. The first is via trust and empowerment – flexibility is generated when decisions about work are delegated to a significant degree to the workers themselves. The other road is via exchangeability – flexibility is achieved when the organization becomes independent of its individuals. These ways manifest themselves in the occurrence and spread of working hours and the workplace, and in ways of working and in social relations. Research during the last 50 years has shown the negative consequences of flexibility via exchangeability, for example, for stress and health, intellectual development, and quality of life in general. But that research is not a reason for assuming that the opposite, that is, work development, empowerment, and social integration, has the corresponding positive consequences. But this knowledge has not prevented this type of job to be repeatedly re-created. At the same time there is an increase in a different type of job where work requirements are of a different kind – boundaryless work. In companies each kind of work exists side by side but in different proportions in a pragmatic way that will promote the company's flexibility. In practice, there is no sharp distinction between the two types of jobs. Boundaryless work is common especially in the so-called knowledge-intensive sectors.

One purpose of this book and the research it is based on has been to identify and describe the requirements of boundaryless work and the strategies individuals use in this kind of work. When the traditional organizational framework is broken up the individual will be forced to define, initiate, plan, and assume responsibility for work to a much higher extent than in the traditional work organization. In the same way the individual is forced to plan and take responsibility for their private life. Whether an individual will have a good job or not will very much depend on whether the individual can handle the new requirements and regulate time, place, and tasks. A job to a lesser extent can be evaluated according to its demands. Whether the work is good or bad depends also on how the individual deals with these requirements. For those who fail in the regulation of boundaries, work is likely to invade life. The result may be work-life conflicts, a constant lack of recovery, and the accompanying stress and health consequences.

However, despite the perceived uncertainty and stress and the sometimes lack of transparency and rules, almost no one wants to go back to a more externally regulated traditional work situation even if there may be some exceptions. In an ongoing study of people on long-term sick leave, some with qualified work who had boundaryless work conditions expressed a wish for a very traditional and stable work organization when they return to work (Mellner, Astvik, and Aronsson, in preparation).

But if there is no way back to the traditional external regulation of the work, what new forms and instruments can be developed to compensate or replace the steering force of the traditional rules? We can discern at least three such stabilizing factors or arenas of new tools, strategies, and norm formations.

In this book we have extensively described the boundary stabilization that occurs through the individual strategies that create and form the boundaries between work and life outside work. Two main strategies have been discussed. There is a separation or segmentation strategy that may give a similar result to the traditional rules, but it is the individual who chooses the strategy and takes decisions concerning the boundaries in space and time. One example is the freelance journalist who, along with some other colleagues, rents a room and works there Monday through Friday from 8:00 a.m. to 16:00 p.m. and thus inserts himself into the dominant social rhythm of the society he lives in. The second strategy is called integration strategy, which means that the individual mixes paid work and other activities to suit his own needs over the day, week, and year.

A second arena for regulation is the workplace and the norms created in the interaction between employees, and between management and employees. Norm formations can include work efforts, reasonable hours of work, and the relationship between boundaryless and stationary working. It may also be about sending out important emails that cannot be answered without people lengthening their working hours and answering emails from home. There is not much research on this norm formation, and our knowledge is mostly of an episodic nature.

When the conditions for the traditional external regulation decrease or disappear, new so-called soft techniques for regulation enter and increase in importance and use. There is an arsenal of instruments such as steering goals, frequent follow-ups, selection procedures, career development, individual contracts, etc. These soft regulation instruments have so far not encountered any resistance. Trade unions as well as companies and the government support use of these instruments and other quality management techniques. A successful application of such techniques means that the individual psychologically internalizes the company's requirements, standards, goals, values, etc.

But there are also indications that tighter control technology is on the way back, albeit in new forms. Information technology as we have seen, allowing the transcending of time and space boundaries, also has another side, namely that it can integrate the planning, management, monitoring, and control of work processes, and generate data about people's work behavior in a way that far surpasses all previous forms of control systems.

In this context it may be interesting to use some concepts from the scientist Frances Fukuyama, namely, low trust and high trust organizations. In his book, *Trust: The Social Virtues and the Creation of Prosperity* (1995), Fukuyama analyzes different societies from a trust perspective. The thesis is that if a culture contains strong norms of trust this increases the pressure on people living in the culture to think and act in a confident manner. In a culture of mistrust the reverse pressure appears. Trust is reciprocal. One must rely on others, but also act in such a way that one is worthy of others' trust.

Fukuyama categorizes communities and organizations in the degree of trust and talking about high trust and low trust organizations. From this perspective, different economic systems, management systems, and production technologies are considered and analyzed. The degree of individual control of the work situation is dependent on these systems. The more detailed these systems are, the less control is left to the individual or to the collective. Fukuyama regards Taylorism with its precision and its detailed external regulation as a typical low trust system. Taylorism had universal acclaim, but was probably a creation of its time and not well supported in the United States. There was strong opposition among workers when scientific management was introduced, and it was only accepted when it turned out to give workers better pay opportunities.

Detailed command and control systems therefore signal distrust or lack of trust. Trust and distrust are built into an organization's reward, information and control systems, and systems for decision making. If these control systems take a significant volume of resources, they undermine trust and foster mistrust. The companion of limited trust is regulation by contract and law.

Information technology gives us transparency, but may also be the basis for overall control and monitoring of work processes, including individual work and work performance. One clear example of this is work in call centers where individual work performance can be totally monitored, recorded, and documented. This type of control and surveillance has so far mostly been in industrial work, but has now also entered the service work sector, such as call centers.

The work process for professional occupational groups has been subject to such control and regulation. Assessment of quality has been more a matter of collegial evaluation and critique. What we now can observe is that even in those groups where autonomy has been a keyword there is a request for increased time and performance reports. The collected data creates comprehensive and detailed documentation, useful for many purposes and for different types of regulation of professional work. This monitoring and management of professional groups is a recent phenomenon. The reaction in these groups could be a perception that the management lacks confidence in their competence and loyalty, which may trigger a spiral of reciprocal distrust. A very interesting research question for the future is whether these constant increased demands for documentation contribute to the creation of low trust organizations in other sectors than those who have long been characterized by Taylorism and monitoring. The question may even be whether *documentation society* might be a more appropriate name than *information society* for this emerging society.

References

Aaker, D. A., 1991. *Managing Brand Equity*. New York: Free Press.
Aaker, D. A., 1996. *Building Strong Brands*. New York: Free Press.
Aglietta, M., 1979. *A Theory of Capitalist Regulation: The US Experience*. London: NLB.
Ahrne, G. and Roman, C., 1997. Hemmet, barnen och makten [Home, children and power]. *Swedish Government Reports*, No. 1997:139. Stockholm: Ministry of Labour [In Swedish].
Allvin, M., 1997. *Det individualiserade arbetet [The Individualisation of Work: On the Two Practices of Modernity]*. Stockholm, Sweden: Symposion [In Swedish].
Allvin, M., 2001. Distansarbete: Ett instrument för frihet eller kontroll? [Telework: An instrument of freedom or control?]. *Arbetsliv i omvandling*, **10**. Stockholm: Swedish National Institute for Working Life [In Swedish].
Allvin, M., 2004. The individualisation of labour. In C. Garsten and K. Jacobsson, eds, *Learning to be Employable*. Houndsmills, Basingstoke: Palgrave Macmillan.
Allvin, M., 2008. New rules of work: Exploring the boundaryless job. In K. Näswall, J. Hellgren, and M. Sverke, eds, *The Individual in the Changing Working Life*. Cambridge: Cambridge University Press, pp. 19–45.
Allvin, M. and Aronsson, G., 2000. Frilansare [Freelancers: A survey and interview study of freelance journalists' working conditions]. Report to The Swedish Union of Journalists' congress, Fall 2000, Swedish National Institute for Working Life [In Swedish].
Allvin, M. and Aronsson, G., 2003. The future of work environment reforms: Does the concept of work environment apply within the new economy? *International Journal of Health Services*, **33**(1), 99–111.
Allvin, M., Aronsson, G., Hagström, T., *et al.*, 1998. *Gränslöst arbete eller arbetets nya gränser [The new boundaries of work]*. *Arbete och Hälsa*, **21**. Stockholm: National Institute for Working Life [In Swedish].
Allvin, M., Jacobson, A., and Isaksson, K., 2003. Att avgränsa det gränslösa sjuksköterskearbetet. En intervjustudie om sjuksköterskors villkor och

valmöjligheter i bemanningsbranschen [Delimiting the unlimited work of nurses: An interview study of the conditions and choices in the staffing business]. *Arbetsliv i omvandling*, **12** [In Swedish].

Allvin, M., Mellner, C., Movitz, F., and Aronsson, G., 2010. The diffusion of flexible jobs – Estimating the incidence of low-regulated working conditions, submitted.

Allvin, M., Wiklund, P., Härenstam, A., and Aronsson, G., 1999. Frikopplad eller frånkopplad [Unattached or disconnected: On the meanings and consequences of boundaryless work]. *Arbete och hälsa*, **2** [In Swedish].

Alvesson, M., 1995. *Management of Knowledge-Intensive Companies*. Berlin: Walter de Gruyter.

Alvesson, M. and Kärreman, D., 2001. Odd couple: Making sense of the curious concept of knowledge management. *Journal of Management Studies*, **38**(7), 995–1018.

Ambjörnsson, R., 1989. The conscientious worker: Ideas and ideals in a Swedish working class culture. *History of European Ideas*, **10**(1), 59–67.

Amiot, C. E., de la Sablonnière, R., Therry, D. J., and Smith, J. R., 2007. Integration of social identities in the self: Toward a cognitive-developmental model. *Personality and Social Psychology Review*, **11**(4), 364–388.

Antonovsky, A., 1979. *Health, Stress and Coping*. San Francisco: Jossey-Bass Publishers.

Arendt, H., 1958. *The Human Condition*. Chicago: University of Chicago Press.

Argyris, C., 1986. Skilled incompetence. *The Harvard Business Review* (Sep.–Oct.), 71–81.

Aronsson, G., 1989. Swedish findings on control and health. In S. L. Sauter, J. Hurrell, and C. L. Cooper, eds, *Job Control and Worker Health*. Chichester: John Wiley & Sons Ltd, pp. 76–88.

Aronsson, G., 1999. Paid by time but judged by results: An empirical study of unpaid overtime. *International Journal of Employment Studies*, **7**(1), 1–15.

Aronsson, G., 2004. Health and development opportunities for those in fixed-term employment. In R. Gustafsson and I. Lundberg, eds, *Worklife and Health in Sweden*. Stockholm: National Institute for Working Life and Swedish Work Environment Authority, pp. 225–248.

Aronsson, G. and Göransson, S., 1999. Permanent employment but not in a preferred occupation. *Journal of Occupational Health Psychology*, **4**(2), 152–163.

Aronsson, G. and Gustafsson, K., 1999. Kritik eller tystnad: En studie av arbetsmarknads- och anställningsförhållandens betydelse för arbetsmiljökritik [Criticism or silence]. *Arbetsmarknad och Arbetsliv*, **5**(3), 189–206 [In Swedish].

Aronsson, G. and Gustafsson, K., 2005a. Sickness presenteeism: Prevalence, attendance-pressure factors and an outline of a model for research. *Journal of Occupational and Environmental Medicine*, **47**(9), 958–966.

Aronsson, G. and Gustafsson, K., 2005b. Vacation – Still an issue of workers' protection. An empirical study of vacation and recuperation. *International Journal of Health Services*, **35**(1), 143–169.

Aronsson, G., Dallner, M., and Gustafsson, K., 2000. Yrkes- och arbetsplatsinlåsning: En empirisk studie av omfattning och hälsokonsekvenser [Locked-in, in the occupation and the working place. An empirical study of prevalence and health consequences]. *Arbete och Hälsa*, **5** [In Swedish].

Aronsson, G., Dallner, M., and Gustafsson, K., 2002. Work environment and health in different types of temporary jobs. *European Journal of Work and Organizational Psychology*, **11**(2), 151–175.

Aronsson, G., Dallner, M., Lindh, T., and Göransson, S., 2005. Flexible pay but fixed expenses: Personal, financial strain among on-call employees. *International Journal of Health Services*, **35**(3), 499–528.

Aronsson, G., Gustafsson, K., and Dallner M., 2000. Sick but yet at work. An empirical study of sickness presenteeism. *Journal of Epidemiology and Community Health*, **54**(7), 502–509.

Aronsson, G., Gustafsson, K., and Mellner, C., 2010. Sickness presence, sickness absence, and self rated health. *International Journal of Workplace Health Management*, submitted.

Ashforth, B. E., Kreiner, G. E., and Fugate, M., 2000. All in a day's work. Boundaries and micro role transitions. *Academy of Management Review*, **25**(3), 472–291.

Ashkenas, R., 1995. *The Boundaryless Organization: Breaking the Chains of Organizational Structure*. San Francisco: Jossey-Bass.

Astvik, W., 2002. Svåra möten i omsorgsarbete [Managing stressful encounters in care work]. *Arbete och Hälsa*, **17**. Stockholm: National Institute for Working Life [In Swedish].

Astvik, W., 2003. *Relationer som arbete [Relating as a Primary task. Prerequisites for Sustainable Caring Relations in Home-care Service]*. PhD, National Institute for Working Life, Stockholm, Stockholm University [In Swedish].

Atkinson, J., 1984. Flexibility, uncertainty and manpower management. IMS Report No. 89. Brighton: Institute of Manpower Studies.

Atkinson, J. and Meager, N., 1986. Changing working patterns: How companies achieve flexibility to meet new needs. Report for the National Economic Development Office, NEDO, Institute for Manpower Studies.

Atkinson, J. Rick, J., Morris, S., and Williams, M., 1996. Temporary work and the labour market, Report No. 311. Brighton: The Institute for Employment Studies.

Avery, C. and Zabel, D., 2001. *The Flexible Workplace: A Sourcebook of Information and Research*. Westport, CT: Quorum Books.

Babiak, P., 1995. When psychopaths go to work: A case study of an industrial psychopath. *Applied Psychology: An International Review*, **44**(2), 171–188.

Bäck-Wiklund, M., 2002. The family and the welfare state: A route to defamilialization. In R. Liljeström and E. Ozdalga, eds, *Autonomy and Dependence in the Family*. Istanbul/London: Swedish Research Institute in Istanbul and Routledge/Curson.

Barley, S. R. and Kunda, G., 2006. *Gurus, Hired Guns, and Warm Bodies: Itinerant Experts in a Knowledge Economy*. Princeton, NJ: Princeton University Press.

Barling, J., Kelloway, E. K., and Frone, M. R., eds, 2005. *Handbook of Work Stress*. Thousand Oaks: SAGE Publications.

Barnett, R., 1999. Learning to work and working to learn. In D. Boud and J. Garrick, eds, *Understanding Learning at Work*. London: Routledge.

Barnett, R. C. and Hyde, J. S., 2001. Women, men, work, and family: An expansionist theory. *American Psychologist*, 56(10), 781–796.

Barnett, R. C., Marshall, N. L., and Pleck, J. H., 1992. Men's multiple roles and their relationship to men's psychological distress. *Journal of Marriage and the Family*, 54, 358–367.

Baruch, G. K. and Barnett, R. C., 1986. Role quality, multiple role involvement, and psychological well-being in midlife women. *Journal of Personality and Social Psychology*, 51, 578–585.

Baudrillard, J., [1968] 1996. *The System of Objects*. London: Verso.

Baudrillard, J., [1970] 1998. *The Consumer Society: Myths and Structures*. London: SAGE.

Bauman, Z., 1998. *Work, Consumerism and the New Poor*. Buckingham: Open University Press.

Bauman, Z., 2000. Ethics of individuals. *Canadian Journal of Sociology*, 25(1), 83–96.

Beardwood, B., Walters, V., Eyles, J., and French, S., 1999. Complaints against nurses: A reflection of 'the new managerialism' and consumerism in health care. *Social Science and Medicine*, 48(3), 363–374.

Beck, U., 1992. *Risk Society. Towards a New Modernity*. London: SAGE Publications.

Beck, U., 1994. The reinvention of politics: Towards a theory of reflexive modernization. In U. Beck, A. Giddens and S. Lash, eds, *Reflexive Modernization: Politics, Tradition and Aesthetics in the Modern Social Order*. Cambridge: Polity Press.

Beck, U., 1999. *What is Globalization?* Cambridge: Polity Press.

Beck, U., 2000. *The Brave New World of Work*. Cambridge: Polity Press.

Beck, U. and Beck-Gernsheim, E., 1995. *The Normal Chaos of Love*. Cambridge: Polity Press.

Beck, U. and Beck-Gernsheim, E., 2002. *Individualization: Institutionalized Individualism and its Social and Political Consequences*. London: SAGE.

Beck-Gernsheim, E., 1996. Life as a planning project. In S. Lash, B. Szerszynski and B. Wynne, eds, *Risk, Environment and Modernity*. London: SAGE.

Beck-Gernsheim, E., 2002. *Reinventing the Family: In Search of New Lifestyles*. Cambridge: Polity Press.

Belkic, K., Schwartz, J., Schnall, P., et al., 2000. Evidence for mediating econeurocardiologic mechanisms. *Occupational Medicine*, **15**(1), 117–162.

Bell, D., 1973. *The Coming of Post-Industrial Society. A Venture in Social Forecasting.* New York: Basic Books.

Berggren, C., 1992. *Alternatives to Lean Production: Work Organization in the Swedish Auto Industry.* Ithaca, NY: ILR Press.

Bergström, G., Bodin, L., Hagberg, J., et al., 2009a. Sickness presenteeism today, sickness absenteeism tomorrow? A prospective study on sickness presenteeism and future sickness absenteeism. *Journal of Occupational Environmental Medicine*, **51**(6), 629–638.

Bergström, G., Bodin, L., Hagberg, J., et al., 2009b. Does sickness presenteeism have an impact on future general health? *International Archive of Occupational and Environmental Health*, **82**(10), 1179–1190.

Bergström, O. and Storrie, D. W., eds, 2003. *Contingent Employment in Europe and the United States.* Cheltenham: Edward Elgar.

Berntsson, L., Krantz, G., and Lundberg, U., 2005. Total workload: The distribution of paid and unpaid work as related to age, occupational level and number of children among Swedish male and female white-collar workers. *Work and Stress*, **15**(2), 209–215.

Björnberg, U., 2004. Making agreements and managing conflicts. *Current Sociology*, **52**(1), 33–52.

Blomgren, M. and Sahlin-Andersson, K., 2007. Quests for transparency: Signs of a new institutional era in the healthcare field. In T. Christensen and P. Laegreid, eds, *Transcending New Public Management: The Transformation of Public Sector Reforms.* Burlington, VT: Ashgate, pp. 155–177.

Blood, R. O. and Wolfe, D. M., 1960. *Husbands and Wives: The Dynamics of Married Living.* Glencoe, IL: The Free Press.

Bourdieu, P., 1986. The forms of capital. In J. G. Richardson, ed, *Handbook of Theory and Research for the Sociology of Education.* Westport, CT: Greenwood Press.

Braverman, H., 1974. *Labor and Monopoly Capital: The Degradation of Work in the Twentieth Century.* New York: Monthly Review Press.

Brown, J. S. and Duguid, P., 1991. Organizational learning and communities-of-practice: Toward a unified view of working, learning, and innovation. *Organization Science*, **2**(1), 40–57.

Burt, R. S., 2000. The network entrepreneur. In R. Swedberg, ed., *Entrepreneurship: Social Science View.* Oxford: Oxford University Press.

Campbell, C., 1989. *The Romantic Ethic and the Spirit of Modern Consumerism.* Oxford: Blackwell Publishers.

Canivet, C., Ostergren, P.-O., BongKyoo, C., et al., 2008. Sleeping problems as a risk factor for subsequent musculoskeletal pain and the role of job strain: Results from a one-year follow-up of the Malmö shoulder neck study cohort. *International Journal of Behavioral Medicine*, **15**, 254–262.

Cannon, W. B., 1914. The emergency function of the adrenal medulla in pain and the major emotions. *American Journal of Physiology*, **33**, 356–372.

Caplan, R. D., 1983. Person-environment fit: Past, present, and future. In C. L. Cooper, ed., *Stress Research: Issues for the Eighties*. New York: John Wiley & Sons Inc.

Carlzon, J., 1987. *Moments of Truth*. Cambridge, MA: Ballinger Publishing Co.

Cascio, W. F., 1997. Learning from outcomes: Financial experiences of 311 firms that have downsized. In M. K. Gowing, J. D. Kraft, and J. Campbell Quick, eds, *The New Organizational Reality: Downsizing, Restructuring, and Revitalization*. Washington, DC: American Psychological Association.

Casey, B., Metcalf, H., and Millward, N., 1997. *Employer's Use of Flexible Labour*. London: Policy Studies Institute.

Castells, M., 1996. The information age. Economy, society and culture, Vol. **1**. *The Rise of the Network Society*. Oxford and Malden, MA: Blackwell.

Castells, M., 2001. *The Internet Galaxy: Reflections on the Internet, Business, and Society*. Oxford: Oxford University Press.

Castells, M., 2003. *The Internet Galaxy: Reflections on the Internet, Business, and Society*. New York: Oxford University Press.

Castells, M., [1998] 2009. The information age. Economy, society and culture, Vol. **3**. *End of the Millenium*. Oxford and Malden, MA: Blackwell.

Caverley, N., Cunningham, J. B., and MacGregor, J. N., 2007. Sickness presenteeism, sickness absenteeism, and health following restructuring in a public service organization. *Journal of Management Studies*, **44**(2), 304–319.

Cherniss, C. and Adler, M., 2000. *Promoting Emotional Intelligence in Organizations. Guidelines to Help You Design, Implement and Evaluate Effective Programs*. Baltimore: ASTD Press.

Clark, B. K. and Fujimoto, T., 1991. *Product Development Performance: Strategy, Organization, and Management in the World Auto Industry*. Boston, MA: Harvard Business School Press.

Clark, S. C., 2000. Work/family border theory: A new theory of work/family balance. *Human Relations*, **53**(6), 747–770.

Clarke, J. and Newman, J. E., 1997. *The Managerial State: Power, Politics and Ideology in the Remaking of Social Welfare*. London: SAGE.

Coates, D., 2002. *Models of Capitalism: Debating Strengths and Weaknesses*. Aldershot: Edward Elgar Publishing.

Cohen, F. and Lazarus, R. S., 1973. Active coping processes, coping dispositions, and recovery from surgery. *Psychosomatic Medicine*, **35**, 375–389.

Cohen, S., 2005. The Pittsburgh common cold studies: Psychosocial predictors of susceptibility to respiratory infectious illness. *International Journal of Behavioral Medicine*, **12**, 123–131.

Cohen, S. and Syme, S. L., eds, 1985. *Social Support and Health*. Orlando: Academic Press.

Cohen, S., Doyle, W. J., Cuneyt, M., et al., 2009. Sleep habits and susceptibility to the common cold. *Archive of Internal Medicine*, **169**(1), 62–67.

Conway, N. and Briner, R. B., 2005. *Understanding Psychological Contracts at Work. A Critical Evaluation of Theory and Research*. New York: Oxford University Press.

Cooper, C. L. and Dewe, P., 2004. *Stress: A Brief History*. Oxford: Blackwell Publishing.

Cortada, J. W., ed., 1998. *Rise of the Knowledge Worker*. Boston: Butterworth-Heinemann.

Csikszentmihalyhi, M., 1990. *Flow: The Psychology of Optimal Experience*. New York: Harper & Row.

Czarniawska, B., 1997. *Narrating the Organization: Dramas of Institutional Identity*. Chicago: The University of Chicago Press.

Czarniawska-Joerges, B. and Gagliardi, P., 2003. *Narratives We Organize by. Advances in Organization Studies*. Amsterdam: John Benjamins Publishing Co.

Dean, M., 2009. *Governmentality: Power and Rule in Modern Society*, 2nd edn. London: SAGE Publications Ltd.

Dencik, L., 1996. Familjen i välfärdsstatens förvandlingsprocess [The family in the transformation of the welfare state]. *Dansk Sociologi*, **7**(1), 58–82 [In Danish].

Dicken, P., 2003. *Global Shift: Reshaping the Global Economic Map in the 21st Century*. London: SAGE.

DiMaggio, P., ed., 2003. *The twenty-first-century firm: Changing Economic Organization in International Perspective*. Princeton, NJ: Princeton University Press.

Drucker, P., 1954. *The Practice of Management*. New York: Harper & Row.

du Gay, P., 1996. *Consumption and Identity at Work*. London: SAGE.

du Gay, P. and Salaman, G., 1992. The cult(ure) of the customer. *Journal of Management Studies*, **29**(5), 615–633.

Eby, L. T. Casper, W. J., Lockwood, A., Bordeaux, C., and Brinley, A., 2005. Work and family research in IO/OB: Content analysis and review of the literature 1980–2002. *Journal of Vocational Behavior*, **66**(1), 124–197.

Edwards, R., 1979. *Contested Terra in: The Transformation of the Workplace in the Twentieth Century*. New York: Basic Books.

Ehn, P., 1988. *Work-Oriented Design of Computer Artifacts*. Stockholm: Arbetslivscentrum.

Ekstedt, E., 1999. *Neo-Industrial Organising: Renewal by Action and Knowledge Formation in a Project-Intensive Economy*. London: Routledge.

Ekstedt, M., 2005. Burnout and sleep. PhD. Stockholm: Karolinska Institutet.

Elden, M. J., 1981. Political efficacy at work: The connection between more autonomous forms of workplace organization and a more participatory politics. *The American Political Science Review*, **75**(1), 43–58.

Ellström, P.-E., 2001. Integrating learning and work: Problems and prospects. *Human Resource Development Quarterly*, **12**(4), 21–436.

Ellström, P.-E., 2002. Time and the logics of learning. *Life Long learning in Europe*, 7(2), 86–93.

Elvin-Nowak, Y., 1999. Accompanied by guilt. Modern motherhood the Swedish way. PhD. Stockholm University.

Erera, P. I., 2001. *Family Diversity. Continuity and Change in the Contemporary Family*. London: SAGE.

Ester, P., Halman, L., and de Moor, R., eds, 1994. *The Individualizing Society: Value Change in Europe and North America*. Tilburg, NE: Tilburg University Press.

European Foundation for the Improvement of Living and Working Conditions, 2006. *Mobility in Europe. Analysis of the 2005 Eurobarometer Survey on Geographical and Labour Market Mobility*. Luxembourg: Office for Official Publications of the European Communities.

European Foundation for the Improvement of Living and Working Conditions, 2007. *Fourth European Survey on Working Conditions*. Luxembourg: Office for Official Publications of the European Communities.

Eurostat, 2009. Population and social conditions: Labour market latest trends – 1st Quarter 2009 data (Eurostat Data in Focus, 35/2009). European Commission.

Faludi, S., 2000. *Stiffed: The Betrayal of the American Man*. New York: William Morrow and Company Inc.

Fayol, H., 1916. *General and Industrial Management*. London: Pitman.

Felstead, A. and Jewson, N., 2000. *In Work, at Home. Towards an Understanding of Homeworking*. London: Routledge.

Fernandez, R. M., Castilla, E. J., and Moore, P., 2000. Social capital at work: Networks and employment at a phone center. *American Journal of Sociology*, 105(5), 1288–1356.

Fischer, D., Rooke, D., and Torbert, B., 2001. *Personal and Organizational Transformations: Through Action Inquiry*. Boston, MA: Edge/Work Press.

Fleming, P. and Spicer, A., 2004. "You can checkout anytime, but you can never leave": Spatial boundaries in a high commitment organization. *Human Relations*, 57(1), 75–94.

Fligstein, N., 1990. *The Transformation of Corporate Control*. Cambridge, MA: Harvard University Press.

Forseth, U., 2005. Gender matters? Exploring how gender is negotiated in service encounters. *Gender, Work and Organization*, 12(5), 440–459.

Foucault, M., [1974] 1991. *Discipline and Punish: The Birth of the Prison*. London: Penguin Books.

Frankenhaeuser, M., 1983. The sympathetic-adrenal and pituitary-adrenal response to challenge: Comparison between the sexes. In T. M. Dembroski, T. H. Schmidt and G. Blümchen, eds, *Biobehavioral Bases of Coronary Heart Disease*, pp. 91–105. Basel and New York: Karger.

Frankenhaeuser, M. and Johansson, G., 1981. On the psychophysiological consequences of understimulation and overstimulation. In L. Levi, ed.,

Society, Stress and Disease, Vol. IV, Working Life. London: Oxford University Press, pp. 82–89.
Frankenhaeuser, M., Lundberg, U., Fredrikson, M., et al., 1989. Stress on and off the job as related to sex and occupational status in white-collar workers. *Journal of Organizational Behaviour*, **10**, 321–346.
Fredrickson, B. L., 2003. The value of positive emotions. *American Scientist*, **91**, 330–335.
Fredrickson, B. L., 2004. The broaden-and-build theory of positive emotions. *The Royal Society*, **359**, 1367–1377.
Fredrickson, B. L. and Branigan, C., 2005. Positive emotions broaden the scope of attention and thought-action repertoires. *Cognition and Emotion*, **19**, 313–332.
Freire, P., 1970. *Pedagogy of the Oppressed.* New York: Herter & Herter.
Frese, M. and Zapf, D., 1994. Action as the core of work psychology. In C. Triandis, M. D. Dunette and M. H. Leaetta, eds, *Handbook of Industrial and Organizational Psychology*, Vol. **4**. Palo Alto: Consulting Psychologists Press Inc., pp. 271–340.
Frone, M. R., 2003. Work-family balance. In J. C. Quick and L. E. Tetrick, eds, *Handbook of Occupational Health Psychology.* Washington, DC: American Psychological Association.
Frone, M. R., Russel, M., and Barnes, G. M., 1996. Work-family conflict, gender, and health-related outcomes: A study of employed parents in two community samples. *Journal of Occupational Health Psychology*, **1**(1), 57–69.
Fukuyama, F., 1995. *Trust: The Social Virtues and the Creation of Prosperity.* London: Hamish Hamilton.
Gardiner, J., 1997. *Gender, Care and Economics.* Eastbourne: Anthony Rowe Ltd.
Gardner, H., 1983. *Frames of Mind. The Theory of Multiple Intelligences.* New York: Bantam Books.
Garsten, C., 1999. Betwixt and between: Temporary employees as liminal subjects in flexible organizations. *Organization Studies*, **20**(4), 601–617.
Garsten, C. and Jacobson, K., eds, 2004. *Learning to be Employable: New Agendas on Work, Responsibility and Learning in a Globalizing World.* Houndsmills, Basingstoke: Palgrave MacMillan.
Giddens, A., 1990. *The Consequences of Modernity.* Cambridge: Polity Press.
Giddens, A., 1991. *Modernity and Self-Identity: Self and Society in the Late Modern Age.* Cambridge: Polity Press.
Giddens, A., 1992. *The Transformation of Intimacy: Sexuality, Love and Eroticism in Modern Societies.* Stanford, CA: Stanford University Press.
Goff, S. J., Mount, K., and Jamison, R. L., 1990. Employer supported child care, work/family conflict, and absenteeism: A field study. *Personnel Psychology*, **43**(4), 793–809.
Goffman, E., 1959. *The Presentation of the Self in Everyday Life.* Plats: Ancor Books.

Goleman, D., 1995. *Emotional Intelligence.* New York: Bantam Books.
Goleman, D., 2007. *Social Intelligence. The New Science of Human Relationship.* London: Arrow Books.
Göransson, S., Aronsson, G., and Melin, B., 2002. *Vilja och villkor – en studie om långtidssjukskrivnas situation* [Motivation and opportunities – a study of people in long term sickness absence]. In *SOU*, **5**. Handlingsplan för ökad hälsa i arbetslivet. Stockholm: Allmänna förlaget [In Swedish].
Granovetter, M., 1973. The strength of weak ties. *American Journal of Sociology*, **78**(6), 1360–1380.
Granovetter, M., 1983. The strength of weak ties: A network theory revisited. *Sociological Theory*, **1**, 201–233.
Granovetter, M., 2000. Economic sociology of firms and entrepreneurs. In R. Swedberg, ed., *Entrepreneurship: The Social Science View.* Oxford: Oxford University Press.
Grey, C. and Garsten, C., 2001. Trust, control and post-bureaucracy. *Organization Studies*, **22**(2), 229–250.
Gronning, T., 1997. The Emergence and institutionalization of Toyotism: Subdivision and integration of the labour force at the Toyota Motor Corporation from the 1950s to the 1970s. *Economic and Industrial Democracy*, **18**(3), 423–455.
Grönroos, C., 1990. *Service Management and Marketing: Managing the Moments of Truth in Service Competition.* Lexington, MA: Lexington Books.
Guest, D., 2004. Flexible employment contracts, the psychological contract and employee outcomes: An analysis and review of the evidence. *International Journal of Management Reviews*, **5/6**(1), 1–19.
Gustafson, S. B. and Ritzer, D. R., 1995. The dark side of normal: A psychopathy-linked pattern called aberrant self-promotion. *European Journal of Personality*, **9**(3), 147–183.
Gustafsson K., 2008. Working conditions, compensatory strategies, and recovery. PhD. Department of Psychology, Stockholm University.
Hacker, W., 1986. *Arbeitspsychologie*, Vol. **41**. Stuttgart: Verlag Hans Huber.
Hacker, W., Plath, H. E., Richter, P., and Zimmer, K., 1978. Internal representation of task structure and mental load of work: Approaches and methods of assessment. *Ergonomics*, **21**(3), 187–194.
Hagström, T., ed., 2003. *Adult Development in Post-Industrial Society and Working Life.* University of Stockholm Department of Education.
Hagström, T. and Gamberale, F., 1995. Young people's work motivation and value orientation. *Journal of Adolescence*, **18**(4), 475–490.
Hagström, T. and Hanson, M., 2003. Flexible work contexts and human competence: An action-interaction frame of reference and empirical illustration. In A. Bron and M. Schemmann, eds, *Knowledge Society, Information Society and Adult Education: Trends, Issues, Challenges.* Münster: Lit Verlag, pp. 148–180.

Hagström, T. and Kjellberg, A., 2000. Work values and early work socialization among nurses and engineers. In K. Isaksson, C. Hogstedt, C. Eriksson and T. Theorell, eds, *Health Effects in the New Working Life*. London: Plenum Press, pp. 311–328.

Hagström, T. and Kjellberg, A., 2007. Stability and change in work values among male and female nurses and engineers. *Scandinavian Journal of Psychology*, 48(2), 143–151.

Hagström, T., Backström, T., and Göransson, G., 2009. Sustainable competence: A study of a bank. *The Learning Organization*, 16(3), 237–250.

Hakim, C., 2000. *Work-Lifestyle Choices in the 21st Century: Preference Theory*. Oxford: Oxford University Press.

Hakim, C., 2003. A new approach to explaining fertility patterns: Preference theory. *Population and Development Review*, 29(3), 349–374.

Hallsten L., 2005. Burnout and wornout concepts and data from a national survey. In C. Cooper and A. Antonion, eds, *Research Companion to Organizational Health Psychology*. Northampton: Edward Elgar Publishing, pp. 516–536.

Hallsten, L., Josephson, M., and Torgén, M., 2005. Performance-based self-esteem. A driving force in burnout processes and its assessment. *Arbete och Hälsa*, 5. Stockholm: National Institute for Working Life.

Hallsten, L., Lundberg, I., and Waldenström, K., 2005. Low mental wellbeing – Trends in and outside the labour market. In R. Gustafsson and I. Lundberg, eds, *Worklife and Health in Sweden 2004*. Stockholm: National Institute for Working Life and Swedish Work Environment Authority, pp. 159–181.

Halman, L., 1995. Is there a moral decline?: A cross-national inquiry into morality in contemporary society. *International Social Science Journal*, 47(3), 419–439.

Hammer, M. and Champy, J., 1993. *Reengineering the Corporation: A Manifesto for Business Revolution*. New York: Harper Business.

Hansen, L. H., 2001. *The Division of Labour in Post-Industrial Societies. Gothenburg Studies in Sociology*. Göteborg: Department of Sociology.

Hanson, M., 2004. Det flexibla arbetets villkor: Om självförvaltandets kompetens [Self-governing competence for flexible work]. PhD. Department of Education, Stockholm University. *Arbetsliv i omvandling*, 8 [In Swedish].

Harrison, B., 1994. *Lean and Mean: The Changing Landscape of Corporate Power in the Age of Flexibility*. New York: Basic Books.

Hartig, T., Johansson, G., and Kylin, C., 2003. Residence in the social ecology of stress and restoration. *Journal of Social Issues*, 59(3), 611–636.

Hartig, T., Kylin, C., and Johansson, G., 2007. The telework tradeoff: Stress, mitigation vs. constrained restoration. *Applied Psychology: An International Review*, 56(2), 231–253.

Harvey, M., 1999. Economies of time: A framework for analysing the restructuring of employment relations. In A. Felstead and N. Jewson, eds, *Global Trends in Flexible Labour*. London: MacMillan Press.

Hasselbladh, H. and Bejerot, E., 2007. Webs of knowledge and circuits of communication: Constructing rationalized agency in Swedish health care. *Organization*, **14**(2), 175–200.

Hendry, C., 1995. *Human Resource Management: A Strategic Approach to Employment*. Oxford: Butterworth-Heinemann Ltd.

Henry, J. P., 1992. Biological basis of the stress response. *Integrative Physiological and Behavioral Science*, **1**, 66–83.

Hirdman, Y., 1990. Genussystemet [The gender system]. In O. Petersson, Y. Hirdman, I. Persson, J. P. Olsen and A. Westholm, eds, Demokrati och Makt i Sverige: [Democracy and Power in Sweden]. Swedish Government Reports No. SOU 1990:44. Stockholm: Allmänna förlaget [In Swedish].

Hirschman, A. O., 1970. *Exit, Voice, and Loyalty: Responses to Decline in Firms, Organizations, and States*. Cambridge, MA: Harvard University Press.

Hobfoll, S. E., 1998. *Stress, Culture, and Community: The Psychology and Philosophy of Stress*. New York: Plenum Press.

Hochschild, A. R., 1983. *The Managed Heart: Commercialization of Human Feeling*. Berkeley, CA: University of California Press.

Hochschild, A. R., 1997. *The Time Bind: When Work Becomes Home and Home Becomes Work*. New York: Henry Holt & Co.

Holmes, T. H. and Rahe, R. H., 1967. The social readjustment rating scale. *Journal of Psychosomatic Research*, **11**(2), 213–218.

Hudson, M., 2002. Flexibility and the reorganisation of work. In B. Burchell, D. Ladipo, and F. Wilkinson, eds, *Job Insecurity and Work Intensification*. London: Routledge.

Hutchins, D., 1988. *Just in Time*. Aldershot: Gower.

Huws, U., 2003a. The making of a cybertariate? Virtual work in a real world. In U. Huws, ed., *The Making of a Cybertariate? Virtual Work in a Real World*. London: The Merlin Press.

Huws, U., 2003b. Who's waiting?: The contestation of time. In U. Huws, ed., *The Making of a Cybertariat: Virtual Work in a Real World*. London: The Merlin Press.

Huws, U., 2003c. Material world: The myth of the weightless economy. In U. Huws, ed., *The Making of a Cybertariat: Virtual Work in a Real World*. London: The Merlin Press.

Inglehart, R., 1990. *Culture Shift: In Advanced Industrial Society*. Princeton, NJ: Princeton University Press.

Inglehart, R., 1997. *Modernization and Postmodernization: Cultural, Economic, and Political Change in 43 Societies*. Princeton, NJ: Princeton University Press.

Inglehart, R., 2007. Mapping global values. In Y. Esmer and T. Pettersson, eds, *Measuring and Mapping Cultures: 25 years of Comparative Value Surveys*. Leiden and Boston: Brill, pp. 11–32.

Inglehart, R. and Welzel, C., 2005. *Modernization, Cultural Change, and Democracy. The Human Development Sequence.* Cambridge: Cambridge University Press.

Israel, J., 1971. *Alienation: From Marx to Modern Sociology.* Boston: Allyn & Bacon.

Jahoda, M., 1979. The impact of unemployment in the 1930s and in the 1970s. *Bulletin of the British Psychological Society*, **32**, 309–314.

Jahoda, M., 1981. Work employment and unemployment. Values, theories and approaches in social research. *American Psychologist*, **36**(2), 84–191.

Jameson, F., 1991. *Postmodernism or the Culture Logic of Late Capitalism.* London: Verso.

Johannisson, K., 2006. Modern fatigue: A historical perspective. In B. Arnetz and R. Ekman, eds, *Stress in Health and Disease.* London: Wiley, pp. 1–19.

Johansson, G. and Aronsson, G., 1991. Psychosocial factors in the workplace. In G. Green and F. Baker, eds, *Work, Health, and Productivity.* Oxford: Oxford University Press.

Johansson, H., Windhorst, U., Djupsjöbacka, M., and Passatore, M., eds, 2003. *Chronic Work-Related Myalgia. Neuromuscular Mechanisms Behind Work-Related Chronic Muscle Pain Syndromes.* Gävle University Press.

Johnson, J. V. and Hall, E. M., 1988. Job strain, workplace social support and cardiovascular disease: A cross-sectional study of a random sample of the Swedish working population. *American Journal of Public Health*, **78**, 1336–1342.

Johnson, J. V., Stewart, W., Hall, E. M., et al., 1996. Long-term psychosocial work environment and cardiovascular mortality among Swedish men. *American Journal of Public Health*, **86**(3), 324–331.

Johnson, M., 1997. On the dynamics of self-esteem. Empirical validation of basic self-esteem and earning self-esteem. PhD. University of Stockholm.

Kahn, R. L., Wolf, D. M., Quinn, R. P., et al., 1964. *Organizational Stress: Studies in Role Conflict and Ambiguity.* New York: John Wiley & Sons Inc.

Kakar, S., 1970. *Frederick Taylor: A Study in Personality and Innovation.* Cambridge: MIT Press.

Kaplan, R. and Norton, D., 1996. *The Balanced Scorecard.* Boston: Harvard Business School Press.

Karasek, R., 1979. Job demands, job decision latitude, and mental strain: Implications for job redesign. *Administrative Science Quarterly*, **24**(2), 285–308.

Karasek, R. and Theorell, T., 1990. *Healthy Work: Stress, Productivity, and the Reconstruction of Working Life.* New York: Basic Books.

Keat, R. and Abercrombie, N., eds, 1991. *Enterprise Culture.* London: Routledge.

Kegan, R., 1994. *In Over our Heads. The Mental Demands of Modern Life.* Cambridge, MA: Harvard University Press.

Kegan, R., 2003. Hidden curriculum of adult life: An adult developmental perspective. In T. Hagström, ed., *Adult Development in Post-Industrial*

Society and Working Life. Stockholm Lectures in Educology No. 2. Department of Education, Stockholm University, pp. 21–48.

Kelly, K., 1997. New rules for the new economy: Twelve dependable principles for thriving in a turbulent world. *Wired*, 5 September.

Kenney, M. and Florida, R., 1988. Beyond mass production: Production and the labor process in Japan. *Politics and Society*, 16(1), 121–158.

Kern, H. and Schumann, M., 1984. *Das Ende der Arbeitsteilung? Rationalisierung in der Industriellen Produktion: Bestandsaufnahme, Trendbestimmung.* München: Verlag C.H.

Kern, H. and Schumann, M., 1987. Limits of the division of labour: New production and employment concepts in West German industry. *Economic and Industrial Democracy*, 8, 151–170.

Keynes, J. M., 1936. *The General Theory of Employment, Interest and Money.* Cambridge: Cambridge University Press.

Kivimäki, M., Head, J., Ferrie, J. E., *et al.*, 2005. Working while ill as a risk factor for serious coronary events: The Whitehall II study. *American Journal of Public Health*, 95, 98–102.

Klein, N., 2000. *No Logo.* London: Flamingo.

Kocakülâh, M. C. and Austill, A. D., 2007. Balanced scorecard application in the health care industry: A case study. *Journal of Health Care Finance*, 34(1), 72–99.

Kohlberg, L., 1969. Stage and sequence: The cognitive-developmental approach to socialization. In D. A. Goslin, ed., *Handbook of Socialization Theory and Research.* Chicago, IL: Rand McNally and Company, pp. 347–481.

Kohlberg, L. and Armon, C., 1984. Three types of stage model used in the study of adult development. In M. L. Commons, F. A. Richards, and C. Armon, eds, *Beyond Formal Operation. Late Adolescent and Adult Cognitive Development.* New York, NY: Praeger, pp. 383–394.

Kohn, M. L., 2006. *Change and Stability. A Cross-National Analysis of Social Structure and Personality.* Boulder and London: Paradigm Publishers.

Kohn, M. L. and Schooler, C., 1983. *Work and Personality: An Inquiry into the Impact of Social Stratification.* Norwood, NJ: Ablex Publishing.

Kreiner, G. E. Hollensbe, E. C., and Sheep, M. L., 2009. Balancing borders and bridges: Negotiating the work–home interface via boundary work tactics. *Academy of Management Journal*, 52(4), 704–730.

Kunda, G., 1992. *Engineering Culture: Control and Commitment in a High-Tech Corporation.* Philadelphia: Temple University Press.

Kylin, C., 2007. Coping with boundaries. PhD. Stockholm University.

Lager, A. and Bremberg, S., 2009. Association between labour market trends and trends in young people's mental health in ten European countries 1983–2005. *BMC Public Health*, 9, 325.

Länsisalmi, H., Peiro, J. M., and Kivimäki, M., 2000. Collective stress and coping in the context of organizational culture. *European Journal of Work and Organizational Psychology*, **9**(4), 527–559.

Lasch, C., 1977. *Heaven in a Heartless World: The Family Besieged*. New York: W. W. Norton & Co.

Lasch, C., 1996. *The Revolt of the Elites and the Betrayal of Democracy*. New York: W.W. Norton & Co.

Lazarus, R. S., 1981. The stress and coping paradigm. In C. Eisdorfer, D. Cohen, and P. Maxim, eds, *Models for Clinical Psychopathology*. New York: Spectrum.

Lazarus, R. S., 1991. Psychological stress in the workplace. In P. L. Perrewé, ed., *Handbook on Job Stress: A Special Issue of the Journal of Social Behaviour and Personality*, Vol. **6**, pp. 1–20.

Lazarus, R. S. and Eriksen, C. W., 1952. Effects of failure stress upon skilled performance. *Journal of Experimental Psychology*, **43**(2), 100–105.

Lee, C. and Powers, J. R., 2002. Number of roles, health, and well-being in three generations of Australian women. *International Journal of Behavioral Medicine*, **9**(3), 1995–2015.

Lee, D. R., 1996. why is flexible employment increasing? *Journal of Labour Research*, **17**(4), 543–551.

Lee, M. J., 1993. *Consumer Culture Reborn: The Culture Politics of Consumption*. London: Routledge.

Legge, K., 1995. *Human Resource Management: Rhetorics and Realities*. Houndsmills, Basingstoke: MacMillan Business.

Legge, K., 2005. *Human Resource Management: Rhetorics and Realities (Anniversary Edition)*. Houndsmills, Basingstoke, and Hampshire: Palgrave Macmillan.

Leidner, R., 1991. Serving hamburgers and selling insurance: Gender, work, and identity in interactive service jobs. *Gender and Society*, **5**(2), 154–177.

Leidner, R., 1993. *Fast Food, Fast Talk: Service Work and the Routinization of Everyday Life*. Berkeley: University of California Press.

Levi, L., 2002. *Stressen i mitt liv [Stress of my life]*. Stockholm: Natur och kultur [In Swedish].

Lewis, J., ed., 2007. *Children in Context. Changing Families and Welfare State*. London: Edgar Elgar.

Lidwall, U., Marklund, S., and Skogman Thoursie, P., 2005. Sickness absence in Sweden. In R. Å. Gustavsson and I. Lundberg, eds, *Worklife and Health in Sweden 2004*. Stockholm: National Institute for Working Life.

Lindgren, K.-A., ed., 2009. *How Stress Influences Musculoskeletal Disorders*. 9th Physiatric Summer School. Helsinki: Orton Foundation.

Lindh de Montoya, M., 2000. Entrepreneurship and cullture: The case of Freddy, the strawberry man. In R. Swedberg, ed., *Entrepreneurship: The Social Science View*. Oxford: Oxford University Press.

Lipietz, A., 1992. *Towards a New Economic Order*. Cambridge: Polity Press.

Littler, C. R., 1978. Understanding Taylorism. *British Journal of Sociology*, **29**(2), 185–202.

Littler, C. R., 1982. *The Development of the Labour Process in Capitalist Societies*. London: Heinemann Educational Books.

Long, S., 1999. The tyranny of the customer and the cost of consumerism: An analysis using systems and psychoanalytic approaches to groups and society. *Human Relations*, **52**(6), 723–743.

Luber, S. and Leicht, R., 2000. Growing self-employment in Western Europe: An effect of modernization? *International Review of Sociology*, **10**(1), 101–124.

Luhmann, N., 1979. *Trust and Power*. Chichester: John Wiley & Sons.

Luhmann, N., 2000a. *Vertrauen. Ein Mechanismus der Reduction socialer Komplexität*. Stuttgart: Lucius & Lucius.

Luhmann, N., 2000b. Familiarity, confidence, trust: Problems and alternatives. In D. Gambetta, ed., *Trust: Making and Breaking Cooperative Relations*, Electronic edition. Oxford: Department of Sociology, University of Oxford, pp. 94–107.

Lundberg, U. and Cooper, C. L., 2010. *The Science of Occupational Stress, Health, and Wellbeing in a Rapidly Changing World: A Psychobiological Perspective*. Oxford: Wiley-Blackwell.

Lundberg, U. and Melin, B., 2002. Stress in the development of musculoskeletal pain. In S. Linton, ed., *Avenues for the Prevention of Chronic Musculoskeletal Pain and Disability*. Amsterdam: Elsevier Science, pp. 165–179.

Lundgren, K., 1999. *Life-long learning. The Key to Europe's Economic Revival*. Solna: National Institute for Working Life.

Lury, C., 1996. *Consumer Culture*. Cambridge: Polity Press.

Lysgaard, S., 1961. Arbeiderkollektivet: En studie i de underordnedes sosiologi [Workers collective]. Oslo: Universitetsförlaget [In Norwegian].

Mahon, R., 1994. From Fordism to?: New technology, labour markets and unions. In W. Clement and R. Mahon, eds, *Swedish Social Democracy: A Model in Transition*. Toronto: Canadian Scholars' Press.

Martin, R. E. and Freeman, S. J., 1997. Mergers and acquisitions, downsizing, and privatization: A North American perspective. In M. K. Gowing, J. D. Kraft and J. Campbell Quick, eds, *The New Organizational Reality: Downsizing, Restructuring, and Revitalization*. Washington, DC: American Psychological Association.

McCall, L., 2001. *Complex Inequality: Gender, Class and Race in the New Economy*. New York: Routledge.

McCall, L., 2005. The Complexity of intersectionality. *Signs: Journal of Women in Culture and Society*, **30**(3), 1771–1801.

McEwen, B. S., 1998. Stress, adaptation and disease: Allostasis and allostatic load. *Annals of the New York Academy of Sciences*, **840**, 33–44.

McKevitt, C. and Morgan, M., 1997. Illness doesn't belong to us. *Journal of the Royal Society of Medicine*, **90**(9), 491–495.

McKevitt, C., Morgan, M., Dundas, R., and Holland, W. W., 1997. Sickness absence and 'working through' illness: A comparison of two professional groups. *Journal of Public Health Medicine*, **19**(3), 295–300.

Meissner, M., 1971. The long arm of the job: A study of work and leisure. *Industrial Relations*, **10**(3), 239–260.

Mellner, C, Astvik, W, and Aronsson, G., in preparation. Return to work after long-term sickleave through work turn-over.

Melucci, A., 1989. *Nomads of the Present: Social Movements and Individual Needs in Contemporary Society*. London: Radius.

Mészáros, I., 1975. *Marx's Theory of Alienation*, 4th edn. London: Merlin Press.

Mezirow, J., 2000. Learning to think like an adult: Core concepts on transformation theory. In J. Mezirow and Associates, eds, *Learning as Transformations: Critical Perspectives on a Theory in Progress*. San Francisco, CA: Jossey-Bass, pp. 3–33.

Mezirow, J., 2003. Issues in transformative learning. In T. Hagström, ed., *Adult Eevelopment in Postindusrial Society and Working Life. Stockholm Lectures in Educology*. Series no. 2. Stockholm: Department of Education, Stockholm University, pp. 49–65.

Micheletti, M., 2003. *Political Virtue and Shopping: Individuals, Consumerism, and Collective Action*. New York: Palgrave.

Morgan, C. and Murgatroyd, S., 1994. *Total Quality Management in the Public Sector*. Buckingham: Open University Press.

Morrison, E. W. and Robinson, S. L., 1997. When employees feel betrayed: A model of how psychological contract violation develops. *Academy of Management Review*, **22**(1), 226–256.

Mortimer, J. T. and Lorence, J., 1979. Work experience and occupational value socialization: A longitudinal study. *American Journal of Sociology*, **84**(6), 1361–1385.

Moss Kanter, R., 1977. *Men and Women of the Corporation*. New York: Basic Books.

Moss Kanter, R., 1989. *When Giants Learn to Dance: Mastering the Challanges of Strategy, Management, and Careers in the 1990s* London: Simon & Schuster.

Murdock, G. P., 1949. *Social Structure*. London: Collier-MacMillan Ltd.

National Research Council, 1999. *The Changing Nature of Work: Implications for Occupational Analysis*. Washington, DC: National Academy Press.

Nippert-Eng, C. E., 1996. *Home and Work: Negotiating Boundaries through Everyday Life*. Chicago: University of Chicago Press.

Normann, R., 2001. *Service Management: Strategy and Leadership in Service Business*, 3rd edn. Chichester: John Wiley & Sons, Ltd.

NUTEK, 1996. *Towards Flexible Organisations*. Stockholm: NUTEK.

O'Driscoll, M. P., 1996. The interface between job and off-job roles: Enhancement and conflict. *International Review of Industrial and Organizational Psychology*, **11**, 279–306.

OECD, 2002. *OECD Employment Outlook*. Paris: Organisation for Economic Co-operation and Development.

OECD, 2006. *OECD Employment Outlook*. Paris: Organisation for Economic Co-operation and Development.

Olin Wright, E., 1997. Rethinking, once again, the concept of class structure. In J. R. Hall, ed., *Reworking Class*. Ithaca: Cornell University Press.

Olmsted, B., 1996. Special issue: Flexible work arrangements. *Career Planning and Adult Development Journal*, 12(3).

Olmsted, B. and Smith, S., 1994. *Creating a Flexible Workplace: How to Select and Manage Alternative Work Options*. New York: Amacom.

Orlikowski, W. J., 2002. Knowing in practice: Enacting a collective capability in distributed organizing. *Organization Science*, 13(3), 249–273.

Ouchi, W. G., 1981. *Theory Z: How American Business can Meet the Japanese Challenge*. Reading, MA: Addison-Wesley.

Pakulski, J. and Waters, M., 1996. *The Death of Class*. London: SAGE.

Parker, S., 1981. The work–leisure relationship under changing economic conditions and societal values. In B. Gardell and G. Johansson, eds, *Working Life*. New York: John Wiley & Sons Ltd.

Piaget, J., 1977. *The Development of Thought. Equilibration of Cognitive Structures*. Oxford: Basil Blackwell.

Piaget, J., 1982. *The Childs Conception of the World*. London: Granada.

Piore, M. J. and Sabel, C. F., 1984. *The Second Industrial Divide*. New York: Basic Books.

Piotrkowski, C. S., 1979. *Work and the Family System*. New York: Free Press.

Pollert, A., 1991. The orthodoxy of flexibility. In A. Pollert, ed., *Farewell to Flexibility?* Oxford: Blackwell.

Portes, A., 1998. Social capital: Its origins and applications in modern sociology. *Annual Review of Sociology*, 24, 1–24.

Putnam, R. D., 1993. *Making Democracy Work: Civic Traditions in Modern Italy*. Princeton, NJ: Princeton University Press.

Putnam, R. D., 2000. *Bowling Alone: The Collapse and Revival of American Community*. New York: Simon & Schuster.

Rabinbach, A., 1990. *The Human Motor: Energy, Fatigue, and the Origins of Modernity*. Berkeley: University of California Press.

Rasmussen, J., 1986. *Information Processing and Human-Machine Interaction: An Approach to Cognitive Engineering*, Vol. 12. Amsterdam: North-Holland.

Reich, R. B., 1992. *The Work of Nations: Preparing Ourselves for 21st-Century Capitalism*. New York: Vintage Books.

Repetti, R. L. and Crosby, F., 1984. Gender and depression: Exploring the adult role explanation. *Journal of Social and Clinical Psychology*, 2, 57–70.

Repetti, R. L., Matthews, K. A., and Waldron, I., 1989. Employment and women's health: Effect of paid employment on women's mental and physical health. *American Psychologist*, 44, 1394–1401.

Ritzer, G., 1996. *The McDonaldization of Society*. Thousand Oaks, CA: Pine Forge Press.

Robinson, P., 1999. Explaining the relationship between flexible employment and labour market regulation. In A. Felstead and N. Jewson, eds, *Global Trends in Flexible Labour*. London: Macmillan Press, pp. 84–89.

Robinson, S. L. and Rousseau, D. M., 1994. Violating the psychological contract: Not the exception but the norm. *Journal of Organizational Behaviour*, 15(3), 245–259.

Rooke, D. and Torbert, W. R., 2005. Seven transformations of leadership. *Harvard Business Review*, April.

Rosvold, E. O. and Bjertness, E., 2001. Physicians who do not take sick leave: Hazardous heroes? *Scandinavian Journal of Public Health*, 29(1), 71–75.

Rousseau, D. M., 1995. *Psychological Contracts in Organizations: Understanding Written and Unwritten Agreements*. London: SAGE.

Rousseau, D. M. and Schalk, R., 2000. Learning from cross-national perspectives on psychological contracts. In D. M. Rosseau and R. Schalk, eds, *Psychological Contracts in Employment. Cross-National Perspectives*. London: SAGE, pp. 283–304.

Royle, T. and Towers, B., eds, 2002. *Labour Relations in the Global Fast-Food Industry*. London: Routledge.

Ryff, C. D. and Singer, B., 1998. The contours of positive human health. *Psychological Inquiry*, 9(1), 1–28.

Sahlin-Andersson, K. and Engwall, L., 2002. *The Expansion of Management Knowledge: Carriers, Flows, and Sources*. Stanford, CA: Stanford Business Books.

Sànches-Runde, C. J. and Pettigrew, A. M., 2003. Managing dualities. In A. M. Pettigrew, R. Whitington, L. Melin, C. Sànches-Runde, F. A. J. van der Bosch and T. Nomagami, eds, *Innovative Forms of Organizing*. London: SAGE, pp. 242–250.

Sandberg, Å., ed., 1995. *Enriching Production: Perspectives on Volvo's Uddevalla Plant as an Alternative to Lean Production*. Aldershot: Avebury.

Sandberg, T., 1982. *Work Organization and Autonomous Groups*. Stockholm: Liber.

Sapolsky, R., [1998] 2004. *Why Zebras Don't Get Ulcers: An Updated Guide to Stress, Stress-Related Disease and Coping*. New York: W. H. Freeman and Co.

Scandura, T. A. and Lankau, M. J., 1997. Relationships of gender, family responsibility and flexible work hours to organizational commitment and job satisfaction. *Journal of Organizational Behavior*, 18, 377–391.

Schlosser, E., 2001. *Fast Food Nation: The Dark Side of the All-American Meal*. New York: Penguin.

Schwartz, S. H., 2007. A theory of cultural value orientation: Explication and applications. In Y. Esmer and T. Pettersson, eds, *Measuring and Mapping Cultures: 25 Years of Comparative Value Surveys*. Leiden and Boston: Brill, pp. 31–78.

Seligman, M. E. P., 1975. *Helplessness: On Depression, Development, and Death.* San Francisco: W. H. Freeman.

Selye, H., 1956. *The Stress of Life.* New York: McGraw-Hill.

Semmer, N. K., Jacobshagen, N., Meier, L. L., and Elfering, A., 2007. Occupational stress research: The "stress-as-offense-to-self" perspective. In J. Houdmont and S. McIntyre, eds, *Occupational Health Psychology: European Perspectives on Research, Education and Practice,* Vol. 2. Castelo da Maia, Portugal: ISMAI Publishing, pp. 43–60.

Semmer, N. K., Tschan, F., Meier, L., et al., 2009. Illegitimate tasks and counterproductive work behavior. *Applied Psychology: An International Review,* 59(1), 70–96.

Sen, A., 1999. *Development as Freedom.* New York: Random House.

Sennett, R., 1998. *The Corrosion of Character. The Personal Consequences in the New Capitalism.* New York: Norton.

Sennett, R., 2006. *The Culture of the New Capitalism.* New Haven and London: Yale University Press.

Shapiro, C. and Varian, H. R., 1998. *Information Rules: A Strategic Guide to the Network Economy.* Boston: Harvard Business School.

Shingo, S. and Dillon, A. P., 1989. *A Study of the Toyota Production System: From an Industrial Engineering Viewpoint,* rev sub. Boca Raton, FL: Productivity Press.

Siegrist, J., 1996. Adverse health effects of high-effort/low-reward conditions. *Journal of Occupational Health Psychology,* 1(1), 27–41.

Siegrist, J., 2008. Effort-reward balance and health in a globalized economy. *Scandinavian Journal of Work and Environmental Health,* Suppl. 6., 163–168.

Simmel, G., 1903. The metropolis and mental life. In D. N. Levine, ed., *Georg Simmel on Individuality and Social Forms.* Chicago: The University of Chicago Press, pp. 324–339.

Sinnott, J. D., 1994. *Interdisciplinary Handbook of Adult Life Span Learning.* Westport, CT, Greenwood.

Sinnott, J. D., 2003. Complex post-formal thought and its relation to adult learning, life span development, and the new sciences. In T. Hagströmed, ed., *Adult Development in Post-industrial Society and Working Life.* Stockholm Lectures in Educology No. 2. Department of Education, Stockholm University, pp. 78–108.

Smitka, M. J., 1991. *Competitive Ties.* Columbia University Press.

Somech, A. and Drach-Zahavy, A., 2007. Strategies for coping with work-family conflict: The distinctive relationships of gender role ideology. *Journal of Occupational Health Psychology,* 12(1), 1–19.

SOU, 1990. Demokrati och makt i Sverige: Maktutredningens huvudrapport [Democracy and Power in Sweden]. Swedish Government Reports no. 1990:44. Stockholm: Allmänna förlaget.

Stalk Jr, G. and Hout, T. M., 1990. *Competing Against Time: How Time-Based Competition is Reshaping Global Markets*. London: Macmillan.

Starrin, B., Åslund, C., and Nilsson, K., 2009. Financial stress, shaming experiences and psychosocial ill-health – Studies into the finances-shame model. *Social Indicators Research*, **91**(2), 283–298.

Storper, M. and Scott, A. J., 1990. Work organisation and local labour markets in an era of flexible production. *International Labour Review*, **129**(5), 573–591.

Swedberg, R., ed., 2000. *Entrepreneurship: The Social Science View*. Oxford: Oxford University Press.

Swedish National Board of Health and Welfare [Socialstyrelsen], 2003. Utmattningssyndrom: Stressrelaterad psykisk ohälsa [Burnout syndrome – stress-related mental health]. Stockholm [In Swedish].

Taylor, F. W., 1911. *The Principles of Scientific Management*. New York: Harper & Harper.

Taylor, F. W., [1912] 1977. Testimony before the Special House Committee. In F. W. Taylor, ed., *Scientific Management*. Westport, CT: Greenwood Press.

Taylor, R. F., 2004. Extending conceptual boundaries: Work, voluntary work and employment. *Work, Employment and Society*, **18**(1), 29–49.

Tempest, S. and Starkey, K., 2004. The effects of liminality on individual and organizational learning. *Organization Studies*, **25**(4), 507–527.

Tennant, M., 1999. Is learning transferable? In D. Boud and J. Garrick, eds, *Understanding Learning at Work*. London: Routledge.

Theorell, T., 2002. To be able to exert control over one's own situation. A necessary condition for coping with stressors. In J. Campbell Quick and Lois E. Tetrick, eds, *Handbook of Occupational Health Psychology*. Washington, DC: American Psychological Association, pp. 201–219.

Theorell, T., 2004. Democracy at work and its relationship to health. In M. L. Perrewé and D. C. Ganster, eds, *Research in Occupational Stress and Well-Being. Emotional and Physiological Processes and Positive Intervention Strategies*, Vol. 3. Amsterdam: Elsevier, pp. 323–357.

Theorell, T., ed., 2008a. After 30 years with the demand-control-support model – How is it used today. *Scandinavian Journal of Work and Environmental Health*, Suppl. 6.

Theorell, T., 2008b. Anabolism and catabolism – Antagonistic partners in stress and strain. *Scandinavian Journal of Work and Environmental Health*, Suppl. 6, 136–143.

Thompson, E. P., 1967. Time, work-discipline and industrial capitalism. *Past and Present*, **38**, 56–97.

Tidline, T. J., 1999. The mythology of information overload. *Library Trends*, **47**(3), 485–506.

Toffler, A., 1970. *Future Shock*. New York: Random House.

Touraine, A., 1971. *The Post-Industrial Society: Tomorrow's Social History: Classes, Conflicts and Culture in the Programmed Society*. New York: Random House.

Trist, E. L. and Bamforth, K. W., 1951. Some social and psychological consequences of the longwall method of coal-getting. *Human Relations*, **4**(1), 3–38.

Tsoukas, H., 2001. What is organizational knowledge? *Journal of Management Studies*, **38**(7), 973–993.

Tuckman, A., 1994. The yellow brick road: Total quality management and the restructuring of organizational culture. *Organization Studies*, **15**(5), 727–751.

Uchino, B. N., 2009. Understanding the links between social support and physical health: A lifespan perspective with emphasis on the separability of perceived and received support. *Perspectives in Psychological Science*, **4**, 236–255.

Uggla, H., 2000. *Managing the brand-association base: Exploring facets of strategic brand management from the imaginary organization perspective. Based on a Semiotic Study on the ASSESS CD-ROM by American Skandia*. PhD. Stockholm School of Business.

Ursin, H., and Eriksen, H. R., 2004. The cognitive activation theory of stress. *Psychoneuroendocrinology* **29**, 567–592.

Uvnäs-Moberg, K. and Petersson, M., 2005. Oxytocin, a mediator of anti-stress, well-being, social interaction, growth and health. *Zeitschrift Psychosomatic Medicine and Psychotherapy*, **5**(1), 57–80.

Virtanen, M., Kivimäki, M., Elovainio, M., et al., 2003. From insecure to secure employment: Changes in work, health, health related behaviours, and sickness absence. *Occupational and Environmental Medicine*, **60**(12), 948–953.

Volpert, W. 1989. Work and personality development from the viewpoint of the action regulation theory. In H. Leymann and H. Aldershut, eds, *Socialisation and Learning at Work*. Avebury: Gower Publishing Company Limited, pp. 215–232.

von Schéele, F. and Ohlsson, K., 1997. *Variations between Groups of Individuals in an Organisation using Distance Working*. Stockholm: Kommunikationsforskningsberedningen.

Waldron, I. and Jacobs, J. A., 1989. Effects of labor force participation on women's health: New evidence from a longitudinal study. *Journal of Occupational Medicine*, **30**(12), 977–983.

Weber, M., [1934] 2003. *The Protestantic Ethic and the Spirit of Capitalism*. New York: Dover Publications, Inc.

Welzel, C., 2007. Democratization in the human development perspective. In Y. Esmer and T. Pettersson, eds, *Measuring and Mapping Cultures: 25 Years of Comparative Value Surveys*. Leiden and Boston: Brill, pp. 155–186.

Wenger, E., 2000. *Communities of Practice: Learning, Meaning, and Identity*. Cambridge: Cambridge University Press.

Westerlund, H., Kivimäki, M., Singh-Manoux, A., *et al.*, 2009. Self-rated health before and after retirement in France (GAZEL): A cohort study. *Lancet*, **374**(9705), 1889–1896.

Wethington, E., and Kessler, R. C., 1989. Employment, parenthood, and psychological distress. *Journal of Family Issues*, **30**(4), 520–546.

WHO, 2006. *The World Health Report 2006. Working Together for Health*. Geneva: World Health Organization.

Wilensky, H., 1960. Work, careers, and social integration. *International Social Science Journal*, **12**(3), 543–560.

Wilkinson, A., 1997. Empowerment: Theory and practice. *Personnel Review*, **27**(1), 40–56.

Womack, J. P., Jones, D., and Roos, D., 1990. *The Machine that Changed the World*. New York: Rawson Associates.

Wood, S., ed., 1989. *The Transformation of Work*. London: Unwin Hyman Ltd.

Worthington, J., 2006. *Reinventing the Workplace*. London: Architectural Press.

Wurman, R. S., 1991. *Information Anxiety: What to Do when Information Doesn't Tell You What You Need to Know*. London: Pan.

Zanders, H., 1994. Changing work values. In P. Ester, L. Halman, and R. de Moor, eds, *The Individualizing Society: Value Change in Europe and North America*. Tilburg: Tilburg University Press, pp. 129–154.

Zedeck, S. and Mosier, K. L., 1990. Work in the family and employing organization. *American Psychologist*, **45**(2), 240–251.

Zuboff, S., 1988. *In the Age of the Smart Machine*. Oxford: Heinemann.

Index

abortion 145–6
absenteeism 166–7, 195, 205–6, 209–11
adaptive energy 169
adbusting 139
administrative resources 41–2
adrenaline 183, 188
Aglietta, Michel 123–4
alienation 72, 87, 200–30
allostatic stress model 184–9
altered significance of work 104–7
altruism 86, 105, 116
Alvesson, Mats 43–4
American lifestyle consumption 123
anabolic processes 184, 207
anonymous money 164
anxiety 208–10
Arendt, Hannah 153
arthritis 188
artificial insemination 145
artisan production 33–4
Astvik, Wanja 84–5, 213–14
Atkinson, John 34–5, 57, 62–3
autoimmunity 188
autonomy 105–6, 112–15, 122

backlash 88
bad jobs 60–2

balance between catabolic and anabolic processes 184
balance in life 158–61
Bamford, Ken 36
Barnett, Ronald 108–9
basic family form 144–5
Baudrillard, Jean 141–2
Bauman, Zygmunt 121, 143
Beard, George 163
Beck, Ulrich 102–3, 147–8
Beck-Gernsheim, Elizabeth 147–8
behavioral tactics 131–3
being locked-in 202–4
"being someone else" 142
being "with the times" 106
Bell, Daniel 98–101, 103
benchmarking 54
bodily reactions to stress 182–9
  allostatic stress model 184–9
  catabolic and anabolic processes 184
  see also fight or flight response
border theory 130
boundaries 130–3, 199–200
  behavioral tactics 131–3
  boundaryless work 24, 194–5, 222, 225–6
Bourdieu, Pierre 89

Work Without Boundaries: Psychological Perspectives on the New Working Life, First Edition. Michael Allvin, Gunnar Aronsson, Tom Hagström, Gunn Johansson, and Ulf Lundberg.
© 2011 John Wiley & Sons, Ltd. Published 2011 by John Wiley & Sons, Ltd.

boycotting   139
Braverman, Harry   49, 72
Bremberg, Sven   208, 212
bullfighting   83
burnout   84, 210–11
buying parts   63

call centers   32
Calvinist values   70, 117
cancer   209, 212
Cannon, Walter   168, 172
cardiovascular disease   176
Carlzon, Jan   33, 83
Castells, Manuel   11, 100–1, 103
casual employment   57–8, 200–3, 224
catabolic processes   184, 207
CATS *see* cognitive activation theory of stress
change-over time   30
Chernobyl   103
choosing path to flexibility   62–5
citizenry spirit   91
classic theory of entrepreneurship   111
classification mechanisms   153–5
Clinton, Bill   99
coalmining   36
Coca-Cola   44, 140
cognitive activation theory of stress   171
cognitive knowledge demands   71–4
  space for action and control   72–4
Cohen, Sheldon   188
Cold War   169
collaboration   65–6
collective theory   176
Coming of Post-Industrial Society   98
commitment to work   130, 181–2
common language   45
communal knowledge   107
company "organization"   43
compensation   127–8, 193

competence   174–5
competence profile   12
competing spheres   129–30
compromise   49
conditions outside work life   134–8
confidence   91–2
  see also trust
conflict   158–61
conflict theory   129
conflicting demands of service work   83–5
constellations   51
consumption aesthetic   143
consumption society   134–8
  new relations   137–8
  sovereign customer   136–7
contingent employment   58
  see also casual employment
contrasting activities   154
control   72–4
conviviality   147
cooperation   41
  see also spontaneous cooperation
coping with boundaries   130–3
coping mechanisms   171, 213–14
corporate practices   43–7
Corrosion of Character   118–19
cortisol   183, 188
craftsmanship   120
Csikszentmihalyhi, Mihaly   159–60
culture jamming   139
"customer in the center"   33

de Montoya, Monica Lindh   112
defense   213–14
delegating production   18
Delta Airlines   56
demand–control model   173–7
demand–control–support model   178, 185, 209
Dencik, Lars   148–9
departmental meetings   42

deregulation of working life 126, 193, 218–19
detraditionalization 126
diabetes 188
diagnosis-related groups 54
diaries 155
dimensions of knowledge 69–122
  cognitive knowledge demands 71–4
  conclusion 120–2
  existential knowledge demands 107–20
  social knowledge demands 81–97
  societal knowledge demands 97–107
  tacit knowledge 74–81
direct work 48
discontent 118
  see also "exit or voice"
discursive change 19–20
disintegration of family as institution 145
distributed operations 51
distribution of inequalities 4–7
division of labor 35, 64
divorce 172
documentation society 228
"doing" work 143, 153
double deregulation 126
double diaries 155
doubly locked-ins 203
Drach-Zahavy, Anat 132–3
DRG see diagnosis-related groups
drifting 39
Drucker, Peter 35–6
du Gay, Paul 45
dumbing-down 173

early industrialism 69
EBM see evidence based medicine
economic depression 168–9
economic emergency 201–2

economic flexibility 34
economic recession 223–5
Edwards, Richard 81–2
effort–reward–imbalance model 177–9
Ellström, Per-Erik 74
emancipating pedagogy 109
embeddedness 115
emergency duty 50
emotional intelligence 85
emotional labor 84
empirical change 19
employability 110–12
employee knowledge 42–3
employment security 57–8
empowerment 35–42, 58, 219
  administrative resources 41–2
  managing indefinable jobs 40–1
  unlimited/indefinable jobs 38–40
empty individuality 142
Enlightenment 70
entrepreneurship 110–12
equilibrium 185
Ericsson 17–18
Eriksen, Hege 171
European Working Conditions Survey 193–4
everyday democracy 174
evidence based medicine 54
exhaustion syndrome 163–5, 182, 210–12
existential knowledge demands 107–20
  autonomy 112–14
  employability and entrepreneurship 110–12
  exit or voice 117–20
  place for morals 114–17
  supercomplexity and metacognition 108–10
"exit or voice" 117–20
external regulation 225–8

"face to the world" 44
Faludi, Susan 143
familiarity knowledge 76
family friendly organizational arrangements 129
family and negotiation 146–8
fast-food industry 21, 84, 159
Fayol, Henri 21, 28
"feed forward" 78
feedback 78
Felstead, Alan 156
fight or flight response 168, 183–7
  see also bodily reactions to stress
fire-fighting 187
fitness 151, 154
"five o'clock beer" 44
flexible boundaries 131
flexible firm 34
flexible offices 51
flexible production 29, 33, 35
flexible work 29–58, 223–5
  empowerment 35–42
  individual control and regulations 42–7
  substitution 48–58
  in times of recession 223–5
flexitime 130–2
Flextronics 17–18
follow-ups 42
Ford, Henry 66, 123–4
forms of regulation 225–8
Foucault, Michel 70
"fourth world" 101
franchising 100
Frederickson, Barbara 215–16
"free floating" sexuality 145
freeing oneself of work 191–7
  intensifying work 193
  transcending personal health limits 194–7
  transcending time related framing of work 193–4

freelance journalism 63, 154, 156–61, 227
Freire, Paulo 109
Freudenberger, Herbert 210
Frone, Michael 129
front personnel 83
Fukuyama, Francis 227–8
functional flexibility 34, 62

gainful employment 133–4, 211–12
Gardner, Howard 85
Garsten, Christina 93
GAZEL 210
general adaptation syndrome 169
Giddens, Anthony 92–3, 103, 113, 146
Goffman, Erving 86
Goleman, Daniel 85–6
good jobs 60–2
good work 173–7, 194
Gramsci, Antonio 123
Granovetter, Mark 89–90
greenhouse effect 166
Greenpeace 139
Grey, Chris 93

Hakim, Catherine 156
Hallsten, Lennart 211
Hamburger University 83
Harley-Davidson 44
Harvey, Mark 153
"Health Behaviour in School-aged Children" (WHO) 208, 212
Hegel, Georg Wilhelm Friedrich 72
"helping jobs" see service work
heterogenization of working life 220–1
hierarchy 28, 151–2
highly qualified workers 150–2
hiring parts 63
Hirschman, Albert 117–18
"hitting the wall" 182

Index

Hochschild, Arlie R.   55–6, 84, 87, 149–50, 158–9
Hoff, Ted   11
Holmes, Thomas   170
Home and Work   154
homeostasis   185
household chores   153–4, 159
"humanist" division of labor   35

ill health   163–216
   new ill health   205–12
   new work life as source of stress   189–205
   stress models for work life   172–89
   stress as social problem and research area   167–72
   work environment and possibility space at work   212–16
illegitimate tasks   179–81
   see also ill health; stress
indefinable jobs   38–41
   managing   40–1
independence   48
indirect work   48
individual control   42–7
individual strategies   155–8
individualization of working life   219–20
Industrial Revolution   69
inebriation   69
inequality   4–7, 221–2
informality   44
information anxiety   78–9
information recycling   81
information society   99–100, 228
information technology revolution   11
Inglehart, Ronald   114–15
insecurity   200–3, 212–13
   being locked-in   202–3
insourcing   100, 136, 198
inspection   52
institutional change   19

institutionalized practices   43
Intel   11
intensification of nervous life   164
intensifying work   193
Internet selling   32
intrapreneurialization   100, 136

Jagannath   103
Jewson, Nick   156
job decision latitude   174
job numbers   65–8
job-sharing   50
Journal of Mental Science   164
just-in-time learning   77–8

kaizen   30
kanban   30
Karasek, Robert   128–9, 174–5
   see also demand–control model
"karoshi"   191
Kelly, Kevin   37
key competences   57
Keynes, John Maynard   123–4
knowledge management   81
knowledge society   98–9

labor-intensive services   64
Lager, Anton   208, 212
language   43–7
Lankau, Melenie J.   130
Lazarus, Richard   171–2
lean organization   50
learned helplessness   175
leaving work   117–20
Leidner, Robin   87
liaisons   89–90
   see also social capital
life change unit score   170
lifelong learning   79
"lines of demarcation"   131
   see also work–life balance
liquid boundaries   61

Littler, Craig   49
locked-in-ness   202–4
loss of moral motivation   203–5
Luhmann, Niklas   91–2
Lundgren, Kurt   77
Lysgaard, Sverre   192

McDonald's   55, 83, 87, 140
McEwen, Bruce   184
management by objectives   36
managing flexible work   25–68
managing indefinable jobs   40–1
managing lean organization   50
mapping   42
market aesthetic   141–3
  work and consumption
    aesthetic   143
market capitalism   49, 123
marketization   137
markets   7–13
Marx, Karl   49, 70, 72, 123
Maslach, Christina   210
Matthews, Karen   133–4
MBO *see* management by objectives
mechanisms of classification   153–5
Melucci, Alberto   140
memory disruption   211
mental ill health   133, 206–12
  exhaustion syndrome   210–11
  physical problems   211–12
  tiredness, sleeping disorders   207–8
  worry, anxiety   208–10
meta-learning   79–81
metacognition   108–10
Mezirow, Jack   109
"Mobility in Europe"   203
modernization theory   114–17
"moment of truth"   83
moral motivation   203–5
moral supermarket   138–41
  "nomads of the present"   140–1
morals   114–17

Morrison, Elizabeth Wolfe   95
Moss Kanter, Rosabeth   111
Murdock, George Peter   144
mutual dependence   63
mutually favored spheres   133–4

narcissism   152
narrative movement   120
national pride   204
negotiation   146–8
neo-liberalism   136, 177
network family   148–9
network society   100–1
"networks of networks"   140
neurasthenia   163–5
  see also exhaustion syndrome
neuroscience   86
new economy   37
new family   144–9
  family as forum for
    negotiation   146–8
  network family   148–9
new ill health   205–12
  mental ill health   206–12
new public management   181
new relations   137–8
new vs. old work   18–22
new work   1–24
  new inequality   4–7
  new markets and structures   7–13
  the "new" in "new work"   16–18
  new vs. old work   18–22
  new work life   13–15
"niched" goods   31
Nike   64, 140
"nine-to-five job"   2
Nippert-Eng, Christena   154–6
no buffer   30
"nomads of the present"   140–1
non-regulated working
  conditions   67–8
noradrenaline   183

Normann, Richard 32–3
nuclear family 144–5
numbers of jobs 65–8
numerical flexibility 34, 62

offense to self 179–81
  see also ill health; stress
opposition 221–2
"organization" of the company 43
organizational learning 79–80
organizing living 149–58
  highly qualified worker 150–2
  individual strategies and universal attitudes 155–8
  new mechanisms of classification 153–5
"ornamental culture" 143
outcome expectancy 171–2
outsiderness 135
outsourcing 63, 100, 159, 198
overcommitment 179
overexertion 167–8
overstimulation 174

part-time work 50
participation 80
pathological loss of energy 163
patient satisfaction 53
performance based self-esteem 179
performance of work 52–4
permeable boundaries 131
personal chemistry 197
personal health limits 194–7
personnel fostering 151
personnel productivity 55
person–role conflict 179–81
physical health problems 211–12
Piaget, Jean 109
Piore, Michael 29–30, 33, 35, 64–5
place for morals 114–17
place of work in life 123–62
  competing spheres 129–30
  conflict and balance in life 158–61
  coping with boundaries 130–3
  individual matter 162
  market aesthetic 141–3
  moral supermarket 138–41
  mutually favored spheres 133–4
  new conditions outside work 134–8
  new family 144–9
  organizing living 149–58
  separate spheres 126–9
playing the social game 87, 89, 97, 119–21, 152
poka yoke 30
pollution 102
possibility space 212–16
post-bureaucratic organization 137
post-Fordism 124–5
post-industrial society 97–104
  information society 99–100
  knowledge society 98–9
  network society 100–1
  risk society 101–4
post-modernization 114–15
power 223–5
precarious employment 58
  see also casual employment
precariousness 200–3
"presence despite illness" *see* sickness presence
protesting about work 117–20
psychiatric disorders 206
psychological contracts 93–7
psychopaths 86, 152
Putnam, Robert 91

quality circles 30, 36

Rahe, Richard 170
rationalizing 64
re-organization 42
Reagan, Ronald 136, 177
Reaganomics 60

recession 223–5
reciprocal trust 227–8
redistribution 118
regulations 42–7
　corporate practices, symbols, language 43–7
Reich, Robert 99–101, 103
rejection 84
relativization of norms 199
renaissance of artisan production 33–4
Repetti, Rena 133–4
requirements theory 176
research into stress 167–72
resistance 169, 222
resource theory 176
rewards 178
risk society 101–4
Robinson, Sandra L. 95
Rolls-Royce 44
Rousseau, Denise 94
routines 78, 80
rules of work 25–68
　flexible work 29–58
　separate paths 60–8
Ruskin, John x

Sabel, Charles 29–30, 33, 35, 64–5
Salaman, Graeme 45
SAS 33, 83
Scandinavian Airline Systems see SAS
Scandura, Terri A. 130
Schumpeter, Joseph 111
Schwartz, Shalom S. 115
scientific management 54
Second World War 114, 123, 168–9, 172
secularization 114
segmentation 127–8
self-contained market 101
self-determination 48, 147

self-esteem 197, 200–1
self-generating communities 89
self-perception 181
self-realization 105, 114
Selye, Hans 168–9, 172
Semmer, Norbert 179–81
Sen, Amartya 214
Sennett, Richard 118–20
sensorimotoric ability 73
separate paths to flexibility 60–8
　choosing path to flexibility 62–5
　good and bad jobs 60–2
　number of jobs 65–8
separate spheres 126–9
separation 148
service work 82–7
　conflicting demands of 83–5
　social competence 85–7
sex hormones 184–5, 188
sickness presence 2, 194–7, 205–6, 209–11
Siegrist, Johannes 178–9, 189
significance of work 104–7
Simmel, Georg 164
situated learning 80
slavery 103
SLE see systemic lupus erythematosus
sleeping disorders 189, 207–10
social autism 86
"social black holes" 101
social capital 89–91
social changes 18–20
social competence 85–7, 197–9
social conflicts 197–200
social corrosion 86
social knowledge demands 81–97
　all work is service work 82–7
　spontaneous cooperation 87–98
social management 57
social networks 88–9
social polarization 101

social problems 167–72
  war and economic
    depression 168–9
  wealth and welfare 169–72
social readjustment rating scale 170
social relations 54–7
socialization 96–7, 176
socialization theory 176
societal knowledge demands 97–107
  altered significance of work 104–7
  post-industrial society 97–104
socio-technical school 36
somatic diseases 211
Somech, Anit 132–3
source of stress 189–205
  freeing oneself of work 191–7
  insecurity, precariousness,
    alienation 200–3
  loss of moral motivation 203–5
  social conflict 197–200
sovereign customer 136–7
space for action 72–4
spillover 127–8, 133
spontaneous cooperation 87–97
  psychological contracts 93–7
  social capital 89–91
  social networks 88–9
  trust 91–3
stagflation 9
stagnation 168
Statistic Sweden 66, 207
status control 189
strains 222–3
streamlining 64
stress 163–216
  see also ill health
stress hormones 182–9
stress models for work life 172–89
  bodily reactions to stress 182–9
  effort–reward–imbalance
    model 177–9
  illegitimate tasks as stressors 179–81

time pressure 181–2
work environment and good
  work 173–7
structural changes 7–13
subcontracting 18, 63, 100
subjective complaints 211
substitution 48–58
  casual employment 57–8
  managing lean organization 50
  performance of work 52–4
  social relations 54–7
  working hours 50–1
  workplace 51–2
supercomplexity 108–10
Survey of Living Conditions
  (ULF) 207
Swedish Employers'
  Confederation 31
Swedish National Patient Safety
  Agency 53
Swedish Railways 32
"switching off" 222
symbol-handling professions 99
symbolic markers 154–5
symbols 43–7
sympathetic nervous system 182–3,
  187–8
symptoms 222–3
systemic lupus erythematosus 188

tacit knowledge 74–81
  what we need to know in flexible
    work 75–81
Taylor, Frederick 21, 48–9, 60, 66, 72,
  149, 159, 228
telecommuting 17, 36, 132, 151
telemarketing 32
temporary constellations 51
temporary employment *see* casual
  employment
Terkel, Studs ix
Thatcher, Margaret 34, 136, 177

Theorell, Töres   128–9, 174–5
theory of cognitive development   109
Thompson, Edward P.   25
Thomson, Dr. Symes   164
time economies   153
time environment   192
time pressure   181–2
"time to market"   1
time-limited employment   57–8
times of recession   223–5
The Time Bind   150
tiredness   207–10
Toffler, Alvin   170
total quality management   52, 54
TQM *see* total quality management
training programs   42
transactional contract   95–6
transcending personal health limits   194–7
transcending time related framing of work   193–4
transformative learning theory   109
trimming   50
Trist, Eric   36
trust   91–3, 225–8
Trust   227

Uddevalla plant   31, 64
  see also Volvo
understimulation   174
universal attitudes   155–8
UNIX   11
unlimited jobs   38–40
unregulated working conditions   67
urgent matter of separation   162
Ursin, Holger   171
US Army   104–5
usefulness   120

Viking Line   142
virtual reality   86
Volvo   31, 64

Waldron, Ingrid   133–4
war   168–9
way forward   217–28
  deregulation of working life   218–19
  flexibility in times of economic recession   223–5
  heterogenization of working life   220–1
  individualization of working life   219–20
  new inequality   221–2
  new strains and symptoms   222–3
  trust or external regulation   225–8
wealth   169–72
Weber, Max   70, 117
welfare   169–72
welfare capitalism   123
well-being   166–7, 184, 191, 213
Welzel, Christian   114
what is new about "new work"   16–18
what we need to know in flexible work   75–81
  information anxiety   78–9
  just-in-time learning   77–8
  meta- and organizational learning   79–81
Whitehall II Study   196
WHO *see* World Health Organization
Wilensky, Harold L.   128
Wired   37
"women's jobs"   145
work aesthetic   143
work environment   173–7, 212–16
  and good work   173–7
work life   13–15, 69–122, 163–216
  stress models   172–89
work motivation   199
work rules *see* rules of work
work task   28
workaholism   197
Working   ix
working hours   50–1

work–life balance   130–2
workplace   51–2
work's place life   123–62
World Health Organization   208
worry   208–10
"wrong decisions"   121

xenophobia   102

"yuppie flu"   211

zero-sum game   6
Zuboff, Shoshana   20–1